'on Mennonite Church
,0 County Road 44
hen, Indiana 46528

In Harmony with Creation

Benton Mennonite Church
15350 County Road 44
Goshen, Indiana 46528

In Harmony with Creation

Seeking God's Face in Mennonite Camping

Edited by
Larry and Mary Jane
Breneman Eby

Mennonite Camping Association
Elkhart, Indiana
2006

To order copies of *In Harmony with Creation*,

to inquire about it,

or for permission to reprint excerpts (except in brief reviews),

please contact:

Mennonite Camping Association (MCA), office@mennonitecamping.org

1-574-523-3043, fax 1-574-239-1892, P.O. Box 1245, Elkhart, IN 46515

For an overview of Mennonite Camping Association (MCA),
please see www.mennonitecamping.org

Dedication

To Oswald (Ozzie) H. Goering, outdoor recreation teacher, friend and encourager; Virgil Brenneman, former Executive Secretary of MCA and primitive camping enthusiast; and Helen and James Reusser, who describe church camping as the "church of the out-of-doors."

Their vision and love for God's creation has been inspiring to us in the production of this book.

Table of Contents

In Harmony with Creation
Seeking God's Face in Mennonite Camping, 1980-2006

Foreword

This book, *In Harmony with Creation*, is a valuable addition to the growing literature witnessing to the importance and value of the Mennonite camping experience. As such, it should be on the reading list of church leaders and be placed in church libraries where it is available to church members.

It follows the work of Jess Kauffman who wrote the book, *A Vision and a Legacy* (Faith and Life Press, 1984), which traces the history of the Mennonite camping movement from its beginnings through 1980. Another important book related to camping is Tim Lehman's *Seeking the Wilderness* (Faith and Life Press, 1993), which emphasizes the important role that wilderness experiences can play in the development of spiritual life and the understanding of God's creation.

Adding to and complementing those publications, *In Harmony with Creation* is important in updating the history of the Mennonite camping movement to the present. It identifies and describes the contributions of some of the historical and current leaders of the camping movement in the Mennonite church.

One cannot help but be inspired as one reads the chapters by present-day Mennonite camping leaders telling of their own camping experiences and the positive influence these had on their lives. The importance of the lasting effects of Christian camping on thousands of others has been attested to by countless testimonies and stories. Research is now in progress under the leadership of the National Council of Churches Committee on Outdoor Ministries and the Religiously Affiliated Camps of the American Camp Association to gain empirical, measurable evidence of these effects.

Authors Larry and Mary Jane Breneman Eby are well qualified to give the leadership needed for the production of this book with their long history of interest in the outdoors and their extensive participation in a wide range of nature-related activities. Mary Jane made valuable contributions in her role as president and member of the Mennonite Camping Association (MCA) board.

Both Larry and Mary Jane have actively participated in leadership roles at Drift Creek Camp in Oregon.

Oswald H. Goering
Moundridge, Kansa
June 2005

Preface

A few years ago, Ozzie Goering, president of Mennonite Camping Association in the early 1980s, suggested to the MCA Board that it might be time for their history to be updated while a few "old-timers" like him were still around. Jess Kauffman's book, *A Vision and a Legacy: The Story of Mennonite Camping, 1920-80*, had been published by Faith and Life Press in 1984.

The board asked if we might be interested in taking on this new assignment. They knew we had written the history of Oregon's Drift Creek Camp, *Spirit Roots: Celebrating the Vision* (2000). Our agreement to undertake the new MCA project has resulted in the book you now hold in your hands.

Many people have shared in the production of this book. Our thanks go out to them.

· The Mennonite Camping Association Board for their confidence that we had the abilities to do another book. Also for their eagerness to make a copy available to the congregations of Mennonite Church Canada and Mennonite Church USA.

· To Ozzie Goering for suggesting the book and writing a foreword.

· To Wilbur Kauffman and the staff of Kauffman & Associates for the fantastic graphic design as a contribution to the project.

· To Paul M. Schrock of Schrock Media Enterprises for his project management and editorial work and, especially, for his encouragement and support to two struggling authors.

· To Jennifer Gingerich, Tim Lehman, Darryl Neustaedter-Barg, and David Helmuth for major chapter writing. Most of them have full-time jobs, but their enthusiasm for this book is evident in the high quality of what they have written.

· To the many camping directors, administrators, staff persons, board members, and camping enthusiasts who encouraged us and took time out from their busy schedules to write, assemble, and send materials to us for use in the pages that follow. The quality of materials contributed has directly impacted the effectiveness of the book. For any lack of complete or accurate credit, we apologize.

Larry and Mary Jane Breneman Eby
Albany, Oregon
March 2006

Introduction

But turn to the animals, and let them teach you; the birds of the air will tell you the truth. Listen to the plants of the earth, and learn from them; let the fish of the sea become your teachers. Who among all these does not know that the hand of Our God has done this? In God's hand is the soul of every living thing; in God's hand is the breath of all humankind.

Job 12:7-10 The Inclusive Hebrew Scriptures

Reflecting on God through God's creation, as the writer of Job suggests, the writers, compilers, and editors of this book believe the history of Mennonite Camping Association (MCA) is "living history." It has been formed, recorded, and written in the hearts, minds, and journals of thousands of persons who have been and are being impacted by the programs of the camps, retreat centers, and special institutions that are Mennonite Camping Association.

For the most part, this book is not a chronological account of people and events. Rather we attempt to present a panorama of our camps across two countries during the last twenty-five years as a way to show what has happened and what may yet come to be.

Primary questions considered in shaping **In Harmony with Creation** and choosing the contents were: How is the camping experience unique? What does it offer that is distinct from the other activities connected with *church*? How does the environment of nature impact the camping program and experience? Is the Mennonite camp and retreat ministry different in its goals and offerings? How does it fit into the Mennonite, Anabaptist, and Christian spiritual experience?

As reports of the institutions, information from many web sites, and reflections of persons impacted by the camping experience are presented, let them tell you the history, past and present, of Mennonite Camping Association. It is in these that the living history of the organization reaches uniqueness as an expression of our faith specially learned and lived in the great panorama of God's creation.

Additionally, the chapters, "Since Before I Was Born," "Rooted in Relationships," "Knowing God in This Place," "Music, It's What We Remember," "For the Love of Camping and Retreating," and "Foresight and Faithful Stewardship" include people who have had significant experiences in and helped shape the camping and retreat ministries that are in all cases Mennonite and in some ways perhaps uniquely so. Jess Kauffman in **A Vision and Legacy** (Faith and Life, 1984) wrote a thorough history of the various movements, programs, and persons that dreamed of and formed camps and programs for and by Mennonites to that point. In this new book, **In Harmony with Creation**, we have not attempted to repeat his story or style.

Rather in the form of an anthology, the pages of the chapter "Camping and Retreating in Places Apart" tell the current living history of each member camp as portrayed in the facilities and programs, in the mission or vision statements of the institutions, and perhaps most especially in the accounts and anecdotes that testify to the effectiveness of these missions and visions.

Many of the MCA camps and retreats have their own web sites which are listed in Chapter 6. You may want to browse in some of these for more photographs and information on their purposes and programs.

Not everything in this new book may appeal to everyone. Theological issues are raised, reflections on persons' meaningful encounters in a camp or retreat setting are related, some serious, others humorous. There are suggestions for writing camp histories, for thinking about what is unique about camping, about Mennonite camping, and suggestions for programming. There are stories about new or recovered faith, adventure, and odes to the grandeur of God's creation, and the effectiveness of special camps.

It is the fervent wish of the authors that this contribution to Mennonite literature will help, not only to record the past and present, but also to shape the future of ourselves and our camps and retreat centers. We hope thousands of children, youth, and adults can encounter God in a special way that can be experienced best in a place apart, *In Harmony with Creation*—a place where God is celebrated, observed, cherished, and preserved in word, in song, and in fellowship with God and each other—in God's creation.

Chapter 1

Since Before I Was Born
Reflections on experiences at Drift Creek Camp by Jennifer Gingerich

[God] said, "Go out and stand on the mountain before the LORD, for the LORD is about to pass by." Now there was a great wind, so strong that it was splitting mountains and breaking rocks in pieces before the LORD, but the LORD was not in the wind; and after the wind an earthquake, but the LORD was not in the earthquake; and after the earthquake a fire, but the LORD was not in the fire; and after the fire a sound of sheer silence. When Elijah heard it, he wrapped his face in his mantle and went out and stood at the entrance of the cave. Then there came a voice to him...

1 Kings 19:11-13a (NRSV)

I believe God often speaks to us in the silent moments, if we allow silence to happen. Our lives are constant whirrs of activity and they seem to get only busier and busier. How can the Holy Spirit be present in our everyday life if we do not make space to hear that still, small voice?

Drift Creek Camp is one of the key places where I have experienced God. It is a place to which I retreat with intention and excitement. I seek sanctuary among the peaceful silence of the trees and mountains.

I have been going to camp since before I was born. My mom and dad volunteered in the kitchen for the summer camp program three months before my birth, and I have been going there at least once a year ever since. I'm quite sure no one has thrown up on the road to Drift Creek Camp as often as I have. A long, winding, forest-service road makes the ten-mile trip to camp a long and sickly one. But after navigating through the 127 tight curves that make up the picturesque drive and arriving in the plot of land leased by the camping association, you know the trip was worth it.

Drift Creek Camp is tucked away in the Coastal Range Mountains of Western Oregon just about a half-hour east of Lincoln City. The spot is idyllic. Drift Creek begins in the mountains above the camp and flows down to the Pacific Ocean. The creek makes a large loop that encircles the camp property and gives it a flowing boundary. The water splashes over rocks and crags as it winds its way through the mossy, temperate rain forest. The rushing of the creek provides a musical backdrop to every activity or fireside event. Giant trees tower two hundred feet overhead—hemlock, Sitka spruce, alder, and Douglas fir, to name a few. Salmon berries and huckleberries line the trails and roadway and tree cones are scattered all over the earthen floor. A glorious abundance of bracken, sword, and deer fern enhance the picture even more. Mosses drape like shaggy icicles from branches and give a soft cover to tree trunks and rocks.

The trails meander under the tapestries of moss and through the magnificent, towering trees. They go alongside and through creeks, up mountainsides, and over fallen "nurse logs"; dead, decaying logs on whose crumbling bodies new generations of trees and other rain forest flora have their beginnings. The main camp trail leads around the creek loop past green and brown, moss-covered, A-frame cabins each named after an Oregon river. It also goes past a huge, old-growth tree that my cabin mates and I lovingly named "Groovy Biff" during one summer during camp. The name had no specific meaning. It was just what came to our adolescent minds as a "groovy" name, using a then favorite group word. Trail walkers hear the whir and hum of

the camp generator providing our electricity. Small creatures scurry around—little chipmunks, rabbits, and squirrels. Slow-moving, slimy banana slugs inch along the forest floor. I have seen many deer at camp. Along the forest service road I have even observed a porcupine, raccoons, skunks, elk, and an adolescent bobcat. It would be a shame not to mention the malicious mosquitoes and horrid horseflies.

A trail just east of the large, A-frame lodge leads up a ridge into a cathedral of trees where the amphitheatre lies. The wooden benches stagger down the hillside and a large, uneven stump sets the stage.

I have a favorite place within the camp loop. It lies on a rocky beach next to the creek. A huge boulder sits in the creek. I get to it by crossing a log. Water flows and gurgles around me as I lie on my rock, staring up at the trees, listening to the breeze making the branches sing. And if my thoughts remain quiet enough, I sometimes hear that still, small voice— the sound of sheer silence.

Being in this environment opens one up to the wonder of the Creator. With the beauty of the camp, it is hard not to sense God's presence. The natural world has always been a key way for me to connect with God and experience my faith. Retreating to the peace and simplicity of the camp setting allows space for God to work in my life.

It is not only the beauty of nature and silence that makes being at Drift Creek Camp wonderful. One can always seek these things in any natural setting where one finds beauty, and this is right and good! But what makes Drift Creek Camp (and many other camps, Mennonite or not) unique and wonderful also has to do with the people. God speaks to us in silence, but also in the wisdom of shared experiences. Whether going for summer camp and meeting campers and counselors, or the annual retreat, I always meet wonderful people. The camp directors, the caretakers, and all those retreating make the camp what it is. Seeking God in community is a beautiful thing.

"Being in this environment opens one up to the wonder of the Creator. With the beauty of the camp, it is hard not to sense God's presence."

I have experienced God through people in many places around the world, but a unique combination occurs when a community of people searches for truth in the natural world with lots of space for fellowship and reflection. I believe many people have powerful spiritual experiences in camp settings because of an intentional withdrawal into an environment where seeking and praising God, asking questions, and developing faith is encouraged. The common experience, simple solitude, and silence are often a catalyst for intense growth.

Camp provides opportunities for spiritual development at many age levels. I already mentioned that I have been going to camp all my life. In my early years before I was summer camp age, I attended the annual meetings and the fishing retreats every fall and spring with my family. I played with other young children who also came for the occasion. We hiked, jumped on the beds (for shame!), played games, ate together, worshiped with the adults, and much, much more. We enjoyed candy, created "arts and crafts," played hide-and-seek and truth or dare, and usually ended up getting in some minor trouble. I also remember those retreats as one of the only times of the year that I was allowed to stay up past my usual bedtime. Eleven o'clock seemed deliciously late when I was four years old.

One of these retreat years, I think I was in junior high by then, the new activities center was completed. The children and youth who were present were allowed to put messages and artifacts (such as tree cones) into a time capsule that is positioned in one of the high beam corners of the structure.

As soon as I reached the age when summer camp was a possibility, I packed a month ahead of time in anticipation and excitement. I didn't touch the things I had packed so they would be all ready to go. Camp was the most exciting time of the year, giving me some freedom and independence. When we arrived at camp we could pick a friend with whom to sign up for a cabin and settle in. Often my cabin mates became my closest friends for the week. Many continued as friends the next year and beyond.

Every morning we had the option of getting up early and jumping in the frigid creek water at the swimming hole after singing the "Polar Bear Song:"

> *It's summertime at Drift Creek*
> *And it's forty degrees below.*
> *The polar bears go swimming*
> *Because they love it so.*
> *So early in the morning*
> *They break through ice and snow.*
> *It's summertime at Drift Creek*
> *And it's forty degrees below!*
> *GGRRRRRRRRRR!*

Those who went in every morning received a special prize at the end of the week. The cabin with the most Polar Bears each day won the Polar Bear award which entitled them to take Boris, the stuffed polar bear, back to their cabin until the next morning. In my younger years I thought this was just super. As I got older I decided a shower was good enough for me. Jumping into 45-degree water in the coolness of Oregon mornings can really knock the wind out of you.

"As soon as I reached the age when summer camp was a possibility, I packed a month ahead of time in anticipation and excitement."

We had chapel every morning in the amphitheatre (think "cathedral of trees" once more!) as long as it wasn't raining, in which case we held it in the indoor chapel. We sang praises to God (some songs more theologically sound than others) and heard a brief meditation by the camp pastor. My favorite times were the planned silence, either together in the amphitheatre or when the pastor sent us into the woods to meditate or pray in personal silence. These were sacred moments of discovery and solace.

Then there was always the good food, cabin cleanup, announcements, quiet time, lots of activities, free time, and all-camp games. And don't forget the talent shows! We reveled in tubing down the creek, the Wet Hike, Hike to the Rock, Hike to the Giants, nature walks, Ultimate Frisbee, soccer, kickball, volleyball, basketball, arts and crafts, singing with Carlos, and the list goes on and on. Activity times provided outlets for rampant energy and fellowship with other campers. Every year we would take one afternoon of the week to have "Olympics" in which we were divided into teams that competed in silly activities like the chubby bunny marshmallow contest, spinning your body around a baseball bat with your forehead on the bat and then trying to run, and the water-balloon toss which always ended with one of the counselors getting doused. The favorite all-camp activity was the treacherous game of Capture the Flag. Nothing beat running around with faces painted and trying to capture the flag of the other team. Plenty of people (myself included) received anything from minor scrapes to torn muscles or broken bones, but it was still always so fun.

Fireside concluded every glorious day either outside around the fire ring close to the creek or in the Activities Center if it was raining, not unusual in the coastal rain forest. Everyone bundled up, applied their mosquito repellant, and came to sing their hearts out. Singing was always one of the most moving times for me. Hearing all our voices together creating

harmonies and praising the God of love was an incredible experience. I distinctly remember sitting at the fire ring staring up into the treetops and singing, "How lovely on the mountains are the feet of them..." and feeling God present right there with us. Counselors sometimes shared their stories or the camp pastor provided us with thoughtful homilies and I never left a week of camp unchanged. I was filled with a spirit of awe and wonder at those firesides. I sensed God's work among us and in me.

"I distinctly remember sitting at the fire ring staring up into the treetops and singing, 'How lovely on the mountains are the feet of them...' and feeling God present right there with us."

There were also the difficult parts of summer camp—those tumultuous years of adolescence with all its stresses, the campers or counselors who made you feel left out, and other such rough times. But even the hardships brought opportunity for growth. I experienced more grace in the trials at camp than in the difficult relationships back at school. I attribute this to the staff and the safe environment created at camp.

The summer counselors were always so cool and significant to me. I looked up to them as mentors and wanted to be like them someday. Upon reaching the age that I could start volunteering as a summer counselor, I convinced my parents to give me a few more weeks off from helping them in our nursery business so that I could work at Drift Creek. I worked at Drift Creek Camp every summer I could through late high school and college, which ended up being five summers in all. My roles ranged from dishwasher along with junior counselor my first summer all the way to program director in my final summer. New activities were introduced over time. Some of the key changes in the years I worked at camp were initiatives (group dynamic exercises and challenge courses), the climbing wall, and "Stories with Jen."

Drift Creek Camp allowed me the opportunity to develop leadership skills and overcome old insecurities. I was able to use the gifts I have been given and share them with others. I learned from fellow staff members and we supported and rejoiced with one another through the good times as well as the tenuous days. It was always an honor to share the hope, peace, love, and joy of Jesus Christ with campers and other staff members.

At some point along the way, my extended families also began having reunions at Drift Creek Camp. Everyone would unload at camp for a weekend and play games, hike trails, reacquaint themselves with one another, and take full advantage of the marvelous setting. These were always times of fun and fellowship, experiencing the Spirit through common ties and, as ever, God's creation. Two of my cousins also decided to get married at camp, so I had the joy of being in weddings in that setting that were really just a big reunion of friends coming to celebrate the joining of loved ones!

All I have experienced at Drift Creek Camp has been foundational in forming and molding my theology and who I am. The memories I hold from camp remind me how I have grown over the years, as well as how I have come to know our Creator more fully through my experiences. Going to camp always means going to God. Through the firesides, stories told and shared, songs, friendships, activities, and sitting among large trees in silence I have found a God who loves me and wants a personal relationship with me. I have known God through the people I have met and the friendships formed. I have known God in the beauty of creation.

I will continue to go back to Drift Creek Camp at least once a year, simply to visit its natural beauty and to experience God's presence there. Each time I retreat to that sacred location, I am encouraged to make space in my life to listen again for God's voice in the silent moments.

Chapter 2

Where in the World of Nature Do We Find God?

By Larry Eby

"Wouldn't this be a great place to have a condo?" The question left us almost speechless. Our only immediate response could be, "But it wouldn't be the same!"

The setting was Drift Creek Camp in the Oregon Coastal Mountains rain forest. We were hosting a men's rental group. Overwhelmed by the awesome beauty around us, the speaker meant it as a compliment. Yet we felt somehow that the idea showed a misdirected appreciation. We recalled another person who questioned us about our recycling program. This led to a conversation about our appreciation of nature and the need for wilderness, something in abundance in the Drift Creek environment. This person's question was, "But what good is wilderness if no one sees it?" Our spontaneous but perhaps inspired answer was, "But the animals see it."

As people get farther away from the land and focus more on material advancement, increasingly nature is viewed for its utilitarian value to humans. This is reflected in the above questions. Nature and the earth's resources are seen as the raw material for humans to use as they wish,

This idea is reflected in a different way when we think that the **primary** reason for the camp experience is to get people into a setting where they can be intellectually and emotionally more receptive to the ideas we want to teach them. At Drift Creek Camp we hosted rental groups who used the camp to preach to vulnerable adolescents the message of the gospel as accepting Jesus as an escape from hellfire. These groups spoke of the beauty around them but gave little affirmation for what nature might teach them of the love of the Creator. A more common, more subtle motif can be expressed in camp singing such as "our God is an awesome God that rules in heaven above with power and love." Both situations use the awesome setting of nature to make a point that at best misunderstands or misinterprets the presence of a loving, creating God all around us, placing the Creator in some remote heavenly scene.

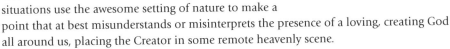

"This person's question was, 'But what good is wilderness if no one sees it?'"

Is this human-centered viewpoint what the Genesis writer had in mind with these words in *Genesis 2:15, "The Lord God took the (hu)man(s) and put them in the garden of Eden to till it and keep it."* In the verses before and after that God creates the rest of the cosmos and sees it to be good. Humans are to care for it and in doing that to share it with all creation.

Mennonite camping began at a time when concern for the environment took a back burner to spiritual nurture and evangelism as the focus of the camp experience. The development of the environmental movement in the last half of the 20th century carried over into the Mennonite Church and was especially nurtured, developed, and promoted by camping people. With the organization of the Mennonite Camping Association in 1960, nature as a place to encounter God and learn about God gained attention.

As noted in *A Vision and a Legacy* by Jess Kauffman, in 1970 a group of nearly one hundred persons from the inter-Mennonite camping community met in a Conference on Camping Philosophy. Their full statement of nine main points on pages 140-141 of that book is comprehensive and God-centered, with emphasis on the uniqueness of the camp experience.

A condensed statement from that conference follows:

Christian camping focuses on learning through relationships in the context of experiencing nature as interpreted and understood in the light of God's Word. Thus programming and counseling take seriously: First, the opportunity of confronting campers with Jesus Christ and commitment to his way of life. Second, interpersonal relationships in real life situations as an agenda for growth in understanding, acceptance of others, wholesome attitudes toward oneself, the church, and the world. Third, the natural environment, cultivating appreciation for it, developing skills in using it, caring for it with a sense of stewardship, and responding in worship to the God who created it.

*(From **A Vision and a Legacy** by Jess Kauffman, Newton, Kan.: Faith and Life Press, 1984, p. 142)*

> *"...the camp environment adds the third element, namely land, and that creates a unique but important aspect of the church's ministry. Proclamation and nature of the land are provided in the camp setting. "*

In the years since that Conference, Mennonites have paid more attention to the place of the environment in the Anabaptist/Mennonite scene. The development of the Mennonite Environmental Task Force and presently the Mennonite Creation Care Network have created forums for developing, sharing, and reflecting on God and creation in relation to our spiritual experience and to the environment. This book includes some of these ideas in the major chapters by Tim Lehman, Jennifer Gingerich, and Darryl Neustaedter-Barg. Reflections of other persons connected with Mennonite teaching and other institutions follow.

Ted Hiebert in an address in 1995 at a Mennonite-sponsored Creation Summit stressed the profound meaning of the creation story, especially the second one in Genesis 2, with humans formed out of the topsoil of the earth, the same substance from which all surrounding life was formed. Humans were to care for and till the soil for the benefit not only of themselves but so that all of creation could be valued and preserved.

Gayle Gerber Koontz at a Mennonite Camping Association annual meeting at Amigo Center in Michigan suggested a similar idea. She used the phrase, "dust between our toes," to emphasize the relationship of humanity to the world. She suggested camping as a unique and powerful way to experience our primal connection to our origin from the things nature is made of. (See **Theology of Mennonite Camping** by Jim Penner in Chapter 8 of this book.)

In Chapter 4 Tim Lehman speaks of Mennonite Camps as "knowing places," different for each of us in our settings and different to us at different times.

In *A Theology for Christian Camping* (Newton, Kans.: 1977) Helmut Harder asks, "What is unique about the camp setting compared to other places of worship and religious education?" He resonates with Lehman's idea of "knowing places," Hiebert's of humans as of one substance with all surrounding life, and Koontz' "dust between our toes." Harder believes that in the camp setting one particular biblical theme is highlighted—the interrelationship of God, persons, and land. Each ingredient is appropriate. God is essential in a church camp. The interrelationship of persons influences our programming. These two things are normative in most church programs but the camp environment adds the third element, namely land and that creates a unique but important aspect of the church's ministry. Proclamation and nurture of the land are provided in the camp setting.

Harder acknowledges that some camping programs have the same agenda as other church programs such as Sunday school or vacation Bible school. So why have camping? He believes that camping provides the foundation for a Christian understanding of the relationship among God, persons, and land:

· God is Creator. The emphasis is on God's current as well as past presence with creation.

- The creation is orderly; everything has its time, place, and purpose. Teaching campers to respect their natural settings supports the creative program God has in mind for the universe.
- People are to have dominion over creation. We are to care for it within our power to do so. The earth is a trust from God. The camp setting provides the opportunity to teach campers by word and example to live upon the earth as persons who are thankful for the Creator's gift, the earth.
- To have dominion is to serve. We are placed upon this earth to serve each other for mutual benefit.
- Sin is still sin. There is a temptation to disregard the Creator and attempt to raise ourselves above our God-given level.
- The promise is fulfilled. Genesis 1 still stands as God's intension for the created world. The fulfillment of the promise comes through Jesus Christ who lived perfectly in the created order. He expressed a respect for all God's creatures.
- More fulfillment is to come. We anticipate a new heaven and a new earth. We await the peaceable kingdom of God in which the full community of love will be realized. We take comfort that Jesus has gone before us to prepare the way.

Harder asks, "How can the Christian camp develop these concepts?" He suggests the camp setting should provide a context for the learning experience in which the Christian church can:

- Communicate its biblical understanding of the theology of creation.
- Lead campers to express an attitude of praise/humility and obedience/responsibility toward their Creator.
- Invite campers to express their repentance for having fallen from the purpose God has for humankind, and to receive forgiveness through Jesus Christ.
- Train campers to express responsible attitudes toward the created world in the context of fostering the harmony in nature intended by God.
- Provide a setting where Christian attitudes of caring and sharing can be learned and experienced.

In the *Educational News Bulletin* (General Conference Mennonite Church), James Ruesser defined camping as an integral part of the Christian education program of the church alongside Sunday school, summer Bible school, and weekly instruction. But it ought not duplicate, or be an extension of these other arms of the church. **Church camping is "the church of the outdoors"**. Because of its unique setting, camping holds unique opportunities in the church's education program. The effective camp program will take full advantage of the uniqueness of the camp experience to lead children, young people, and adults to commit themselves to following Christ as disciples.

"Teaching campers to respect their natural settings supports the creative program God has in mind for the universe."

In James' interpretation, the uniqueness of camping is:

- Its situation in nature. The camper's week at camp is probably the only time during the year that many children and young people live (eat, sleep, and play) in the out-of-doors, close to God's creation. Fifty-one weeks are spent in the midst of human creation. The week at camp presents the unique opportunity to discover again the beauty, usefulness, and harmony of God's handiwork.
- A concentrated 24-hour-a-day experience. A week at camp provides as much time for Christian education as is available in a year of Sunday school.
- Controlled Christian community living. The camper eats, sleeps, talks, works, and worships with his/her own age group and with mature Christian leaders, away from the influences, sights, and sounds of the usual secular, materialistic culture.

· A relaxed atmosphere. Campers are offered relief from the pressure and routine of their normal home and school life. Camp should be a retreat from the complex and human-made world of modern civilization to the simple and God-given world of nature.

"Everything that happens at camp is program," Reusser says, "worship, a nature hike, a cookout, sleeping, swimming, classes, a campfire challenge, deep sharing after the lights are turned out at night." The fact that camp provides a total natural living situation makes possible many types of experiences that can lead to Christian growth. Thus a campfire where campers learn to cooperate and to depend on each other may be more significant in learning about fellowship and group living than a discussion or a vesper speaker. A quiet half-hour contemplating the wonders of the constellations or the intricacies of a flower may inspire more true worship and awe for God than a planned worship service, assuming that theological understandings are provided.

> *"Everything that happens [at camp] is program," Reusser says, "worship, a nature hike, a cookout, sleeping, swimming, classes, a campfire challenge, deep sharing after the lights are turned out at night."*

Reusser discusses the Objectives of Camping as developed by the GCMC Retreat Committee. Like any educational experience, the camp program must have clear objectives.

General Objective. Church camping fosters personal growth by providing an experience of Christian living through which campers share understandings of Christian principles and teachings, commit themselves to Christ, and develop their own program of personal growth and Christian action.

· Specific Objective 1. The church camp endeavors to bring the camper into a personal, living relationship with God, to foster Christian growth, and to provide resources for growth.
· Specific Objective 2. The church camp endeavors to provide a 24-hour-a-day experience in peer-group living based on the Christian concept of love for Christ and a respect for individual worth through which the camper may gain a sense of values by simple living in small groups and may become a responsible member of the church and his/her community.
· Specific Objective 3. The church camp endeavors to provide an experience of living in the out-of-doors through which campers may discover the laws of God operating in the universe and develop a keener awareness and appreciation of God's handiwork as they acquire new skills, knowledge, and enjoyment in contacts with nature, thereby gaining a deeper appreciation for God as Creator and Sustainer.
· Specific Objective 4. The church camp endeavors to provide time and stimulus for contemplation seemingly not always possible in other aspects of life; to provide ways and to develop habits, skills, and motives for Christian service and leadership in each camper.

The experiences that result in the achievement of these objectives at camp do not just happen; they must be planned. We must discover how to motivate campers to want these experiences, and provide opportunities for them to respond and become involved.

In "Beyond the Printed Word: The Reality of Camp Curriculum" (see Chapter 8 of this book), Eleanor Snyder writes about camp curriculum having three important parts: the printed resource materials (What do they teach? Are they consistent with our theology and values?), the curriculum of the camp staff (What the child sees the child does. What the child does the child is.), and God's creation. (The latter provides natural opportunities for children to meet God through exploration of the great outdoors, through experiences of prayer, singing, playing, journaling, sitting in silence, and observing God's world.)

Camping, if done in relationship and a consciousness of our presence in connection to the natural environment, can sensitize us to experiences that turn the ordinary into the extraordinary, or perhaps the awesome into something that can communicate to us in

extraordinary ways. One of the incredible aspects of the globe on which we live in contrast to the other known planets is the atmosphere of moisture crucial to all of life. This atmosphere includes the clouds that billow in remarkable ways into the sky. One late summer evening, as Larry was traveling west across the North Dakota plains on Amtrak's Empire Builder passenger train, a beautiful sunset spread itself across the western sky. The following words express his feelings for The Moment:

"Suddenly my eyes were captured by a scene that I could only receive as a gift that turned into the following verse."

PRAIRIE SUNSET RELECTIONS
By Larry Eby, 1995

In the Western Dakota sky
broken clouds reflect the retreating sunlight

One, the silhouette of a happy pig, appears…
but only for a moment; the sun's angle changes.

And the pig? Out of alignment.
Just another grey wisp of condensed moisture.

Gone its moment in the sun. For that fleeting moment
reflecting to receiving eyes revealed beauty,
the art of nature.

We also are creation's art;
in proper alignment, reflecting beauty,
catching rays of the Creator;
out of alignment, dull, just one of the crowd.

Finally, the full sun falls into view,
too bright for human eyes.

Is the true nature of the Creator best seen in reflection?

"Camping, if done in relationship and a consciousness of our presence in connection to the natural environment, can sensitize us to experiences that turn the ordinary into the extraordinary, or perhaps the awesome into something that can communicate to us in extraordinary ways."

Chapter 3

Rooted in Relationships, MCA 1980-2005

This is a shared chapter written in successive segments, the first by David Helmuth who in his role with Mennonite Board of Congregational Ministries (MBCM) represented the Mennonite Church on the MCA Board. The second author, Mary Jane Eby as President-elect, President, and Past-president was on the MCA Board for six years during the nineties. From those experiences, researching many documents and interviewing people they have written the following anecdotally-illustrated commentary on relationships between Mennonite Camping Association and the camping/ecology movement in the Mennonite Church for the past 25 years.

First by David Helmuth

Orie O. Miller in a letter to Paul Mininger in 1934 wrote: "Our young people are in need of help and in most communities are not getting it."

In 1984, Armond Ball wrote in *Camping Magazine:* "Today's child who will come to camp this summer is more afraid than has been the case for several decades…what a challenge we face in the way we deal with children in terms of their attitudes and their feeling of safety, trust and peace." What would Armond have written today?

MCA, which began in 1960, brought together camps and their personnel to continue responding to the needs not only of children and youth but also eventually of adults across the life span.

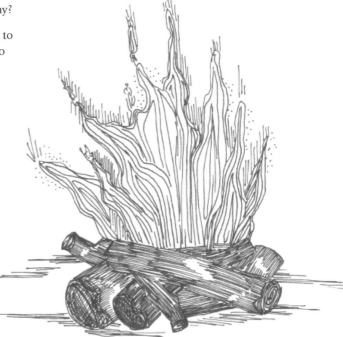

In 1977, Mennonite camp visionary, Virgil Brenneman, then executive secretary of the MCA, summarized the value of church camps and retreat centers as:

1. Church camping is education—a setting for Christian nurture.
2. The church camp is an extraordinary leadership training resource for the church.
3. The Christian camp is an opportunity to help the church meet the challenges of the "new leisure."
4. The camping program is uniquely suited to model the church's goals with regard to the simple life-style, conflict resolution, the building of community, the teaching of stewardship of creation and an awareness of a responsibility regarding natural resources.

From 30 Camps to Nearly 100!

From the beginning, MCA was an interMennonite organization and during the '80s it grew quickly adding camps from both the U.S. and Canada. The quarterly *MCA Newsletter* provided the communication link for sharing ideas, concerns, special needs, and special programs including the fast developing bi-annual Regional Meetings of the MCA. The May '83 newsletter reported that if all our Mennonite camps in North America were used to capacity on any given day there may be as many as 10,000 campers in attendance with 3000 staff required!

Ongoing Concern and Involvement with Christian Education

During the 1981 meeting of the district Christian Education Cabinets of the Mennonite Church prior to the General Assembly at Bowling Green, Ohio, Christian education leaders expressed a strong interest in dialogue with camp leaders on a more regular and formal

way. This interest was affirmed, supported and facilitated by MBCM (Mennonite Church) and Commission on Education (General Conference Mennonite Church) staff.

During the decade of the '80s there were numerous meetings with dialogue between church and camp leaders in relation to Christian education; often these meetings were held in a camp setting. Churchwide Christian education staff often planned teacher training events and curriculum planning sessions including the training of writers for the new Jubilee Sunday School curriculum at a camp facility making good use of the environment and other resources in the camp setting.

During the '80s camp leaders made various efforts to develop a curriculum for use by camps. One such effort was reported in 1982. "Camps with Meaning", a trio of camps in Manitoba made an offer of the curriculum they had developed called *"Freed by the Spirit"* to all MCA camps. Later in 1989 several of our MCA leaders participated in Passage 2000, an interdenominational event for leaders in outdoor ministries. *"Come Follow Me"* was the first series developed under the umbrella title of *"Sow Seeds: Trust the Promise."* This apparently was used by some of our camps. *(Editor's note: See Jim Penner's account of such a meeting in Chapter 7.)*

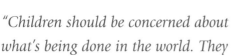

"Children should be concerned about what's being done in the world. They are going to inherit it!"

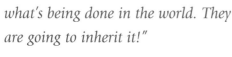

Concern for the Environment

In 1982, the May issue of the *MCA Newsletter* told the story of 10 year old Manuela Pinho de Azevedo Sousa from Brazil. She had been "sounding off" at protest demonstrations and T.V. interviews since she was 7 years old. She said, "Children should be concerned about what's being done in the world. They are going to inherit it! If adults keep destroying the environment, there won't be anything left for us when we're grown up." (As she talked she played with her teddy bear and pet turtle.) Later Manuela, with the help of her parents who are professionals, founded a group called, "Children in Defense of Nature". What happened to Manuela is that someone listened to her.!

It was this ongoing concern for a wide range of environmental issues that led MCA and Outdoor Ministries of the Church of the Brethern to co-sponsor the 1982 Christian Camping Convention held at Camp Amigo near Sturgis, Michigan. The theme was "Toward a Peaceable Kingdom" with Don Miller, professor of Bible and Christian Education at the Church of the Brethern Seminary in Chicago as the main plenary sessions input person.

There was great response from the 124 registered participants from 36 camps along with 15 college and seminary students from several Mennonite and Church of the Brethern colleges and seminaries. The 12 workshops offered were resourced by college and seminary personnel including David Augsberger and others from Associated Mennonite Biblical Seminary. It was an important event that seemed to nudge MCA camps more fully into our common Anabaptist theological underpinnings! During the '80s this concern and interest was kept alive in some of our camps, especially since some of the MCA Board Members attended events of the American Camp Association which offered workshops and resources in this area of concern.

Food, Fellowship, Fun, and a Practical Tip from Jess

Once while I was at Rocky Mountain Camp for a MCA event in the early eighties, Jess Kauffman, Virgil Brenneman, and I along with several others took our tents, food and gear one afternoon to hike into the mountains behind the camp. We hiked, cooked our evening meal over the fire, talked, fellowshipped and had fun together after the day's meetings. The afternoon was warm but the evening and the next morning were chilly with water freezing overnight. While several of our group of five went skinny dipping, Jess and I got the

morning fire ready for breakfast as the day dawned. I gathered wood and was looking for some birch bark to start the fire when Jess pulled out a small can with kerosene-soaked sawdust in it. "Here", he said, "this is simpler and more effective." Placing several table-spoons of sawdust under the tepee of wood, the fire started and the sawdust served as a wick until the other wood ignited! Cool, I thought! Ever since, both at home with the fireplace as well as in many camping experiences, I remember Jess when I build a fire! To be with outdoor/camp pioneers like Jess and Virgil is to experience a presence and feel reverence for what the outdoors is all about! What a privilege!

MCA Camps – A "Safe" Setting for the Discussion of "Unsafe" Issues

Often there were meetings of persons concerned for and working with some of the predominate issues of the decade such as "integration", human sexuality, the role of women in church leadership, abortion, payment of war taxes, *etcetera*.

Laurelville Mennonite Church Center in particular, operated by an association without official ties to a church conference, programmed and hosted events that invited participants that often were on the margins of the church and society. There were a host of these: a retreat for the deaf, retreat for families with children with disabilities, singles' retreat, persons with same sex orientation who struggled with this issue and with their relationship to the church of which they were a part. MCA, through camps like Laurelville and others, made a significant contribution to the life of the larger church. (LMCC became something of our "Camp David"!)

The year Regional Meetings did not meet was the year for the church-wide MCA Camping Convention. The MCA Board members really "stepped to the plate" during the '80s after having a half-time executive secretary for five years (1974-1979). By this time MCA camps realized, to a greater extent, the importance of MCA and, in particular, of having a regular newsletter to keep the camps in touch with each other. MBCM, via the availability of some staff time, was an important element in keeping this important work going, especially after there was no paid executive secretary due to lack of sufficient funding support. MBCM staffers, Marlene Kropf and Evon Castro, played an important role in keeping camp membership fees up to date as well as helping the *MCA Newsletter* get published and to all the camps, especially during this transition time and they are still involved with MCA today. The General Conference Commission on Education was also very supportive to our camps and to the work of MCA, especially providing funds through their budget.

"The 80s were a time of increasing numbers of retreats of all kinds in many camps, some of which focused more on retreat planning than on the more traditional age-specific camp programs."

The '80s were a time of increasing numbers of retreats of all kinds in many camps, some of which focused more on retreat planning than on the more traditional age-specific camp programs. According to Marlene Kropf, there were women's retreats, men's retreats, and quite a number of contemplative spirituality retreats.

Surviving and Thriving Through the Wilderness

"Outdoor wilderness living, canoeing and back packing helped me survive and even thrive through a very difficult time of my life," said good friend Virgil Brenneman. I asked him to explain.

"My wife, Helen, became ill with Multiple Sclerosis at a fairly young age. We, with our four children, enjoyed many auto camping trips together in settings of state and national parks, and national forest camp grounds across the country. All of that ended when Helen

was no longer able to travel. As her illness progressed, and the prospect of her needing nursing home care loomed over our heads, I faced a very difficult change in my life, feeling lost and lonely and discouraged. But when I took up wilderness trips with canoes on water, or backpacks in forests or mountains, I experienced healing and strong survival desires. I continued to hike, camp, canoe, and walk or bike, and that was my survival...yes, even more, I thrived despite and maybe because I had a serious problem – a diseased heart. The continued discipline of staying in shape, carrying all my gear and food but much more, the fellowship of community with other outdoor persons became my lifeline! It was physical survival, but also emotional and spiritual survival! Living in the great outdoors is healing. It is a gift!"

"Trucking It" With John Blucker to Meet the Train

We had a great time at the bi-annual meeting of MCA at Camp Mennoscah in Kansas. Rich Oswald, John Blucker (Camp Amigo staff) and I (representing the church-wide Mennonite Board of Congregational Ministries) traveled by train to Newton, Kans., which was fairly close to the camp. We had a wonderful time as we always did, but by the end of the last day, the three of us were ready to travel back East. We were in Newton by 10 p.m. and had a little over an hour to wait for our 11:30 p.m. train. We walked up town and sat down to have coffee and donuts and to reflect on the happenings of the weekend. Suddenly a half hour before our train was due, we heard a whistle and it was an approaching train from the West going East. We were 10-15 minutes from the train station! So leaving our coffee and donuts on the table, we sent our fastest runner (Rich Oswald) on ahead, and John and I trucked along as fast as we could go (slower than Rich). Arriving at the train station, Rich announced that Newton had more than one train going through from the West and this was not it. Ours would come later as scheduled. John did put his big cowboy boots in gear and I could hardly keep up!

"The church hopes for many things from camps. It's only fair that camps should be able to expect certain things from the church as well."

This important decade saw our MCA camps increasingly become more like retreat centers, but at the same time some programmed for off-the-campground events like canoe trips to the Boundary Waters of Minnesota via Wilderness Wind camp and other kinds of wilderness events like backpack hikes. Biking was popular. Our camps were now doing year-round programming for children and adults. To be sure, all MCA camps had budget concerns, and so to some degree their programs were "market-driven" in order to survive even though there was growing church support for the camping and retreat programs. Some camps during this time saw the opportunity to provide for outdoor education experiences for public schools at the elementary level. This helped with the budget as well as being a valid way of community-based ministry.

Near the 30th birthday of MCA, Marlene Kropf, staff person in Congregational Education, Worship and Spirituality for the MBCM, wrote in the *MCA Newsletter* (1990) that what the church wants from camps is:

1. To be aware of faith development stages and respond accordingly to the unique needs of each stage.
2. To nurture affective as well as cognitive dimensions of faith.
3. To feel free to confront campers with a call to commitment.
4. To keep pastors and other congregational leaders informed about important faith growth that happens at camp.
5. To address "unsafe" issues which are often neglected in local congregations.
6. To provide a hospitable space for ongoing groups in the church (Sunday School classes, church councils, women's groups etc.) to meet together and deepen their faith, and their relationships with each other.

The church hopes for many things from camps. It's only fair that camps should be able to expect certain things from the church as well: prayer support, willing volunteers, capable staff, generous finances, seasoned counsel and wisdom. Then a mutually enriching partnership with the church and the camp can help to fulfill Jesus' call to make disciples and bring glory to God.

The following is written by Mary Jane Eby, but opens with the testimony of a youth couselor, Caitie Picket, "God's Hand is Never Still."

God's Hand Is Never Still
We floated on darkness, where the distinction between the water below and the night sky above was unclear. And as the stars shot and burned down the heavens, my soul sister and I sang to the God who had created all that was beautiful in this world; a God who can shift the foundations of the earth; a God whose hand extends from the center of our hearts to beyond the edges of infinity; a God who became flesh and dwelt among us.

One year ago, my Mom went to be with the Lord. It hurt, but God carried me through that time, and I knew that without God I would have lost hope. And as I stared at the camp application this spring, I could hear myself loud and clear, "Me? A camp counselor? No way, God! Ask someone else, OK?" But God asked for my life, and beyond the excuses my heart knew there was a deep hunger in me to do something that might last longer than a week. I hear the message, "Have I not asked of you, be strong, and courageous. Do not be afraid, or discouraged. For the Lord your God will be with you wherever you go."

Where did the Lord take me in my summer of being a counselor? From sunburns to skinned knees, from laughter to tears, I found even with my many failures, God could use me. I learned that the family of God extends past my church, past my relatives, even around the world. God's hand is never still, though it does not depend on emotional out-pourings or lightening bolts to move hearts in wonderful ways.

Now that I am at College, I praise God as the Healer for healing hearts of those who came to camp with burdens and joys and were able to seek God's face for the first time. The summer camp ministry is a place built on sharing God's love in the context of God's beautiful creation and is a place to experience God's gentle hands of healing.

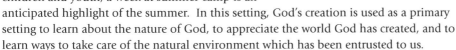

"The summer camp ministry is a place built on sharing God's love in the context of God's beautiful creation and is a place to experience God's gentle hands of healing."

Youth and Camping
"The camping experience for youth is not complete until you have served on staff at a summer camp," stated Jeremy after his dad, Abe Bergen, asked him to reflect on the ways in which camping equips youth for leadership responsibilities in the church. For many children and youth, a week at summer camp is an anticipated highlight of the summer. In this setting, God's creation is used as a primary setting to learn about the nature of God, to appreciate the world God has created, and to learn ways to take care of the natural environment which has been entrusted to us.

Camping ministry is an extension of congregational life that provides an opportunity for campers to get to know Jesus and commit to His way of life. To develop supportive relationships, and to return home with memorable faith experiences.

Leadership Training

There is another benefit of camping ministry – the leadership training that happens for camp staff. Many times one will not notice development of leadership skills as a camp goal or objective. However, the '90s became a time in camp ministry when there was a renewed awareness in recognizing the positive impact leadership responsibilities have for the young staff. Abe Bergen, Director of Youth Ministry, Winnipeg, Manitoba, proposes that youth who become involved as summer camp leaders grow significantly because of these five expectations:

1. Youth become responsible for other people.
   At camp the counselor is expected to be responsible for a cabin of campers for 24 hours a day, five days in a row. They become the ones who take care of hurts, home-sickness, providing comfort and support, This diverse cabin group needs to become a community in one week. Cabin leaders are challenged to become creative, respon-sible and deal with difficult challenges. The staffer is stretched regardless of experience.

"Many teens in camp leadership will have discussed faith issues but being a camp leader may be the first time they are required to verbalize what they believe to others."

2. Youth are required to articulate their faith.
   Many teens in camp leadership will have discussed faith issues BUT being a camp leader may be the first time they are required to verbalize what they believe to others. The opportunities to share their faith are numerous: devotions, Bible lessons, campfire, and the many questions campers ask. Praying in public may be a new experience. While this may produce anxiety, such opportunities to share faith and offer prayers help the young counselors to deepen their own faith.

3. Youth become conscious of being role models.
   Being role models creates some pressure for youth to pay attention to what they say and do. It encourages them to be more intentional in their actions and words.

4. Opportunities to exercise leadership gifts.
   For a variety of gifts such as to lead singing, organize games, lead nature walks, and crafts, spontaneous leadership is required. Youth gain self-confidence which in turn enhances their self-image as their leadership skills emerge.

5. Youth find a place to be needed.
   Young people appreciate feeling their contribution makes a difference. God uses the young counselor to impact the lives of many children and in the process they learn much about responsibility, grow in their faith and develop confidence as leaders.

Sacred Journeys to Sacred Places

In late 1992, MCA participated in a Mennonite Churchwide Christian Education Symposium – Education 2000. Mary Elizabeth Moore, Professor at Claremont, California School of Theology, was a main plenary speaker. The following is a summary of her lecture.

Outdoor ministries have to do with sacred journeys to sacred places. This is a journey outside our normal environments, routines and communities into a new environment, a new routine and a new community. Then we return home again. Camping and outdoor ministries introduce people to a new world, often an idealistic or utopian world.

Camp is a place to be free to try new roles and different ways of relating; and its communal lifestyle is counter-cultural in that it is less structured, hierarchy is minimized and social relations are maximized. Camping and outdoor ministry share the same nature as pilgrimages in the early Christian church, where on the road to sacred places the rich, the poor, the powerful and the humble became an intentional community outside the restrictions of their normal social structures.

"...where on the road to sacred places the rich, the poor, the powerful, and the humble became an intentional community outside the restrictions of their normal social structures."

We think of this as a "sacred place" in camping. The wisdom of the past and the "vision" of the future are bound up in camp as we experience the sense of God pulling us to something more. This model of camp experiences challenges us to have a vision of how we ought to live all the time, encouraging us to reflect on our camp ministries as we are responsible agents of transformation. Our camp ministry needs to point in the direction of God's new creation.

Dr. Moore outlined three gifts she believes Mennonites have to share with the Christian community:

1. Standing against culture as an alternative lifestyle in today's world
2. Making peace central to the gospel
3. Living so as to give an example of what church community can be

"Violence in our world is greater than ever," Moore told participants. *"Mennonites have a vision and a model for peace that can influence the rest of the world."*

Ralph Swartzentruber, Program Director at Camp Hebron, Pa. who attended said, "I will approach curriculum differently because of this conference. It puts things in perspective for me." "I'm psyched and my staff will be excited before summer starts," echoed Jim Penner, Director of Silver Lake Mennonite Camp in Ontario, Canada.

Seeking, Receiving, Reflecting

A question and concern expressed by some persons was "if there is no difference between Mennonite Camp Ministry and all of the other camps out there, there is no reason for our existence." By 1994, as camp leaders responded to an MCA survey, the voices of individuals and camps made it clear that there is a difference. These statements reflected a collective desire to maintain an Anabaptist tradition and theology within camp ministry.

By the winter of 1995, the MCA Board of Directors sensed the need to develop a theology for the Mennonite Camp/Retreat Ministry in the form of a Vision Statement. "It is the Board members' hopes that this Vision Statement will bind us together and give us focus as we strive to do the things we do as camps and retreat centers," said Jim Penner, *MCA Newsletter* Editor. "Camp Ministry meets a need that no other part of the church can meet."

An Invitation to Share the Vision

As Mennonite Camping Association (MCA) celebrated 35 years of promoting Mennonite church camp/retreat interests, I was asked, as the new president, to give leadership to the development of a Vision Statement. Like numerous other organizations who were concerned to bring clarity to their planning, we believed it was important for MCA to also see this as an opportunity to look at the past and build for the future.

"Why does MCA need a vision statement now?" some asked. One hope was to build a sense of shared loyalty. Although we represent diverse camps and retreat ministries, we share the experience of finding importance in being a part of the Anabaptist faith community. A Vision Statement inspires as well as informs and mobilizes us together into the future. A mission statement, by contrast, provides us an identity as the MCA, who we are now and whom we serve.

At the 1996 Biennial Convention the MCA Board of Directors presented a proposed Vision Statement for discussion by the assembled members. Additionally camp leaders were encouraged to take the statement back to their Boards of Directors for study and discussion and were asked to submit comments to be addressed at the 1997 Regional gatherings.

The regional MCA meetings in 1997 were filled with lively discussions with many suggestions (a few are listed below) that have been included in the final Vision Statement.

1. One person advised that we may not need a Vision Statement but a "Vision!"
2. "Real vision is best stated, not on a wall poster, but a live part of camp ministry."
3. "Live your Vision" before you plaster it all over your camp/retreat center.

"Though the VISION has been carefully written and chosen, it is not set in stone," commented MCA president, Mary Jane Eby at that time. "The statement is one that will and must change over time. As language changes we face the challenge of keeping our words contemporary even if the ideas remain the same. In a few years we may need a new vision, a new opportunity to discern our direction along our faith journey."

"Many Strands, One Web," the MCA Vision Statement, 1998

The September to November months are times for spider webs. Dewdrops hang on the threads like tiny ornaments. The sunrise catches the droplets and set the entire filament sparkling like a chandelier. One really cannot touch any part of that web without moving every other part. All parts are interconnected. Can we fathom what's going on 24 hours of each day in all parts of God's creation? There is that connectedness when we confess God as Creator of the universe of which we are one tiny part.

Camps and congregations experience that connection as partners in educational ministry. Both are about nurturing faith and building community.

The Mennonite Camping Association adopted the VISION statement at the March 1998 Biennial Convention at Camp Arnes, Manitoba.

Commenting on the finalizing of the Vision Statement, Mary Jane Eby shared her thoughts: "Hopefully we will not become over-burdened with a concern about our correctness in writing a MCA Vision but to continue to be challenged with a desire to have the Vision of God. Perhaps God's Vision cannot be described in our language of dichotomies, where we are so prone to say; 'this is right and that is wrong, this is productive and that is unproductive.' The essence of camp/retreat ministry is action that invigorates one to 'step forward', to grasp opportunities when another may see problems, to seek solutions when others want to escape. May we ask to see through God's eyes?"

The gospel of Jesus Christ comes only by seeing things as God sees them. May this MCA Vision be a gift for each of us to see through new lenses."
(The full vision statement is in the appendix.)

Going Outside the Boundaries

"Periodically we need to free our spirits and God's Spirit for new insights and understandings. God's creation can nurture our souls, renew our minds, and refresh our hearts, if only we dare to venture outside the boundaries of the classroom" said Ken Hawkley, Director of Young Adult Education, Columbus, Ohio. Listed below are some ways Ken suggested to stimulate discussion and encourage new insight with young adults:

1. Use camps for educating. Take your class to camp! Design your own retreat.

2. Combine work and play. Encourage your class to spend time working at the camp. Great things happen when we work and play together. Learning new things about each other helps to strengthen the bond of friendship. The excellent mix of physical exercise and mental reflection while you work, play, and study the Bible brings spiritual fitness.

3. Capitalize on travel time. Make the drive to camp a time for building relationships.

4. Enjoy nature. Take lots of time outdoors. Plan for worship and study in the midst of God's wonderful creation to smell, listen, watch and feel God's natural wonder.

5. Cemetery. Use the church cemetery as a place to think, remember, share, and contemplate. The Old Testament is about remembering the faithful acts of God. What faithfulness might fit with a stroll through the cemetery?

Setting the Stage—1998

by Eleanor Snyder, Kitchener, Ontario, Director of Children's Education,
General Conference Mennonite Church and GCMC Representative MCA Board
in the sCEne, Winter 1997-98, Eleanor Snyder, Editor, Commission on Education, GCMC

Congregations and camps serve as partners in educational ministry. When people enter camp or retreat settings, they often find connection, meaning, identity, perspective and wholeness. Camping is characterized by transformation. Through Christian community and the beauty of creation, people are changed as they encounter God. Many return to their local churches as more committed disciples. Camping thereby enhances the ministry of the local congregation. So…

What Can Congregations Do to Nurture Faith Through Camping?

1. View church-related camp programs as an important and essential component of Christian educational ministry.

2. Discover and discuss the theological orientation of your church camp. Is the camp's theology consistent with your congregation's? How are children invited to faith? Learn about the curriculum being used for study and reflection.

3. Support your area conference church camp with your prayers and finances.

4. Include children's registration fees as part of your annual education budget or through special camp awareness events. Give every child an opportunity to experience camp.

5. Acknowledge and validate the experiences of transformative faith. Give opportunity for campers to share their stories with the congregation, or Sunday School class. Find appropriate ways to validate the decisions made at camp.

6. Encourage members of your congregation to participate in camp life, as counselors, staff, grandparents, cooks, or other leaders. Subsidize salaries for students who want to be volunteers but need assistance.

"Encourage members of your congregation to participate in camp life, as counselors, staff, grandparents, cooks, or other leaders."

33

As the Page Turns—Heading into the Twenty-First Century

The year 2000 was memorable as Mennonite Camping Association celebrated its 40th anniversary, 1960-2000. Camp Hebron, Pennsylvania hosted the biennial convention as Jonathan Larson from Atlanta, GA, through story-telling, guided participants in recognizing the 'holy moments' of camp/retreat ministry. New at the convention was a special all day seminar for Camp Board members, led by Lee Schmucker. Don Rittenhouse, as MCA president-elect, directed the planning of this special celebrative event, but sadly his life was taken in a car accident prior to this time.

Camps Can Teach Congregations to Think Outside the Box

The family retreat speaker asked us to think back to the first time we had an awareness of God's reality. Deb Schrock, director of Camp Luz, Ohio says: "I recalled when I was nine years old and sitting in the same camp at the same fire circle was the night I said 'yes' to Jesus Christ and experienced a profound awareness of God's love. I then spent 29 years having my faith nurtured by a close connection between church and camp."

"As the transformation of the Mennonite Church has taken place, there are new images, words, and ideas emerging."

As the transformation of the Mennonite Church has taken place, there are new images, words, and ideas emerging. The challenge is to become partners as we learn about "Habits of the missional church." There are Bible Circles, accompaniment, peace building, hospitality, and celebration. We read about the focus of Mennonite Church USA and Mennonite Church Canada to be missional. Deb Schrock comments, "As a camp director, I am eager to see how this transformation will look as each congregation, conference and agency discerns the missional activity of God among, around and through them. Many Mennonite camps are between 40-55 years old. These camps can teach congregations about being missional."

MCA has chosen to remain binational, governed by board members from Canada and the United States, even though there is now a Mennonite Church Canada and Mennonite Church USA. Our MCA gatherings have a spirit of cooperation and appreciation.

Keith Zehr, president of MCA, 2002, says: "In these days of uncertainty and the perceived desire for U.S. domination in the world, I am grateful for what I have learned from my Canadian brothers and sisters in the camping ministry. We seek a common missional vision and we learn from each other."

Dateline, 2002, Goshen College Launches CIP

In the March 5, 2002, *The Mennonite,* a news article introduced an exciting new program at Goshen College, the Camping Inquiry Program. In cooperation with Mennonite Camping Association and selected member camps, an internship program to encourage students to consider ministry in camping and retreat programs was launched. This has great potential to support our member camps and camping in general by introducing college students to camp leadership as a calling and vocation. Two articles near the end of Chapter 8 describe this more fully.

MCA Board of Directors Chooses Liaisons

One reason MCA exists is to present a united voice to the Church of the many member retreat centers, camps, individuals and associations in the Anabaptist faith family. Through this give-and-take, the Church can give ear to the concerns of the camping ministry. The Church can also help camps and retreat centers fulfill their roles of expanding upon and supplementing congregational nurture. With this in mind, the MCA Board periodically chooses two persons to serve as camp and church liaisons.

Deb Schrock

Elsie Rempel is representative of Mennonite Church, Canada. She is from Winnipeg, Manitoba. Elsie is Director of Christian Education and Formation. She envisions an interactive relationship with MCA.

Linford King, Lancaster, Pa. is Mennonite Church USA representative on the MCA Board. He is the Denominational Minister on the Congregational and Ministerial Leadership Team of Mennonite Church USA.

2004 – Biennial Convention, Drift Creek Camp, Oregon
What did I miss?

Corbin Graber, Director of Rocky Mountain Mennonite Camp, Colorado says, "MCA gatherings are a mini-sabbatical that uplift and energize our family by connecting with God and God's wonderful people in Mennonite camping. Brochures and websites cannot equal the opportunity to personally experience the setting, facilities, activities and people that make each camp unique!"

"The chance to network around the tables during meals and free time gave us a look into the way other camps operate, a great time of retreat and communion. Hallelujah!"

Alvie and Will Martens, Directors of Camp Moose Lake, Sprague, Manitoba say, "We enjoyed the convention very much; it was our first! Amy and Jerry Markus, DCC directors, were wonderfully relaxed and generous hosts. (Jerry is MCA President.) Marlene Kropf's sessions on the spiritual discernment of call spoke very deeply to us since we, just six months ago, gave up careers and a home to follow a call to a new way of life at Moose Lake Camp. The chance to network around the tables during meals and free time gave us a look into the way other camps operate, a great time of retreat and communion. Hallelujah!"

Mennonite Camping Association at Charlotte 2005

*Adapted from an article **by Grace Nolt** from Spruce Lake Mennonite Camp, MCA Newsletter Editor*

"What's that noise? Listen! Can you hear it? There it is again."

What you hear—if you could put your ear up against the door of the North American Mennonite Church—is the sound of people talking about their experiences with Mennonite Camping. It's the sound of adults counting the number of Mennonite camps that they and their families have visited. It's the sound of young people hanging out around the campfire playing camp songs. It's the sound of 8-year olds saying, "I get to go to camp for the first time this year," with a big smile and their 6-year old brother saying, "Why can't I go too?!"

What You Hear is the Sound of the Impact on People's Lives Made By Mennonite Camping.

Mennonite Camping Association put our ear against that metaphorical door at Charlotte 2005, the joint convention of Mennonite Church Canada and Mennonite Church USA, through a common exhibit and we were blessed to hear the sounds, that together, all 43 MCA members are making in the life of the church.

"Can't Keep Quiet" was the theme of Charlotte 2005, based on the story of Peter and John appearing before the temple council and their response in Acts 4:20: "We cannot stop telling about the wonderful things that we have seen and heard." And people could not stop telling about their experiences with Mennonite Camps.

Throughout the week, attendees stopped by the exhibit to share their most memorable camping stories and their positive affirmations for their camps. Some talked about making faith commitments at camp, of meeting spouses or best friends at camp, and of volunteering at camp. Some talked of growing in their own faith during a camp summer,

while others spoke of seeing their children mature in faith and leadership as a counselor. Still others had stories to reconnecting with family through reunions held at camping facilities. It was an incredible time of witnessing to the ministry of Mennonite Camping and glorifying God.

The MCA "Forest" Exhibit

The physical exhibit was composed of 900+ square feet of outdoor camping moved inside. It was often referred to during the week as the "MCA forest in the corner of the exhibit hall."

Burlap banners, hung twelve feet high surrounding the exhibit on two and a half sides, stood out in the exhibit hall of table-top booths. Visually the banners also helped to create a sense of rest and isolation among the exhibits. With paint and felt, each banner included the camp logo, name, and state/province. Scattered inside the exhibit, over fifteen trees created the forest itself. An electric campfire in a rock fire ring, masked with partially burned logs and surrounded by 8 camp chairs was the central focal point of the exhibit. Many children actually thought it was a real fire until they got close and then had fun running their hands through the silk "flame". Three guitars and a mandolin were available for anyone to try their hand at.

Additionally a 4-foot high rockfall water fountain burbling away, a CD of birdsong and a sleep machine running cricket sounds helped to create the retreat atmosphere.

The MCA exhibit received extensive publicity throughout the convention. On Tuesday, July 5, the local newspaper, *The Charlotte Observer*, ran an article about the convention and included one photograph—a number of MCA hosts sitting around the campfire playing guitars. The caption referenced Mennonite Camping Association. In addition *mPress*, the convention newspaper published by Goshen College daily during the convention, ran an article and photo on Friday, July 8 concerning the MCA forest.

Finally, *mPress* classified ads were purchased daily to draw attendees' attention to the forest in the corner. The exhibit was hosted by a core group of four staff members from Spruce Lake Retreat: Melissa Beidler, Grace Nolt, Dan Ziegler, and Wendy Ziegler.

Camp, a Ministry Like No Other!

As Mennonite Camping Association celebrates 45 years of outdoor ministry in 2006, exploring the potential and possibilities of nurturing faith through activities that affect the body, mind and soul continue. God's vast outdoor classroom invites us all to participate in the wonder, awe and mystery of the Creator and the entire created world. Storytelling/sharing, counselors who make teaching more real, more present, more "here and now," personal experiences from those whose own faith is still growing, is what camping ministry is all about. Through "seeking God's face, receiving God's love and radiating God's Spirit" there is joy to free our spirits and God's spirit for new insights and understandings. God's creation can nurture our souls, renew our minds and refresh our hearts, if only we dare to venture outside the boundaries of the classroom.

"Stop and consider the wondrous works of God" (Job 37:14).

We are challenged to listen to the stories of children, youth, and adults who remember that moment where the sacred burst through, who changed, who experienced conversions, each in a different way as a result of encounters with the living Jesus. "Faith is not transferred by osmosis," it needs to be lived and wrestled with. Youth need to catch and own their faith in their own space. Camping ministry is an extension of congregational life that provides an opportunity for campers to develop, grow and return home with memorable faith experiences.

"Stop and consider the wondrous works of God" (Job 37:14).

Chapter 4

To Know God in This Place
By Tim Lehman

For no one can lay any foundation other than the one that has been laid; that foundation is Jesus Christ.

1 Corinthians 3:11 (NRSV)

But the one who hears and does not act is like a man who built a house on the ground without a foundation. When the river burst against it, immediately it fell, and great was the ruin of that house.

Luke 6:49 (NRSV)

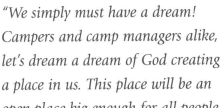

The Dream

We simply must have a dream! Campers and camp managers a like, let's dream a dream of God creating a place in us. This place will be an open place big enough for all people joining together. This is essentially a huge dream, beyond anything you have imagined before. It is literally in us! There is no other place where God will have us and hold us. This earth and our lives upon this earth together are the only real interface we have with God. The dream is now, not later. This dream will shatter all our smaller dreams. God will use us, live in us, and reconcile the world to God through us. We truly are this dream "in Christ" as the apostle Paul has dreamed it and proclaimed it.

> *"We simply must have a dream! Campers and camp managers alike, let's dream a dream of God creating a place in us. This place will be an open place big enough for all people joining together."*

Here is the dream; it will blow your mind and your heart:

Jesus Christ is our foundation…

Jesus lives The Love Story of all time. Christians, our love story is alive, and it is The Love Story of all time. From cover to cover, the Bible witnesses to God's living presence and activity in this world! *"God so loved the world (cosmos), that he gave his only Son…" (John 3:16)*. This is amazingly good news! We live in a wondrous, earthly context which God created in love (OT) and saves in love (NT).

Jesus lives in The Love Story now *(John 1:1-5)*. He always has been and always will be the living presence! He is currently the supreme example of God's presence in this world. It is Jesus who tells us that God's reign is both now and not yet in this world. We simply need real eyes and ears to live it too. *(See the kingdom parables in Matthew 13.)* He brings living and eternal significance to this very moment of life even as we read these words. He tells us that he is *"the way, and the truth, and the life" (John 14:6)*. We therefore live The Love Story with every new day of our lives as we allow Jesus to live in us!

Jesus creates The Love Story. Jesus, the Living Word, began The Love Story *(John 1:3)*! Jesus is not only our Lord, but he created us and our world. Within the mystery of the oneness of God, our Lord and Savior created/creates the forests and the waters, the hills and the valleys, you and me, and life itself! This first century confession of God's unity explodes any attempts to isolate Jesus from our lives spent caring for the earth.

Jesus writes The Continuing Love Story. The author of Hebrews tells us that Jesus is "the exact imprint of God's very being, and he sustains all things by his powerful word" *(Hebrews 1:3)*. Jesus' life is the faithful witness *(Revelation 1:5)* of God's intent for human life on this planet. His death was inevitable, but the "passion of Christ" was and is his life! Jesus is the "first born" of all creation. All creation is reconciled by him through the supreme act of self-giving love – the cross. *(See Colossians 1:15-20.)* Paul in this passage clears the way for us to see clearly the potential for Jesus' continuing life (our lives) lived here in this world.

Jesus Calls Us Into the Love Story

In Jesus we learn who we are. We are the blessed. We are the salt of the earth. Like him we are the light of the world *(See Matthew 5 and John 8:12)*. We are the good seed. We are to be a blessing – to be the teachers and healers of the world. We find the true meaning of our lives in the words, actions, and calling of Jesus. We too were created to be the imprint, the image of God in this life *(Genesis 1:26)*. This is what Paul means when he says that in Christ we are a new creation *(2 Corinthians 5:17)*. We too are called to reconcile the world to God through Christ (his living example).

May it be said of us too that we left our nets immediately *(Mark 1:18)*.

Nothing in the way of camp ministry will transform the world if it is not fixed to this foundation – The Love Story. Anything less is the shifting sand of the world's false foundation. We can throw words like "Anabaptist" and "Mennonite" around for naught if we are not living in Christ's intimate love. In this dreamed of place then is the space for inviting the world to God! For camping people, this dreamed of place is the forest, the water, the grassland, the mountaintop, the hollow, the hillside, the meadow – all the holy ground where we welcome people in Christ's name. Why else would 1 Corinthians 3:11 be the most loved Anabaptist text?

Wow! As a friend of mine likes to say, "If that doesn't light your fire, your wood's wet."

Called to Salvation

While doing some trail work in the woods yesterday, I noticed an eight-point buck cautiously passing through about 40 yards from me. I watched him awhile, then doubled back around to see if I could get closer. There was no wind and that increased my odds. The woods was thick. I thought I lost him. Then he raised his head 20 yards from me. I snorted a few times pretending not to be human. He did not seem to care. We watched each other for about 10 minutes, both curious and a little apprehensive. For me it was another reunion, bringing together two parts of my heart too often separated by a world of the mind.

The Love Story of Christ must get past our heads and into our hearts! If it does, and if it finds lodging, the encounter of all things or anything can bring us to our knees like Paul on the Damascus Road. Paul's experience is not a history lesson. It is presence – God's presence in us. We become the apostle brought low and then sent carrying God's grace in our heart. Our heart becomes a place big enough for all the people in the wilds of this world. Our heart and this world become in fact one place! This is salvation – ours and possibly the world's.

Does this surprise you – that I would take a chance meeting in the woods and turn it into a life text for salvation? Surely you have not forgotten the parables of Jesus. He spoke the language of earth and heaven as one – one simple love story to explain the everlasting kingdom of God. As camping people this is exactly what we must live. We must acknowledge the scene of life playing in front of us, perhaps a hawk flying overhead or sitting on a fencerow. A frog in a swamp singing on a summer's eve will tell us how to speak the right love word to the aching hearts of campers in our charge.

Camp leaders, you have been the poor cousins of the real church leaders long enough. To you God has entrusted the greatest, most profoundly simple parables of life in the everyday. If you will not take the leaves of a tree and transform hearts from this miracle, no one else will. Your specialty is everyday miracles! Mennonite camp leaders, if you will not tell The Love Story from within your life, how will the world ever know Christ's peace? The grace of God flowing out of nature combined with your personal love affair with the nonviolent God, Jesus—this is the life experience you live for.

But here is the rub. The Love Story (salvation story) is more personal than you have yet imagined. Christ present is your one thing. All your intimacy finds its meaning in revelation. *"I am the way, and the truth, and the life" (John 14:6)* defines you and marks your life's journey as the start of eternity. Each word from your mouth, every thought, all desires of your heart sum up your soul-love of Jesus. Here is more than the first and greatest commandment *(Matthew 22:37)*, for you are more than a questioning Pharisee. You have given your heart away to the one who is transforming it. This is your reality. Nothing else in your life is real unless it finds meaning in and through your soul-love of God. Please do not consider this an exaggeration. Simply live it now.

I know what you are thinking. You are trying hard to figure out how the above paragraph can be true of you. Turn off your brain and quietly release the desire of your heart—this is called prayer. Take as long as necessary to deny the lies, stop the shame, put off the doubt, refuse all the false names you and others use to define you. Allow God to clothe you with Christ. Become again a reconciler with Christ of all things *(Colossians 1:20)*.

The buck stayed. I left first. He simply watched as I walked away. I could have tried to get closer. I could have waited him out, but I thought that if I left first it would tell him that I was safe, that I had no agenda beyond respect. Such a small gesture, but it was all I had to give. The beauty of love is in giving whatever we have on hand at the time. I am talking about being present in whatever the moment of the ongoing Love Story. I doubt if any of us can imagine the accumulation of moments in The Love Story that we have missed. We let them pass by because we do not believe that Jesus Christ really is the foundation of our life here and now. We are in danger of missing our own salvation.

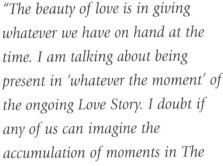

"The beauty of love is in giving whatever we have on hand at the time. I am talking about being present in 'whatever the moment' of the ongoing Love Story. I doubt if any of us can imagine the accumulation of moments in The Love Story that we have missed."

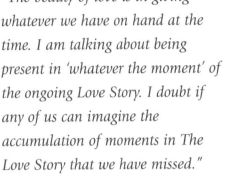

Now I hope that you are ready to hear the rest of this wild but holy dream.

God in This Place in Us

Genesis 1 and 2 do not directly frame the creation stories in terms of God's love. These texts are focused more on God's creative power, the goodness of creation, and God's plan for humans. In Genesis 1:26-30 we, being made in God's image, are clearly told to have dominion. Since God is the creator of life, our task is a life-giving one. Likewise, in Genesis 2:15 the human creation is given the responsibility to serve and guard the garden.

God's intent for us! Do you know God's intent for you? Is this not the most important thing for you to know – in the sense of living it to the hilt? I'll give you a hint. It is all about image.

The word, *dominion*, from Genesis 1 has been co-opted by many generations of Scripture readers causing a huge problem regarding God's intent. For the past two or three centuries, most modern, European/North American Christians have used this term for their own self-centered benefit. All of us first worlders and our ancestors have been caught up in the ideals of modernism. That is, we have lived an ethic of accomplishment; we have been swallowed up by goal-oriented and acquisition thinking. Everything in life comes with a price tag. Value has been placed on creation according to our needs and wants. Many generations of self-proclaimed Christians have left us the legacy of looking at creation as a commodity. This is the undoing of salvation! Self-centered thinking and behaving always separates us from our personal and loving God, something our Bible calls sin. We simply lose ourselves in another story! God always comes looking for us, but many choose not to be found.

This Christianized aggression toward things of the earth was never intended to be the attitude described by the Hebrew creation writers. The creation accounts were to be good news about all of creation, including us humans. Something has to give – it is all about image.

> *"The biblical meaning of **dominion** must now be reclaimed by those of us who live The Love Story and wish to know (in the biblical sense) God in this place. We must become clear about our God given responsibility on this earth because it is an awesome responsibility!"*

The biblical meaning of *dominion* must now be reclaimed by those of us who live The Love Story and wish to know (in the biblical sense) God in this place. We must become clear about our God-given responsibility on this earth because it is an awesome responsibility! It has everything to do with our image. In Genesis 1, only humans receive the direct address of God. God speaks to and commissions us. In a Hebrew world where any image of God was spurned as idolatrous, here alone is the image of God given expression – in the intended responsibility of the human being! Wow! At the dawn of creation, God has given us the greatest of all gifts – that is personal relationship with the divine and freedom to exercise an endowed, divinely ordained, imitated *(Ephesians 5:1)* power! Walter Brueggemann states it like this:

"The human creature attests to the Godness of God by exercising freedom with and authority over all the other creatures entrusted to its care. The image of God in the human person is a mandate of power and responsibility. But it is power exercised as God exercises power. The images the creative use of power which invites, evokes, and permits. There is nothing here of coercive or tyrannical power, either for God or for humankind…The 'dominion' here mandated is with reference to the animals. The dominance is that of a shepherd who cares for, tends, and feeds the animals. Or, if transferred to the political arena, the image of the shepherd king (cf. Ezek. 34). Thus the task of 'dominion' does not have to do with exploitation and abuse. It has to do with securing the well-being of every other creature and bringing the promise of each to full fruition…Moreover, a Christian understanding of dominion must be discerned in the way of Jesus of Nazareth (cf. Mark 10:43-44)…The role of the human person is to see to it that the creation becomes fully the creation willed by God."

Genesis, Interpretation, Walter Brueggemann, pp. 32-33, John Knox Press, Atlanta 1982

Now that is astounding news for all the earth, and for all peoples of the earth! If you and I can withstand the invading river of a self-centered culture, then all life will be blessed. It is all about image! When we understand this, we will know the essential ministry of camping.

Incredibly, we are the image of God in the world. God is known to the world through us. We can live in denial or be honest about our deepest sense of self. Either God is a liar in Scripture or we have been lying in the way we have lived – thinking that we were less than God's very representation to the entire world. Image is everything! We are the standard, the image that God uses to show divine compassion to the world!

Living in the image of God enables us to do anything, be anything, create anything, know anything, hold anything, and release anything. I am talking about God truly in us – let that sink in, whatever time it takes. I am not making this up. The apostle Paul said it first, *"I can do all things through him who strengthens me" (Philippians 4:13).* And we either forget it or disbelieve it. What will it take to make us a believer? Do we still not know the salvation of the Lord?

How is it Possible to Believe Like This?

Jesus knew that image was everything. Everything that we know about his life claims the truth of Genesis 1:26. Simply put, he lived it so that we could too. But we have to choose to believe it willingly if we are going to live it. We have to share this life with Jesus if we wish to share it with campers in our care. It is a heart thing that realigns the head thing. To again borrow from Paul, we must let Christ do it in us. Paul's favorite phrase was *"in Christ"*.

Do you wonder if others through the ages have so thoroughly believed? Is it possible? Think of the many who have given their lives as image. For Christian martyrs (let's say Anabaptist martyrs for those who are Mennonite readers) to go willingly to their death, they had to know the meaning of image. Their lives were Christ's life in the moment and for eternity. They had to live in and on and through The Foundation. They knew the meaning of incarnation/salvation, Christ in them. Whether physically martyred or not, we are given the ultimately joyful invitation to live Christ.

So what makes Mennonite camping people unique among camping ventures, leaders, denominations, and any attempts to imitate us? We are Jesus campers – the very best! We take upon ourselves the life of a traveler of dusty roads, a teacher of earthy parables, a lover of all sinners, a water walker, a homeless wanderer at home with all the earth, a healer of all hurts, a totally nonviolent, nonauthoritarian servant of everyone and everything, a speaker of lilies of the field and sparrows and vineyards, an absolutely forgiving dispenser of forgiveness, a self-acknowledged lover of all enemies and all persecutors, a reconciler of all things unreconciled, and a heart willing to bleed and die simply out of love for those killing him. This is who we become, and in this we become God's image.

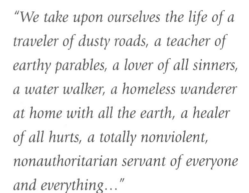

"We take upon ourselves the life of a traveler of dusty roads, a teacher of earthy parables, a lover of all sinners, a water walker, a homeless wanderer at home with all the earth, a healer of all hurts, a totally nonviolent, nonauthoritarian servant of everyone and everything…"

Jesus came to set the record straight – God does love the whole world with a whole heart full of compassion. The gospel accounts are full of snapshots of God's love shown to us in Jesus' teaching, healing, and loving ministry. The most well-known New Testament text is *John 3:16, "For God so loved the world that he gave his only son, so that everyone who believes in him may not perish but may have eternal life."* This text is not a formula to send us to heaven like so many Christians have thought. Eternal life is unending life that starts now! Eternal life is our life lived within the affirmation/confirmation of the life of love that Jesus lived. Jesus' life of love is what is eternal and it is our life! Jesus is the eternal image God intends for you and me!

To know God in such a radical and life-changing way might seem to be too difficult. It is not. In fact, it is altogether easy. We make it difficult; God makes it easy. God has shown us and invited us in. We only need to open ourselves moment by moment to be emptied and refilled—re-created into God's image. Most people choose not to live the life of Christ, but they could choose it.

Mennonite camping folks should know that place is important when it comes to choosing to know God in such a deep way. The times that I have lived in the woods have been my deepest moments of knowing God. Your woods might be a city park, a desert oasis, or a flower garden. Mine has been the north woods of Minnesota. Certainly, all the Mennonite camps that I have visited over the years are blessed with knowing places—places where people can be emptied and refilled—re-created into God's image, Jesus Christ. We must cherish and know these places if we are to stay capable of knowing God. This is simply because so many other places fill us with a secular knowing. Most other places will not empty us and refill us with Christ.

A few days after I met the eight-point buck, I was again doing some trail work in the woods. Since it was late fall, I could see many things normally hidden by the summer foliage or a blanket of snow. Now there were neither snow nor leaves to hide the more subtle beauty of the land. What I discovered was a fresh sense of place and knowing. Though I had been coming to those woods for the past ten years, I literally saw some things for the first time. I sat down just across a small ravine from a huge white pine tree. The ground was carpeted with leaves, but I still could see a deep cut in a rock the size of a truck. I studied the generous way these huge rocks and fissures allowed the pine to grow up from among them.

In these quiet moments, I was overcome by the beauty and the majesty, the simplicity and the splendor of the woods surrounding me. In Matthew 6, Jesus speaks of the lilies of the field and from these lilies admonishes us to seek the kingdom of God. This was no accident of mixed metaphors. Jesus understood that the deepest connections we have are with the earth and things of the earth, because God has always intended us to mirror divinity from within and among creation. We just have to sit down. That is how easy it is to become the image of God. Sit down in awe of all that is around us. Sit down and rest among the lilies of the field or the trees of the forest. Sit down as respite from our worries that have led us to self-imaging. Sit down and *"know that I am God" (Psalm 46:10)*. Sit down and know God in this place! Sit down and allow The Love Story to overpower and re-birth your present sense of self. Sit down.

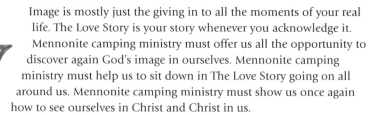

Image is mostly just the giving in to all the moments of your real life. The Love Story is your story whenever you acknowledge it. Mennonite camping ministry must offer us all the opportunity to discover again God's image in ourselves. Mennonite camping ministry must help us to sit down in The Love Story going on all around us. Mennonite camping ministry must show us once again how to see ourselves in Christ and Christ in us.

With this understanding of image, we have confidence that we are a people grounded in and grounded by God's Word – yes, the biblical text, but especially the Living Christ. Our foundation in Christ is the one and only. As we are grounded in the text and the Living Word, we are then also grounded within history and grounded on this earth. A reality of our living in this created world that God loves so much, is that we can only truly understand/ know God in this place—by living, breathing, and dying our discipleship (Menno-speak for Paul's *"in Christ"*) to Jesus, the Living Word. This discipleship is lived within the context where God, in infinite love for us, has placed us—The Love Story. Thus we can say with confidence as did our Anabaptist forbearers—Jesus Christ is indeed our foundation.

Here then is the challenge to Mennonite camp staff, board members, participants, and all the churches and church people that play a supporting role in Mennonite camping. It is time (always time) to live our lives in the self-giving love of the cross of Christ, not in theory—some other world—but in reality and real time which is now – be God's images. Creation, which is all around us at all times, is always the medium for self-giving love, for knowing God, and for living in Christ.

Image is everything if we wish to know God in this place.

We must have a dream! Campers and camp managers alike must dream of God creating a place in us. This place will be an open place big enough for all people to join together.

This is essentially a huge dream, beyond anything we have imagined before. It is literally in us! There is no other place where God will have us and hold us. This earth and our lives upon this earth together are the only real interface we have with God. The dream is now, not later. This dream will shatter all our smaller dreams. God will use us, live in us, and reconcile the world through us. We truly are this dream *in Christ* as the apostle Paul has dreamed it and proclaimed it.

As in Luke 6:49, Jesus would say that our other choice is to become a washout to the river of self-centered culture. And great will be *"the ruin of that house."*

Finally Then, a Few Suggestions

The Mennonite camping movement within the broader spectrum of the Mennonite expression of faith has an awesome task ahead. All involved in Mennonite camping must give themselves to a countercultural movement that will call us all to re-center our lives within The Love Story of God.

What follows and concludes this chapter is a beginning list of ways for camping people to live this purpose. I invite you to live your camping ministry in these following ways. I would also ask that you live your own discoveries within The Love Story. In other words, add to the list with love's abandonment!

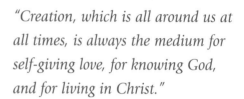

"Creation, which is all around us at all times, is always the medium for self-giving love, for knowing God, and for living in Christ."

Keep Christ's life as the absolute center for your own daily living. In all you do, follow his example as a living witness to the world. Image Jesus in you moment by moment.

Be a person of Sabbath – bask in an ongoing loving relationship with God. Sit down. Consider what it would mean to tithe your time for Sabbath, to allow all of your life to flow from Sabbath! Envision how your camp could lead the Mennonite church in Sabbath keeping.

Share the Living Word of Jesus within every aspect of your camping experience. Strive to make chapel time all the time – moment by moment. Consider integrating worship times into everything. Teach the Living Word as living example 24/7. Use your words and your actions in tandem. Perhaps a separate chapel time should become a category of the past. Would the life of Jesus not fit as well into the swim class, nature study, the breakfast table, and the clean-up duties? Don't reflect our culture's separation of Jesus and life, but show our people how to integrate Christ into everything. This will be possible as you live in Christ yourself.

Explore the ways in your life that you have not lived the fullness of Christ's reconciling kingdom now and coming. Confess honestly the faithless ways that you have lived in this creation. And change what needs to be changed at camp.

Allow Christ to reinstate you into the fullness of divine loving relationship where your task of care and dominion become a defining self-understanding. Commit yourself to a discovery journey in search of the image of God that you may have lost along with most other Christians.

Allow for the message of creation/salvation to expand in your heart. Let it not come from your head. Let it come from God's heart of love into, through, and beyond your heart! Expect a continuing transformation of your concept of God's presence in the world in and through you. Let every day becomes new. Each blade of grass may hold a parable of Jesus.

Learn ways to honor the magnitude of God in Christ Jesus. The experience of church camping has greatly under-accessed a transformative knowledge of Jesus. Most of us have not lived and taught the full extent of the biblical teachings about the magnificence of Christ. Mennonites in particular have sought ways to express Christ's suffering love within human relationships, but we have remained woefully silent about Christ's servant lordship over all things. What might it mean to overlay Colossians 1:15-20 on the Sermon on the Mount in your own process of daily living? How would this revive your camping experience and your teaching to the Mennonite church? How much more would you have to offer a world culture of secular idolatry?

"Let there be nothing in your camping experience that does not image Christ to the world."

Get down on your knees and rededicate your life and the life of your total camping experience to sharing the always personal and never private love of God with all people. Confess when you have made Jesus a commodity to push on the world instead of The Love Story to live within.

Look at your camp buildings, walkways, forests, waters, wildlife, maintenance equipment, personnel, signage, literature, meals, policies, and schedules, and commit yourself to asking how all this serves the majesty of Christ's kingdom now and not yet. Promise your staff and board and constituency that you will open up the future to making all these resources more reflective of Jesus Christ the faithful witness of God's love to the whole world. Let there be nothing in your camping experience that does not image Christ to the world.

Now it is your turn. Image Christ through your own ideas and inspirations.

And so become a reconciler of all things in partnership with Jesus Christ.

Postscript: Christ is our foundation, solid and firm forever. He is also the movement, the shattering, the beginning and the ending, the life force of the future. When you know God in this place, you will experience both the solid forever and the shattering movement forward through the wildness of God's love.

Chapter 5

Music, It's What We Remember

By Darryl Neustaedter-Barg

Preamble: *This is an anecdotal collection of thoughts based on 20 years of leading singing every year at the three camps of Mennonite Church Manitoba: Camps with Meaning. This is meant to be a brief history of musical evolution and a snapshot of where we are now based on my experience at Camps with Meaning. Conversations with people at other camps have shown a similar pattern for many. In this chapter "our camps" or "we" will refer to my Camps with Meaning experience.*

Part 1: The Power and Importance of Song

The mild-mannered camp pastor (let's name him Menno) prepared to step, with some dread, onto the bus taking the week's campers home. The typical "bad camper" (let's name him Jonny) was also to board, and that was only because he had narrowly averted being sent home earlier in the week.

It had appeared to Menno over the course of the week that we camp workers were labouring nearly in vain with this boy. He boisterously resisted all attempts to be "guided" in all areas of camp life, whether Bible sessions, group activities, meal times, or even in exciting activities like kayaking and sail boarding.

So the volume emanating from the doors of the bus was no surprise, until Menno was halfway up the stairs.

It certainly was Jonny's voice, but it was raised in a not particularly pleasant sounding song: "The Lord loves me, and Oh what a wonder I see. A rainbow shines through my window, the Lord loves me..."

Something had connected with Jonny, and it was the message of the love of God as he had learned it during singing that week.

Intuitively, Mennonites and others have long known about the power of song. Song sustained our ancestors through great trials and persecution. Song expressed the joy in our hearts when it was less appropriate to be expressive in public. Song helped a hard day in the field pass. Song continues to be very powerful today.

As a Mennonite people we have also taken the capacity of a song to teach theological content very seriously. Hymnals and collections of songs have long been produced, and certainly in recent efforts, with a serious emphasis on theological expression.

History

Many of our camps began as a specific outreach of a congregation or group of people dedicated to sharing the gospel of Jesus Christ with children in a natural setting. As a people that have found music important, singing was always a part of the program. When our camps began in the 1950s, the songs in the hearts of the camp workers were hymns. But, by the late 1960s and early 1970s, the music had moved to a more contemporary sound. While the history and discussion of how this transition took place is outside the scope of this chapter, the fact that it occurred is very significant.

In a simple sense, the music continued to be the songs in the hearts of those working in the camp setting. At a deeper level, it signaled a move from a group of related works defined by Mennonite church leadership through hymnal creation to a canon of songs

(Editor's Note: This chapter is in two parts. The first is a general discussion of the place of and use of music in the camp setting. The second instructive part is a very practical discussion on Music/Worship leading. But please read both; and the best would be to read them in succession.)

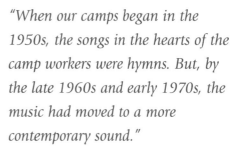

"When our camps began in the 1950s, the songs in the hearts of the camp workers were hymns. But, by the late 1960s and early 1970s, the music had moved to a more contemporary sound."

defined by the local folk tradition in the popular cultural setting. The hymnal was no longer the source of a new song.* By the early to mid-1970s, when I was a young camper, no traditional hymns were being sung. Acoustic guitar and voice were the instruments of leadership, and songs were slowly being added to the Camps with Meaning canon as camp staff brought them to the circle. And so it was for more than a decade. The songs I learned as a camper were the songs I learned to play when I took up the guitar as a young camp staffer in 1985.

The general source of the songs in this period is not entirely clear. The melodies and chord structures for many of the songs definitely had their source in popular music from the later '60s and early '70. One song resource that seems to contain many of the songs we sang is still available. It is *Songs* published by Songs and Creations *(www.songsandcreations.com)*. The website is not attractive, but the book is quite remarkable. The most current version contains over 1100 songs.

While the singing at Camps with Meaning had remained fairly static for a period, a shift was already taking place in the contemporary Christian worship music world. Huge publishers like Word Publishing and specific music publishers like Integrity Music and Maranatha Music were pushing large collections of music that made access to new songs much easier. (One reason these song collections were not heavily adopted by our camps may be that the '80s era music was very keyboard-based. The music translated better on a piano than on a guitar, but guitar was the instrument of choice for most singing at camp.)

Guitar-based music, prolific publishing, and more personalized lyrical content brought the Vineyard Music songs strongly into our use in the early to mid-1990s. Over half of the new songs introduced in our camps in the last ten years are published by Vineyard Music. While there are other networks and publishers of new worship music that are strong in the mix of sources of new contemporary worship music, Vineyard is likely still the largest one.

The songs we sing at camp are not the only significant change over the last 40 years. The way we view them has changed as well. In the days of the traditional hymn, there was a stronger and more formal understanding of the role of music as worship. With a move to a more casual music came a change in attitude on what the music represented. While it may also have been a reflection of cultural attitude toward faith expression, the seventies and eighties saw music much more as an activity at Camps with Meaning. It was something one does to have fun, maybe to learn a bit about God, or to settle down before a Bible lesson or bedtime. Our understanding of worship did not seriously acknowledge that children can worship God through song.

The 1990s brought a renewed and broadened understanding of worship at our camps, even to the point of sitting down and drafting a worship statement. Created by young, 20-something age staff, it is the stepping off point for an exciting era at our camps.

> *Camps with Meaning Worship Vision*
>
> *Worship is making God the first priority in our lives.*
> *In worship the Holy Spirit moves.*
> *We want to be open to this movement.*
> *God desires our worship and longs for us to approach, from whatever place we are at in our faith journey.*
> *Let us approach God honestly and recognize our need for closeness with God.*
> *We want to worship in all areas of our living, seeking connection with God.*
> *We want to transform our music into worship.*
>
> *2001*

The Vineyard network of churches did something that should be noted: they encouraged, mentored and supported their songwriters. They released piles of music. Much of it will be rarely used, but the churches were allowed to decide that—just as many churches sing only a handful of the 6,000 hymns Charles Wesley wrote.

*There are numerous resources that historically detail the change that has taken place in "Church music" up to the late 1970s. For one example, see: Christian Music in Contemporary Witness. Donald Paul Ellsworth, Baker Book House. 1979

While we have acknowledged the importance of music to a great extent, staff leadership has still taken a fairly hands-off stance on the overall selection of songs. Two significant factors affect the place the Camps with Meaning canon is at now on this matter.

The first factor is that we have commissioned our own Bible curriculums for many years. Typically we have asked people within our constituency to create the theological framework, and then they or other leadership staff have filled out the details with skits, stories, and suggested songs.

The second factor which might be even more unique to our camps is the move toward writing our own songs. A small group of musical staff began writing songs on their own, and their passion for music at camp finally brought them together intentionally in 2002 to write songs that would fill certain niches in our program for that summer. We have examined musical style, but most specifically, worked with the theme and biblical texts for the upcoming camp season. The quality has varied, but some have been quite good, and have planted the words of Scripture in the hearts and minds of campers and staff alike.

Who Are We Now, and Why?

A worship vision statement may seem a little ambitious, especially in light of Jonny's bold rendering of a song we've been singing at our camps since the 1970s. Who we are as a singing people, how we create our musical canons at our camps, and thus, how we pass music on to our campers are affected by a number of factors. I suggest three broad categories for exploration here: (1) what I broadly call the folk tradition, (2) technology and location, and (3) leadership.

While folk music may be understood as a genre, I use the term to describe music that is created "by the people." I would include most popular forms of music created by persons that don't have musical training and direct European classical lineage. Most rock, country, electronica, and R&B artists fall into this category. Folk tradition musicians may become very skilled musicians in their genre and beyond, but they seem to have a number of common characteristics that relate to our discussion: (1) they followed and created the music that resonated in their being; (2) they were influenced by a local expression, and learned how to create it by listening to and watching others; (3) they started "doing it" before they were particularly skilled; (4) they were not primarily empowered by an institution or governing body, and they do not follow a set path in the way they choose what song to do next or how they will write a new song.

"Who we are as a singing people, how we create our musical canons at our camps, and thus, how we pass music on to our campers are affected by a number of factors."

So, what are the effects of the folk tradition on the singing community? Each of the characteristics above plays a part in how and what we sing. It may be helpful here to consider the continuum on which we move:

1. Music that resonates in the being. Positive: There is passion and conviction in sharing the song. Most campers can tell when staff are convinced about what they are presenting. The song is chosen and presented with integrity and enthusiasm. Negative: Songs that don't "resonate" are not communicated well. Personal passion is often not a useful grid for thinking about what needs to be communicated musically or theologically. Personal passion by definition is very subjective and individualistic. It can often overlook the needs of others. The sources of music become filtered based on a particular person's interests.

2. Local expression and learning. Positive: There is strong accessibility. I learned to play guitar because I appreciated the music other camp staff were making. The learning is based on mentoring. People actually learn many of the necessary skills to play a guitar or

give musical leadership from other camp staff. It is a culture of learning and improving one's skills. Typically there is limited cost as instruments are shared, and no formal lessons are required. Negative: Styles and skills are limited to the most skilled and experienced player (who may not be very skilled at all). Musicians who are not interested in mentoring others stop the progress and limit the culture of learning and improving. There may be limited appreciation for styles that aren't immediately culturally relevant. There is no objective way to determine whether "we should be doing something better."

3. Started "doing it" before being adequately skilled. (I clearly remember the first time I arrived to work a week at camp and none of my guitar mentors were there. I was moved from the side to the front with the ceremonial words that mark this new milestone in musical leadership, "Well, you know a few chords, don't you?" This was followed by a standard ritual of communication: the song leader puts a song on the overhead and looks at the frightened new guitarist. A vigorous shaking of the head had it rapidly pulled off. A tentative nod, and the song would proceed.) Positive: Nothing hones skills like having to do something "for real." Negative: You are limited to the songs the guitarist knows. The motivation to improve skills or learn a new song might be limited by the leadership or charisma of other staff. (For a while, I got away with not playing a song I didn't like by claiming, "I don't know it." Campers liked it, but other staff didn't really care, so I was not highly motivated to learn it.)

"I was moved from the side to the front with the ceremonial words that mark this new milestone in musical leadership, 'Well, you know a few chords, don't you?'"

4. Direction is personally, communally, or culturally set (related to #1). Positive: Motivation to participate is very high. Passion for the song is real. Stagnation is unlikely. Potential relevance to culture campers are coming from is high. Freedom to follow the moving of the Holy Spirit is high. Negative: Potentially limited variety of songs, even within the generally accepted camp repertoire. Only picking favorites. Potentially limited respect for the work of the community on theological understanding.

I choose the words technology and location to describe another set of factors that shape what we sing (and where we sing, for that matter). *A cappella* (no instruments playing along) singing has long been a part of the Mennonite singing tradition. When the community was close, like many churches were, it was possible to repeat songs enough that they would be committed to memory.

With the coming of the "folk song" in the late 60s, early 70s, and the nature of the camp settings, we make many choices when we have campers for a week at our camps: These vary depending on:

1. Complexity of text. If there are many words, we might need to use technology to keep the words in front of us. This ranges from big pieces of poster board, to overhead projectors, to video projection units with PowerPoint. We can't assume campers know the words.

2. Accompaniment. Some songs don't work with guitars. Others shouldn't have accompaniment at all. Some people feel strongly about using culturally current accompaniment like a band with a drum kit (which usually means a sound system).

3. Location. Singing around the campfire in the evening has long been a feature of many camps. If this is a priority at the camp, it affects song selections and the frequency of repetition. While we often try to have some words on a poster board when we go outside, it is a significant experience and a longer-term gift when campers memorize songs.

All the points above dictate which songs we sing, or the songs we choose dictate which technological elements will be employed.

Many more factors affect what we sing and how. One that should be mentioned yet is leadership. The leaders we choose (or don't choose) shape our singing—leaders on the instruments, leaders who choose the songs, leaders of the group, and leaders who oversee Bible teaching and general spiritual nurture. (This might be all the same person, or many

persons.) The culture and canon of our camp songs can change overnight, or may take years to develop as it has at Camps with Meaning. Good leaders will have the well-being of the campers and staff in mind as the program of the camp proceeds. In a general sense, this means that someone is thinking intentionally about what happens during singing. More specifically, it could mean that someone is thinking about many of the factors mentioned above and beyond.

At our camps, I've done some simple leadership training in the area of music. Many of the young staff who desire to participate in musical leadership are within the "folk tradition" and simply haven't had a chance to think about what's going on when they lead campers in singing.

Where to Now?

If it hasn't been clear to this point, my basic assumptions about what goes on and should go on in singing at our camps follow:

1. Music is a dynamic force in our North American culture. To ignore that is to miss incredible opportunities to engage our campers.
2. Campers can worship God through songs, even at a young age.
3. Campers should sing and have fun while doing it. They should participate, not just listen.
4. Since we are teaching campers about God when we sing songs about God, the words matter.
5. We give campers a unique gift when they memorize songs.
6. We give campers another unique gift when they experience worshipping God together, with their voices, in an outdoor setting.
7. Staff receive a gift when they bring their gifts of leadership in music.

I believe these ends are attainable by balancing the dynamic, positive elements of the "folk tradition" with mature leadership that holds theological and musical perspective. At Camps with Meaning, we are working at this in a few specific ways:

1. Doing workshops with the people who will lead singing, choose songs, and play instruments.
2. Including songs in the Bible curriculum we create.
3. Writing songs which relate directly to the curriculum for the summer.
4. Hiring summer program directors at our camps who have Anabaptist schooling or experience.

Am I biased? You bet. These reflections are my story of the last 20 years. I did not begin playing guitar and leading worship at camp with noble intentions. Really, God works in wonderful and mysterious ways. I started playing because of two guys I looked up to. Their lifestyle choices at the time hardly made them textbook staff, but I learned a lot about playing guitar from them because they gave their time freely to me (if not as generously as they might have to their campers). It took time and community discernment for me even to begin thinking about our music as worship and theological nurture, since that was not the culture around singing at our camps. God has brought our camps a long way. May God do the same for yours.

"Good leaders will have the well-being of the campers and staff in mind as the program of the camp proceeds. In a general sense, this means that someone is thinking intentionally about what happens during singing."

Part 2: Song Leading/Worship Leading

General

1. We will do more to lead people into the presence of God by worshipping than by anything else. We're not trying to get people to sing, we're worshipping God. Your attitude/demeanor makes a big difference. If you're making a joke of the time, that's a pretty big statement. Having fun is good. Inside jokes can exclude. Full staff participation is important.

2. Use words to make clear that this is a time of worship. ("Welcome to this time of worship.") Not every time necessarily, but it's okay to use some words to set the tone. Use language that suggests God is present. Prayer is a good way to do this.

3. Everyone leading should sing. It's important that guitar players (for example) make the songs and text part of their worship experience as well (less fancy playing and more leading).

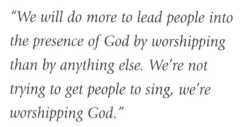

"We will do more to lead people into the presence of God by worshipping than by anything else. We're not trying to get people to sing, we're worshipping God."

Song Selection

4. Variety vs. repetition during the week. This is a fine line which can become skewed for staff over a whole summer. Don't leave campers behind assuming they know something. An overhead-less campfire can be very alienating if you've only heard the songs once. Make an effort to repeat songs so campers can go home knowing some songs and sing them without an overhead.

5. Pick age-appropriate songs with words that will make sense to the campers you have.

6. Move from faster to slower songs to set mood/intimacy; to slow campers down for the Bible instructor or sleep.

7. Look at the words. Most of our songs are "praise," but some speak about discipleship. Include those. Use songs from the curriculum!

8. Some people plan songs from less intimate with God to more intimate. For example, think of moving from "This Little Light of Mine" to "Shine Jesus Shine" to "Here I Am, Lord."

In the Singing/Worship Session

Be super inclusive!! (See #4, 9, 11, and 12.)

9. It's okay/good to spend some time teaching a song. Some songs are harder to learn, especially if they're in serious harmony (for example, "Siyahamba" and "Freedom"). Often these two songs are only fun for staff.

10. Fill the time between songs with something. People lose their focus quickly. Do something to keep the attention forward. (See #11 or 12.)

11. We're singing for worship and fun, but also to learn/teach. Explain words or concepts (codes) so campers can understand (for example, the words to "Shine, Jesus Shine" and "One Tin Soldier." What does "Let Your Light Shine" mean?)

    · Explain where the words to songs come from. Many of our songs are based on biblical passages. Some of these are obvious (Colossians 3:17). But others not ("Fear Not": Isaiah 43; "I Am the Resurrection": John 11:25; "I Am the Bread of Life": John 6:35-40).

    · Sometimes it's confusing whose voice the song is in. For example, "I Am the Bread of Life" switches between Jesus speaking, and us responding; who is "he" in "Holy Lord"?

12. Teach the sign language stuff every week, even though it feels repetitive. Not to know the sign language can be very alienating when everyone else is doing it.

13. Use dynamics (volume changes). These are effective ways of setting mood, highlighting lyrics, or heightening an experience ("somebody's crying"). Peak somewhere. Simple formulas work ("Lord Loves Me"). Guitar players, make use of flat picking, strumming, more aggressive strumming.

Music in Worship

1. We sing because God is great!

O come, let us sing to the Lord; let us make a joyful noise to the rock of our salvation! Let us come into his presence with thanksgiving; let us make a joyful noise to him with songs of praise! For the Lord is a great God, and a great King above all gods. In his hand are the depths of the earth; the heights of the mountains are his also. The sea is his, for he made it, and the dry land, which his hands have formed. O come, let us worship and bow down, let us kneel before the Lord, our Maker! For he is our God, and we are the people of his pasture, and the sheep of his hand. (Psalm 95:1-7)

2. We sing because God has delivered us, and we want others to know that!

I waited patiently for the Lord; he inclined to me and heard my cry. He drew me up from the desolate pit, out of the miry bog, and set my feet upon a rock, making my steps secure. He put a new song in my mouth, a song of praise to our God. Many will see and fear, and put their trust in the Lord. (Psalm 40:1-3)

3. We sing because it sustains us in times of trouble!

The crowd joined in attacking them, and the magistrates had them stripped of their clothing and ordered them to be beaten with rods. After they had given them a severe flogging, they threw them into prison and ordered the jailer to keep them securely. Following these instructions, he put them in the innermost cell and fastened their feet in the stocks. About midnight Paul and Silas were praying and singing hymns to God, and the prisoners were listening to them. (Acts 16:22-25)

4. We sing because the Scriptures invite us to!

Let the word of Christ dwell in you richly; teach and admonish one another in all wisdom; and with gratitude in your hearts sing psalms, hymns, and spiritual songs to God. And whatever you do, in word or deed, do everything in the name of the Lord Jesus, giving thanks to God through him. (Colossians 3:16-17)

"It's okay/good to spend some time teaching a song. Some songs are harder to learn, especially if they're in serious harmony."

Chapter 6

Camping and Retreating in Places Apart

This chapter, a rather lengthy one, is a directory of the member camps of Mennonite Camping Association (MCA) with the vital statistics, description, and history of each camp. Each was invited as well to further personalize their camp through photographs and stories characteristic of the camp life and vision. Realizing that there are constant changes of camp administrators, some names may be different when the book goes to press. But the main information about most camps is constant and ongoing

The stories and information varies. The various camp and retreat centers are a reflection of their locations, water-centered in the upper Midwest, snow camps in the Cascade and Rocky Mountains, warm weather winter retreating in Florida. The emphasis may be on Bible memory, on nature research and education, on a place to teach city children about the great outdoors, to present the good news, and in all cases to experience a greater understanding of God and God's creation and people. Their accounts include Ku Klux Clan encounters and burnt churches, healed relationships with others and with God.

Please read through these to comprehend the breadth of the camps in their location, history, vision, and mission, and the personal contributions of many people who have found direction, purpose, and meaning for life in *these places apart*.

Camp List

Adirondack
  Beaver Camp
  Maple Ridge Center
Amigo Centre
Camp Andrews
Bethany Birches Camp
Bethel Mennonite Camp
Bible Memory Ministries
Black Rock Retreat
Camp Buckeye Retreat Center
Camps with Meaning
  Camp Assiniboia
  Camp Moose Lake
  Camp Koinonia
Camp Camrec
Cove Valley Christian Youth Camp
Crooked Creek Christian Camp
Camp Deerpark Inc.
Drift Creek Camp
Camp Elim
Camp Friedenswald
Harman Mt. Farm Campground
Camp Hebron
Hidden Acres Mennonite Camp and Retreat Centre
Highland Retreat
Camp Keola
Lakewood Retreat
Laurelville Mennonite Church Center
Little Eden Camp
Camp Luz
Menno Haven Camp and Retreat Center
Camp Mennoscah
Camp Men-O-Lan
Merry Lea Environmental Learning Center
Pine Lake Fellowship Camp
Rocky Mountain Mennonite Camp
Shekinah Retreat Center
Silver Lake Mennonite Camp
Spruce Lake Retreat
Camp Squeah
Swan Lake Christian Camp
Camp Valaqua
Wilderness Wind
Williamsburg Christian Retreat Center
Willowgrove Farm
  Fraser Lake Camp
  Glenbrook Day Camp
Woodcrest Retreat
Youth Farm Bible Camp

Beaver Camp

Description

Beaver Camp is situated on picturesque Beaver Lake in the Adirondack foothills of Upstate New York. Activities include swimming, boating, canoeing, fishing and sailing on Beaver Lake, 3 miles of hiking and cross-country ski trails, interpretive nature trails, a challenge ropes course, a ball court, an open play field and a winter tubing hill. Beaver Camp offers a summer and winter youth camping program, guest group rental facility, outdoor education, camp sponsored adult retreats and ropes course rental. Facilities include an historic Adirondack lodge (dining, meeting and dorm rooms), a large pavilion with fireplace, rustic cabins and modern motel rooms.
Capacity: Summer-140, Winter-100.

History

In the mid-1960s, a group of individuals from Upstate and Western New York Mennonite congregations had a vision to create a Christian Children's Camp in the Adirondack Mountains. After looking at various sites, they purchased property on Beaver Lake, a former German-style lodge and boys' camp. In February of 1969, twenty-two people contributed toward the acquisition of the property and became the charter members of the Adirondack Mennonite Camping Association (AMCA). In 1970, Beaver Camp opened for two weeks of 155 campers.

Over the past 34 years Beaver Camp has grown in program, scope and size. Approximately 110,00 people have experienced the ministry of Beaver Camp with an average of 8,000 per year in the last few years.

Mission Statement

The mission of Beaver Camp is to provide facilities and programs, infused by God's love, in which individuals of every age are invited to grow in their relationships with Jesus Christ and others. Our motto is, "Beaver Camp: A Place to Grow." We are committed to excellence in hospitality, quality service and promoting spiritual growth through this organization.

Stories

Dear Beaver Camp:
Thank you for giving me a good and fun week. Before I came to camp, I didn't believe in God but now I do. I also hated camping but now I can stand it a little. I would go back but I would go to Outpost again. Before we went to The Rock I hated canoeing and boats. I liked it until the storm came when we were on Beaver River. We went to an island and, thanks to God and Lydia, we made it even though we were cold and scared. I didn't like water that much but now I will go out in the woods after dark. Even though I didn't like the girls I was with, I had a great time and hope to come back next summer. I hope I see Lydia

8884 Buck Point Road, Lowville, NY 13367
Phone: (315) 376-2640
Fax: (315) 376-7011
Email: info@beavercamp.org
Web page: www.beavercamp.org
Executive Director: Marvin Zehr
Beaver Camp Director: Mike Judd
Director Admin. Services: Emanuel Gingerich
Sponsoring Organization:
Adirondack Mennonite Camping Association

again. The thing I was amazed at was the food. It was good and I liked the fact that Outpost could cut to the front of the line. Thanks, again, for a great time and I hope to go there soon.
-KJ Aug. 2002

Beaver Camp:
Just a note to say "Thanks" to you and your fine staff. Sean and three others from our church have all reported great testimonies of growing in the Lord while at Beaver Camp. You are doing an excellent job! Keep up the good leadership.
-JM – Rochester, 2003

Church Retreat member:
This has been a wonderful place to just be with the Lord. Your hospitality is superb and seeing the young people at prayer and quiet time is inspiring and uplifting. In the words of one of my favorite songs, "This is holy ground…the Lord is here!" Thanks for opening your camp for us and making the retreat possible. I leave refreshed, renewed and energized for the Lord.
-unsigned

Maple Ridge Center

Description

AMCA has recently acquired a Kentucky-style horse ranch in close proximity to the village of Lowville, New York. Here, they will expand their ministry to conjoin family camp experiences with community programs and activities. Acquired through the Pratt Northam Foundation, Maple Ridge Center will offer programs such as thematic day camps, sports camps, an RV cite, winter tubing and ice skating, and guest group events and rentals. The manor will serve as a meeting center for anniversaries, weddings, dinners and receptions. Over time plans are to cultivate a Heritage Farm, a Health & Wellness Center and a multi-purpose center to include music camps, theatre camps, and related recreational activities. As well, Maple Ridge Center is engaging community needs for at-risk youth, cite-based mentoring programs and a volunteer center.

History

With the recent acquisition of Maple Ridge Center, AMCA envisions a unique ministry opportunity with Beaver Camp "coming out of the woods" to embrace and engage the needs of the community. We continue to find new ways to serve people.

Mission

The mission of Maple Ridge Center is to realize the kingdom of God by building people, faith and community. By affirming their value, people are lead to faith and commitment to a faith community. In turn, they can reach out to the needs of the broader community to serve as Christ would. Our motto is, "Maple Ridge Center: Rooted in Faith, Branching out in Service to the Church and Community." We are committed to quality service and intentional spiritual encounters through this organization.

Stories

"Westside Church Newsletter," July, 2000

"Uh, um, Diann, did you know Demario became a Christian today?" The earnest young camp counselor inquired. I was hustling towards the dinner line with our daughters. This news caught me completely off guard. My tired, distracted mind responded, "NO, not now! This is too big! I can't take this in right now! This is not how I pictured it!"

Then I saw Demario, saw the softness in his eyes. I stopped my rushing and took it in. "Demario, Demario is it true?" he answered with a quiet, firm "Yes". "Demario, it's the real thing for you, isn't it?" the same beautiful, "Yes".

7421 East Road, Lowville, New York 13367
Mobile Phone: (315) 486-2227
E-mail: info@mapleridgecenter.org
Website: www.mapleridgecenter.org
Executive Director: Marvin Zehr
Maple Ridge Center Director: Jamie Gleason

"Demario, you are my brother and I am your sister. We will live together forever." We embraced. The loud dinner line had shortened and we were quiet for a moment. "God has not, nor will not ever leave you. Cling to this always."

I saw the words register and was ready to let the moment go. "Better get in there or dinner will be gone." I patted his shoulder and my heart swelled with affection and gratitude while watching his familiar gait as he moved toward the dining hall. I flashed back to the many times I'd stood at the church door after kicking him out, watching him stomp angrily down the street, kicking imaginary objects and yelling to himself. He was so changed, I handed off the girls and walked to the nearby woods, leaning my head against a pine tree while a visceral sigh escaped. "Thank you, God – Thank you, God – Thank you, God." Somewhere inside myself I sensed a fuller conversion; if Demario can bow a knee, anyone can.

Amigo Centre

Description

Amigo Centre is a conference and retreat facility located on 400 acres including a lake in southern Michigan approximately one hour from the Goshen/Elkhart, Indiana area. We are open all year and offer youth and adult programs plus retreats for church, family groups, and outdoor education.

With a 26-room retreat center, cottages, and cabins, we can sleep up to 275 summer and winter. We have handicapped accessible housing and rent to other groups. Activities include canoeing, swimming, tennis, tubing, ice skating, and a gym for indoor activities.

History

Camp Amigo began in 1957 as a children's camp. The first major building, constructed in 1967, included the kitchen/dining hall, lodging, and meeting area. This allowed Amigo to do year-round activities. In the late 1980s it became a retreat/conference center, with more staff and facilities. In 1992 a new 28-room retreat center was opened. In 1994 an activities center with a full-size gym was added. In 1995 our name was changed to "Amigo Centre" to better describe the ministry changes.

Mission

Amigo Centre is a retreat and recreation center for members of Indiana-Michigan Mennonite Conference congregations, their friends, and the wider community.

Our mission is to facilitate the ministry of the church, encourage commitment to Jesus Christ, and assist people of all ages to become the persons God desires. Amigo Centre provides a unique environment where we gather to listen and share, study and reflect, play and recreate, pray and worship, enjoy creation, and experience God's presence.

A number of significant programs support this mission: programs with the conference enhancing the conference activities, and an outdoor/environmental education program with local public and private schools to share our understanding of creation theology and care of the land. All persons who come to Amigo Centre have the opportunity to experience God's creation on a nature hike with one of our staff, relating to our logo, "In Harmony with God and Nature."

Stories

For Amigo Centre, the Outdoor Education has been a vital part of the ministry of the camp for the past 33 years. The roots of the program began under the leadership of camp manager, John R. Smucker in the spring of 1971. Using Title I program money from the government, W. Dale Stutzman, principal at York Elementary and teacher Dan Hochstetler, pursued a dream and coordinated an outdoor

26455 Banker, Sturgis, Michigan 49091-9355
Phone: (269) 651-2811
Fax: (269) 659-0084
E-mail: info@amigocentre.org
Website: www.amigocentre.org
Executive Director: Dana L. Sommers
Sponsoring Organization: Indiana-Michigan Mennonite
Camp Association.

education program for those first sixty 5th graders from York. In his annual report that year Smucker noted that programming for school camps was "one of our untapped horizons to pioneer."

Through the '70s the program grew and in 1979 over 285 students from three Middlebury elementary schools participated in the program. By the mid '80s the number of students being served by the program had nearly tripled and when the Outdoor Education program hit its peak in 1996 nearly 30 schools and 2500 students participated in the program. We are still serving 27 schools (private and public) with a primary focus on students in grades 4-6 from a four county region in Michigan and Indiana. A strong program is also offered for homeschool students in kindergarten through 8th grade.

This experiential program, now called the Outdoor and Environmental Education (OEE) program, continues to exist to support Amigo Center's mission. Through implementation of our strategic plan/program guide, all youth and adult programs camp now offers have an OEE component.

In 33 years the program has grown in many ways through the hard work and vision of so many people. We are trusting that in the years to come many lives will be impacted as individuals experience the wonders of creation and the work of our Creator through various aspects of the Outdoor and Environmental Education program.

Camp Andrews

Description

A rustic facility available for year-round weekend or weekday rental. Food service provided or provide your own. Plan your own program with experienced staff available to help. Activities include archery, a petting zoo, basketball, volleyball, softball, hiking, swimming, fishing, a ropes course, nature study, indoor recreation, and more.

We specialize in serving groups who are reaching urban youth. As a youth camp, we are a rental facility with 150 beds. We are an independent membership group with a board.

History

Camp Andrews received its name from Mr. Harry Andrews, a Lancaster businessman and deacon at St. Paul's Evangelical and Reformed Church who gave $1,000 to the church for young people's work. That church owned and operated the camp until 1973. In that year, the Pulaski Street Mennonite Church in Baltimore, looking for a place to support the youth ministry of the church, bought the property and operated it until 1983.

Since May, 1983, the Camp Andrews Association has been the sponsoring group, formed by persons from Lancaster Mennonite Conference, the Church of the Brethren, and the Amish Mennonite Church. Goals for 1998-2007 are to construct a multipurpose building with dining hall, offices, lodging and meeting rooms, begin a residential program for urban youth, build a lake, and add several cabins, a gym and bathhouse near the existing pool.

Mission Statement

Camp Andrews' purpose is to provide rustic, affordable camp facilities in a natural, Christian environment conducive to bringing urban youth to Jesus.

By providing:

- Youth-friendly facilities with no "chandeliers" to break.
- A natural, peaceful setting where you'll be refreshed.
- Service-oriented staff who will help you plan your program to strengthen your relationships.
- An affordable facility because of the faithful gifts of generous friends.

1226 Silver Spring Road
Holtwood, Pennsylvania 17532
Phone: (717) 284-2624
Fax: (717) 284-2852
E-mail: campandrews@yahoo.com
Website: www.campandrews.org
Administrator: Phil J. Herschberger
Sponsoring Organization: Camp Andrews Association
Memberships: Christian Camp and Conference Association, MCA

Stories

Camp Changed My Life

By Lillian Latshaw, a Honeybrook camper

As a child who came from a nonreligious family, I went to church, but Camp Andrews was the place where I accepted Jesus into my heart. Camp was a place to be accepted. Everyone at camp was always so helpful, like when you wanted someone to listen to Bible memory, or if you had questions about Jesus.

My experience at camp taught me about God, about people, about judgment, and about myself. Camp taught me about the good Christian person I someday hope to be.

Girls and boys return to camp every year because it gets them through the bad times at home. When I am in trouble or scared I sometimes sing camp songs because they always make me feel closer to Jesus. I never leave Camp Andrews the way I arrived. Camp changes my life. I am a better person because I am part of something great. I hope this continues for many more years, because sometimes I just need someone to believe in me.

Bethany Birches Camp

Description

Located on 100 acres of woodland in central Vermont, the 1,700-foot elevation provides a panoramic view of the valley below and several distant mountain ridges. Rustic shelters provide a setting where campers and counselors develop their relationship with Jesus and each other.

The winterized facility provides a setting for adult and family programming. The facilities include a pavilion, kitchen, bathhouse, staff cabin, nine rustic camper shelters, and campsites for tents. The summer program provides an affordable Christian camp experience for local youth ages 6 to 18. Day camp is available for ages 4 to 9. Three snow camp weekends minister to the children in Vermont and New Hampshire.

History

Bethany Birches is owned by the Bethany Birches Camp, Inc., a group of Christians representing several churches in Vermont. The camp was begun in 1965 to provide a local and affordable Christian camp experience for children in Vermont and surrounding states.

Mission

To provide a setting where campers become aware of Jesus Christ and his importance in their lives through worship, Bible lessons, prayer, and fireside chats. To provide a setting where campers and counselors can engage in learning relationships to prepare them for future responsibilities in life.

The summer program is planned in the interest of children where Christian standards guide an integrated program of Bible lessons, worship, nature appreciation, recreation, and living together. The Christian staff shares Jesus Christ as friend and savior, one who makes life worth living. The program focuses around a counselor and his or her six to eight campers.

Stories

Living in the Kingdom

By Ann Moyer

Once upon a time, not so very long ago, a group of people gathered in the green mountains of Vermont to build the kingdom of God.

These people gathered and told their stories to one another, stories of their childhoods and their growing up, stories of their experience of God. They sang together and played together, they hiked and ate and prayed together. Sometimes one or the other was bossy or obstinate or moody. Then they got practice in building the kingdom of God, one disagreement or hurt feeling at a time.

2610 Lynds Hill Road
Plymouth, Vermont 05056-0257
Phone: (802) 672-5220
E-mail: bbc@vermontel.net
Website: www.vtchildrenscamp.com
Executive Director: Brandon Bergey
Sponsoring Organization: Bethany Birches Camp Association.

The first week children came to the community it became apparent there were many opportunities to learn about building God's kingdom. Stories of Jesus' life and teachings were told.

The children understood the kingdom of God. They said it was a place where people are kind to each other, where there is no war, where there is enough space and enough food and shelter for everyone. One of the children told the others he was glad to come to this place in the mountains because he got to have lunch every day. Another child told how he was sent here by a man who paid his fee.

Sometimes there were scraped knees and headaches and tummy aches. Everyone was grateful for the man who washed thousands of dishes, the woman who cooked hundreds of meals and made pretzels with the children when it rained. They were happy to have known the family with two little girls that all the children played with, the retired couple who spent a week helping in the kitchen and on the grounds, the man who came each week to mow. And they knew they were being supported by the prayers of a wider community whose call is also to build the kingdom of God. At the end of their time together, they agreed that God's kingdom is here and now, but still being built.

Bethel Mennonite Camp

Description

Bethel Mennonite Camp is nestled among 300 acres in the beautiful mountains, woods, streams, and unique rock formations of Eastern Kentucky. Facilities are available for personal, small group, or family retreats. Guest rooms accommodate 2 to 4 persons while cabins house up to ten.

Cooking facilities or meal packages are available. Recreation includes outdoor volleyball and basketball, a waterslide, shuffleboard, creek hikes, other hiking, campfires, air hockey, carpet-ball, Ping-Pong, Foosball, and basketball shoot. There is a full summer youth ministry.

History

Bethel Mennonite Camp is a Christ-centered ministry with an emphasis on Bible study and personal commitment to Christ. In addition to the fun young people have while here, scores have come to know Jesus as Lord over the past forty years.

Initially the camping ministry was established to meet the spiritual and social needs of the Mennonite churches of the Appalachian Mountain area. Over the years the camping ministry has expanded considerably to meet a wider variety of needs and to reach out to the larger body of Christ.

Bethel Mennonite Camp is owned by God and overseen by the camp board. We are a nonprofit ministry which operates on donations from churches and caring individuals.

Mission Statement

For individuals to experience life-change through knowing Christ personally as Creator and friend, growing in their relationship to him, and showing him to others.

2952 Bethel Church Road
Clayhole, Kentucky 41317
Phone/fax: (606) 666-4911
E-mail: grow@bethelcamp.org
Website: bethelcamp.org
Administrator: Roger Voth
Sponsoring Organization:
Conservative Mennonite Conference.

Bible Memory Ministries

Description
We are a church-related ministry promoting Scripture memory and verse-related correspondence lessons. We offer twelve weeks of summer camp in six states, fall camps in Michigan and Kansas, and winter camps in Indiana and Ohio. We sponsor skating parties and youth rallies. We lease facilities for our camps.

Our program is divided into several ministries: elementary, middle school, high school, adult, and a video ministry. In addition to the twelve weeks of summer camps, we are used by 135 churches and several home groups in ten states.

History
Bible Memory Ministries began when Harvey and Prudence Birky began helping public school students memorize Scripture. In 1953 this was extended when interested churches enrolled their youth in the program. In 1959 Bible Memory Ministries held their first camp at Perrin Lake, now Amigo Centre. In 1993 they purchased their first building at 109 West Madison Street and moved to their present location in 2002.

Mission Statement
"Changing Lives for Jesus Christ." Bible Memory Ministries helps youth and adults grow in their relationship with God and their understanding of the Bible through Bible memorization, church clubs, correspondence lessons, and camping programs.

Stories
A Prayer for the Campers

We pray for the campers, we call them by name
We present them to the Father in Jesus' name
We ask not for riches, ask not for fame
We pray for their salvation in Jesus' name
May they not be found timid, may they not be ashamed
May they boldly proclaim the gospel in Jesus' name
May they not be found lacking, but be fully prepared
When they stand before Jesus, to receive their reward
We ask for the children, for hundreds of souls
Who are lost without Jesus, outside the fold
Lord, help us to see them with compassion and love
To reach out and lead them to the Good Shepherd above
So we pray for the campers, we call them by name
We present them to the Father in Jesus' name
We ask not for riches, we ask not for fame
We pray for their salvation in Jesus' name

1014 N. Greene Road, P.O. Box 823
Goshen, Indiana 46527-0823
Phone: (574) 533-5388 Fax: (574) 534-6444
E-mail: biblemem@maplenet.net
Website: www.bible-memory.org
Executive Director: Lon Erb
Sponsoring Organization:
Bible Memory Board of Directors

God's Love and Security Didn't Leave
By Elizabeth Rayburn

Bible Memory Camp was awesome as usual. The worship and Bible time were special and very informative. Michael Miller's teen time was very interesting.

I think all of camp was great but campfire was the best part. Every night more and more kids either were giving their lives to Christ or rededicating their lives. On Wednesday night, Michael Miller talked about the crucifixion, about our sins and about how unworthy we really are. Even though we all had heard about the crucifixion, it was just the way that he was explaining it all that made it seem new and incredible. God's presence and his love for us, even as unworthy as we all are, were so powerful that we all cried.

When I left campfire God's love and security didn't leave me. It was still with me the following day and even when we got home. I still felt His love as exhausted as I was. God's love for me will never die. Bible Memory Camp is an awesome week with other youth who love Jesus.

Black Rock Retreat

Description

Located one hour west of Philadelphia in the wooded countryside of Lancaster County, Black Rock is a summer camp and retreat center. It offers comfortable accommodations, including handicapped accessibility, and delicious food for rental groups, as well as an exciting summer camp and outdoor school programs for youth.

We operate year-round as a rental facility with accommodations including 329 beds in motel rooms or bunk cabins, a dining area for 200, six meeting rooms, and a gymnasium. Recreational facilities include a ball field, hiking trails, a ropes course, and outdoor volleyball/ basketball courts. A service-oriented staff is on duty to make your retreat as enjoyable and effective as possible.

History

Black Rock Retreat Center began in 1954 through the efforts of Frank Enck, a local businessman but additionally a pastor and bishop in Lancaster Mennonite Conference. With a heart for the youth of Lancaster City who lacked constructive summertime activities, he purchased twelve acres of natural woodland as a place to gather some of these youth and introduce them to their Creator through God's creation. Frank invited other persons with similar vision to join him in the effort. That was the beginning of Black Rock.

The group also had a vision for adult activities, so over time other facilities and programs were added for these persons. The youth ministry remains the main effort and has expanded to include outdoor education for Christian schools and homeschoolers, and a ropes course. Beginning on a twelve-acre tract with 120 bunks and two double beds, we are now almost 100 acres and include 181 motel-style beds in the Retreat Center Complex.

In the last twenty-five years our Ministry of Hospitality with church retreats, Sunday school classes, and youth groups has become a major emphasis of time, energy, and finances.

Mission Statement

Black Rock Retreat is dedicated to spreading the gospel of Jesus Christ and strengthening his church. We provide quality facilities and a serving staff within the refuge of God's creation, which encourages spiritual growth and restoration.

Black Rock Retreat continues to have a mission for sponsoring youth who cannot afford to pay for this experience in God's awesome creation. Our outdoor education program and ropes course that began in the mid-1980s now accommodates more than twice as many school-aged youth as the summer camp program.

1345 Kirkwood Pike
Quarryville, Pennsylvania 17566-9539
Phone: (717) 529-3232
Toll-free: (800) 858-9299
Fax: (717) 786-6022
E-mail: main@brr.org
Website: www.brr.org
Administrator: Robert M. Bender
Sponsoring Organization:
Black Rock Retreat Association
Other Affiliations: Lancaster Mennonite Conference and
Christian Camp and Conference Association

The Elderhostel program has been the backbone of our adult programming and the Ministry of Hospitality to our guest groups is still our largest outreach to interdenominational and nondenominational groups. Black Rock's most significant contribution is to assist youth of all ages to make life-changing spiritual decisions – a first-time personal commitment to Jesus Christ, a recommitment, or a surrender of their personal life mission to what Christ is calling them to do.

The focus of our entire ministry is on knowing Christ and making him known. We encourage our guests to get out and enjoy the natural surroundings during their time here. Additionally, our outdoor education program staff members teach students about God and creation, imparting biblical principles to them through the beauty of our natural surroundings.

Camp Buckeye Retreat Center

Description

Camp Buckeye Retreat Center is located in the wooded hills of east-central Ohio, Tuscarawas County. Our ninety-one acres of hiking trails are adjacent to hundreds of acres of state property, including two waterfalls and a cave.

Facilities include Agape Center Lodge, seven cabins, and five Adirondacks with accommodations for 100 campers plus staff in summer and 50 in winter. Program focus is for the disadvantaged; the swimming pool a highlight.

Stories

Buckeye Celebrates Twenty Years of Ministry to Families and Youth

Camp Buckeye is celebrating twenty years of ministry. In 1984, through the combined efforts of LeRoy Mullet, Ken Stoltzfus, and Nate Miller, Camp Buckeye was purchased for $130,000. This included ninety-one rolling, wooded acres with a large lodge, a camp manager's cottage, cabins, Adirondacks, a chapel, an amphitheater, and an Olympic-size pool, all in desperate need of repair. The beginnings of the dreams were realized.

Those early days consisted of lots of hard grunt work—cleaning cabins, remodeling the lodge, winterizing facilities, cleaning and repairing the long-unused pool, scrubbing, and work, work, work. The insurmountable things to be done did not deter the enthusiasm with which Nate, an elementary schoolteacher, began plans for summer camps for city kids. He, along with his wife, Vi, a social worker, made numerous contacts with churches, social service agencies, and anyone who would lend them an ear.

The first summer camp was held in 1984—one week of camp with forty-five campers, called Back to Basics. Sheep were sheared, goats milked, wool carded and spun, candles dipped, chickens butchered, suppers cooked at campfires, along with lots of singing and sharing of God's love. Family and friends were recruited for counselors, kitchen staff, craft and recreation directors.

Meantime, Ken and his wife, Elaine, pastored the church, Living Word Fellowship, that utilized the lodge on Sunday mornings. They also pursued programming for adults through various Christian seminars and workshops.

10055 Camp Road NW
Beach City, Ohio 44608
Phone/Fax: (330) 756-2380
E-mail: campbuck@tusco.net
Website: www.campbuckeye.org
Administrator: Jason Stephens
Sponsoring Organization: Grass Roots Ministries

At one point in the camp's history, Kim Kellogg and Mike Pacula joined the ministry efforts by coordinating Christian contemporary concerts, under the name of Grassroots Concerts. Singers such as Silverwind, Michael Card, 2nd Chapter of Acts, Michael W. Smith, and Petra along with Josh McDowell were hosted by Grassroots.

The camp continues to be used all year long for church and family retreats, children's camps such as Bible Memory, Christian Worship Center, Band Camp, Church of God, and Boy Scout troops.

Camps with Meaning

Description

Camps With Meaning is an umbrella organization for three camps—**Assiniboia, Koinonia,** and **Moose Lake.** Camps for children, youth, families, and handicapped adults are offered during July and August. Retreats for enrichment and growth are featured September to June. All facilities are available to school and church rental groups September to June.

Camp Assiniboia

2220 Lido Plage Road Cartier, Manitoba R4K 1A3
Phone: (204) 864-2159
E-mail: campa@mts.ent
Rich Boyd, Manager

Description

Started in 1949, Camp Assiniboia is located sixteen kilometers west of Winnipeg on 160 acres of forest, riverbank, and meadow. Activities include Bible curriculum, singing, crafts, nature discovery, horsemanship, hayrides, swimming, archery, ropes course, volleyball, cross-country skiing, snowshoeing, skating, toboggan slide, broomball, and outdoor meals.

History

Camp Assiniboia began as a result of several factors. Christian summer camping had begun in Manitoba under the auspices of the Canadian Sunday School Mission in the 1930s. Some Mennonite church leaders were concerned that there should be a Mennonite camp program for children of their congregations where the Mennonite point of view and heritage could be imparted.

The leaders of the Mennonite Youth Organization also nourished a vision for a *jugendheim* (youth home) or camp. Willhelm Enns, the leader of the congregation at Springstein in south central Manitoba, had a strong love for youth, and his congregation was concerned that some of their youth were drawn to a local resort known as Sunnyside Beach, where unwholesome activities were deemed to take place.

When this resort came up for sale, Bishop Enns headed an effort to purchase the property and convert it to a camp. The Assiniboine Mennonite Mission Camp was established in 1949 and was operated by a camp association until 1957, when it was given over to the Conference of Mennonites in Manitoba, now Mennonite Church Manitoba (MCM).

200-600 Shaftesbury Blvd.
Winnipeg, Manitoba R3P 2J1
Phone: (204) 896-1616
Fax: (204) 832-7804
E-mail: camps@mennochurch.mb.ca
Website: www.campswithmeaning.org
Executive Director: Bob Wiebe
Sponsoring Organization:
Mennonite Church Manitoba

Camp Moose Lake

P.O. Box 38 Sprague, Manitoba R0A 1Z0
Phone: (240) 437-2091
E-mail: cml@mts.net
Will and Alvie Martens, Co-Managers

Description

Camp Moose Lake is located in southeast Manitoba, 224 kilometers southwest of Winnipeg in Northwest Angle Provincial Forest on Moose Lake. Activities include Bible curriculum, singing, nature discovery, swimming, canoeing, kayaking, boardsailing, basketball, volleyball, archery, broomball, cross-country skiing, snow-shoeing, tobogganing, outdoor meals.

History

Camp Moose Lake in southeastern Manitoba was established in 1957. In part the impetus for its inception, as well as that of Camp Koinonia several years later, was to offer a camping option on a lakeshore and additional camping spaces to the many children who wished to attend Camp Assiniboia.

Another reason was that a number of Mennonite families from the Gretna-Plum Coulee-Altona area had been inspired by the possibilities for camping. These individuals purchased cottage lots at Moose Lake in south-eastern Manitoba, hoping to have a camp for children next door. They formed an association, willing to make their cottages available

continued

for campers and to contribute to the development and guidance of the camp.

The camp and the cottagers were a mutual encouragement to one another, with the camp serving as a site for Sunday worship and the cottagers offering support and guidance. The camp ownership shifted to Camps with Meaning at a later point.

Camp Koinonia

P.O. Box 312 Boissevain, Manitoba R0K 0E0
Phone: (204) 534-2504
E-mail: mheide@mts.net
Matthew and Heather Heide, Co-Managers

Description

Located 272 kilometers southwest of Winnipeg in Turtle Mountain Provincial Park. Activities include Bible curriculum, singing, nature discovery, swimming, canoeing, archery, volleyball, sport- climbing, hiking, mountain biking, hockey, snowshoeing, cross-country skiing, skating, broomball, and outdoor meals.

History

Camp Koinonia began in 1964 near Boissevain in western Manitoba. The Mennonites in this area desired a local camp also. The camp was established as an intentionally wilderness-oriented camp in the Turtle Mountain Provincial Park. There was no electricity in the early years, and several programs took advantage of the out-tripping opportunities of the area. As was the case for all three camps, significant and sacrificial volunteer labor was involved in building the camp.

Camps with Meaning Common History

Over the years the three Camps with Meaning developed from being summer- to year-round camp operations. A significant thrust in this direction took place in the mid-1970s, when winterized lodges were built at each camp. Programming shifted from models borrowed from other Christian camps to programs more reflective of an Anabaptist theology. The three camps were brought under one administration in 1975 under the name "Camps with Meaning" with Terry Burkhalter as the first full-time, overall program director. A significant and unique emphasis implemented during the first ten years of Camps with Meaning was the inclusion of persons with disabilities in the camping program, and on developing a program philosophy which emphasized participation rather than competition. In addition, camps changed from volunteer to salaried staff in key positions such as managers.

In more recent years, physical development of site and facilities has continued. The summer camper demographic served has shifted from a population with a Mennonite concentration in the early years to a population where less than half the summer campers come from Mennonite churches. Guest groups represent a similarly wide range of backgrounds.

Mission Statement

Camps with Meaning is an extension of the congregational life of Mennonite Church Manitoba. It serves these congregations and the larger community by providing facilities and Christian programs in a setting close to nature.

We strive to create an atmosphere conducive to:

· The discovery and the nurture of a meaningful relationship with Jesus Christ and commitment to him and his way of life.

· Affirming the worth of self and others, as well as developing skills in community living.

· Developing an appreciation for the natural environment, learning responsible stewardship of it, and responding in worship to the God who created it.

Our beliefs and practices are based on Anabaptist theology. The camp's primary goal is to further the kingdom of God.

The camp programs have attempted to meet the goals of this purpose statement in several significant ways.

First, the ministry to campers has attempted to balance both "invitational" and "nurturing" elements. It is a source of joy when campers take steps in following Jesus, whether for the first time or as a next step of faithfulness. Camps with Meaning is also cautious to ensure that children do not respond out of a sense of guilt or pressure, and that they adequately understand what following Jesus means. The aim is for a holistic and happy faith experience for campers. One way of accomplishing this is through the creation of a Bible curriculum for the summer program, with a cycle of biblical topics treated over several years. There has also been an emphasis on composing new camp songs which reflect the curriculum.

Second, an ethos of inclusion has developed, starting with children with disabilities and the offering of several camp weeks each summer for adults with mental health challenges. There is a strong sense that camp must be a safe refuge for all who come.

Third, camp programming has de-emphasized competition, instead offering activities in which all campers, including persons with handicaps, can experience success.

Fourth, there has been an intentional emphasis on creation and creation stewardship through a nature activity program in which all campers partake. In addition, an overnight campout is a part of each child's camp session.

Fifth, the camp has acted as an extension of the congregation through offering winter retreats for various

continued

cross sections of the population of Mennonite Church Manitoba, and through bringing persons together from various congregations to serve at camp, where they also learn to know and appreciate each other.

Finally, there is a strong sense among the summer staff that leadership should be based more on consensus than hierarchical models.

Stories

Smoke, the Horse, Legs for the Physically Challenged

By Marlee Chancy

My experience with the Camps with Meaning horsemanship program has spanned seventeen years and includes many special memories. As a camper, I eagerly awaited that special time slot entitled "Horses." My love of all things equine began with those opportunities to groom and ride "my" horse for those few precious minutes a day. Finally, at age 14, I was old enough to attend the trail camp where I could ride all day long for a whole week. It was in those weeks of fun (and pain!) that my confidence in riding really developed.

Later, as a summer wrangler and then full-time horsemanship coordinator, the work was often dirty and tiring (and very cold in the wintertime!) but also fun and rewarding. Highlights included watching campers overcome their fear of going near a horse to sitting proudly in the saddle with big smiles on their faces, evening sleigh rides listening to groups singing Christmas carols with big snowflakes falling around us, and seeing those campers with physical or mental disabilities riding with confidence and grace.

One particularly poignant moment involves a young girl with significant disabilities and a gentle horse named Smoke. This camper loved being around the horses and enjoyed short rides but lacked the physical tolerance to join her cabin mates on a full trail ride on their last day. While waiting for her cabin mates to return, we placed some horse "treats" on her wheelchair tray for Smoke. Watching Smoke happily eat his treats with this young girl's arms wrapped around his neck was a touching moment. Smoke's gentle nature allowed this camper to have some special time with her horse on her last day at camp.

Camping Gives Meaning to the Manitoba Summer

By Brian Petkau

In the early 1970s I worked with the summer camping programs at Camp Assiniboia and Camp Koinonia in Manitoba. Many fond and sustaining memories came from working at those camps, memories associated with canoeing, overnight campouts, performing skits at talent nights, and telling stories in the cabins at night and around campfires. Lifelong friendships were forged with other camp staff during those weeks when everything was done together and focused on the campers. Many of the camp staff later assumed leadership roles in Manitoba churches and conference programs.

Similarly, many campers whom I first met and remembered as being shy or rambunctious nine-, ten-, eleven-, twelve-, thirteen-, or fourteen-year-old young people came to play prominent roles in their local churches, in their communities, and in their chosen professions. To have had the opportunity to experience the relative intensity of those week-long summer camp sessions with staff and campers alike and to see their faith development is a gift and a lasting legacy.

Camp Camrec

Description

Camp Camrec is a retreat center located on 240 wooded acres in the Cascade Mountains of Washington State. Mennonite sponsored retreats and camps, weekend and weeklong, are planned throughout the year. The facilities with a capacity of eighty are also available for rental by nonprofit guest groups.

Activities include hiking, volleyball, softball, basketball, and snow tubing. Forest Service roads are available for mountain biking, cross-country skiing, and snowmobiling. Ski resorts, whitewater rafting, swimming facilities, and tourist attractions are located nearby.

History

Camp Camrec was founded in 1965 by the General Conference Mennonite churches of Washington State primarily as a place to hold summer camps for the youth of the churches. Before the churches built the camp, retreats were held at various rental facilities. The summer camping program is still the primary mission, but as the camp grew, other programs developed with it. We now hold retreats for various segments of our constituency and are also available to member churches for their use. We rent to churches and other not-for-profit groups when member churches are not using the facility.

Mission Statement

Camp Camrec is a place to meet and be met in the harmony of God, people, and nature. It provides an outdoor setting for renewal, fellowship, teaching, and service.

It is dedicated to the enrichment of the lives of members of the Washington Mennonite Fellowship and their guests. It has been dedicated by worship and prayers, and is rededicated by answers to prayers, by lives committed to Christian faithfulness, by friendships made and enriched, by laughter and play, by experiences of compassion and caring, by respectful stewardship and protection of its resources, and by each of us who return from camp refreshed and challenged.

18899 Little Chumstick Creek Road
Leavenworth, Washington 98826
Phone: (509) 548-7245
E-mail: camrec@rightathome.com
Website: www.camrec.wa.us.mennonite.net
Managers: Roger and Carmen Reimer
Sponsoring Organization:
Washington Mennonite Fellowship

Cove Valley Christian Youth Camp

Description
Located in south central Pennsylvania mountains, forty minutes from three major interstates: I-70, I-81, and I-76. Facilities include a kitchen/dining area with meeting room below, eight cabins, a motel unit, and a self-contained motel unit. All are winterized. Recreation: 3.9-acre lake with canoes, swimming pool, a large pond, a ropes course, a ball field, and hiking trails. Total sleeping capacity: 184. Food service option is available. Open yearround.

History
In 1966 several people from the Franklin Mennonite Conference churches purchased a farm in the Little Cove area near Mercersburg, Pa. The first building project was to add to three sides of the original farm house to make a dining room for up to seventy-five people. It was necessary to move a lot of soil in those early years and the donation of two bulldozers, "Samson" and "Little Samson," helped tremendously.

Soon a motel building (twelve rooms) and caretaker's house were built and the first of the eight cabins that now house youth yearround. Recently a second motel, Skyline Family Retreat Center, has become a popular spot for family reunions and small groups to meet and eat – all in the same building. As we continue the minister to the people in this area, we pray that any who come here will be drawn closer to the Lord because of their experience at Cove Valley.

Mission Statement
Cove Valley Christian Youth Camp provides a place and opportunity for Christian teaching and fellowship along with wholesome and guided recreation in a spiritual atmosphere without discrimination of age, sex, or race.

Stories
The Best Kept Secret

By Lee Ebersole (adapted from *MCA Newsletter*, 1991)

"Cove Valley Camp is the best kept secret in Franklin County," [Pennsylvania] a guest said to me at the camp's parking lot overlooking Little Cove Valley. As he walked away I was left scratching my head and thinking, "Was that a criticism or a compliment?"

Cove Valley Camp offers a 164-acre mountain retreat center that is both "back in" and only two hours from Lancaster County, Pa.; Harrisonburg, Va.; Washington, DC; or Baltimore, Md. Approximately sixty-five percent of the site is wooded. There are retreats and camps planned for children and adults in addition to the availability of the camp for persons or groups to come and plan their own program and schedule.

5357 Little Cove Road
Mercersburg, Pennsylvania 17236
Phone: (717) 328-3055
Fax: (717) 328-2350
E-mail: covevalley@pa.net
Website: covevalleycamp.mennonite.net
Executive Director: Allen Eshleman
Sponsoring Organization: Cove Valley Christian Youth Camp Association. Affiliated with Franklin Mennonite Conference

Bird watchers can get an eye- and earful here as many types of birds find refuge in the area. Marian Yoder, a resident employee, has seen 105 different species of birds since coming here five years ago. Pileated and other varieties of woodpeckers can be seen and heard busily pecking at the trees decimated by the gypsy moth infiltration. Five types of flycatchers have been seen as well as other more common birds.

Is it a criticism or a compliment to be considered the "best kept secret in Franklin County"? Well, I'll take it primarily as a compliment. We, in Christian camping, need all the compliments we can get! And I trust that those who come to Cove Valley will have an experience similar to finding a special nugget of treasure.

It is challenging to see the many possibilities of ministry in a retreat setting. While it is a privilege to be considered a wonderful secret, we cannot keep it to ourselves if we desire others to experience spiritual growth through being here. Our goal for Cove Valley Camp is to provide a place and program for Christian renewal and growth to occur. We trust that the Lord will continue to lead us to use this camp for this purpose and to God's glory.

Crooked Creek Christian Camp

Description

A year-round facility located on 300 acres of hills and hardwood timber in southeast Iowa. The camp provides space and services for retreats, family reunions, and children's camping programs. The facilities include a multipurpose retreat lodge with fifteen private sleeping rooms and meeting area, and a second lodge with two sleeping rooms, and eighteen cabins. Activities include a swimming pool, basketball/tennis court, and hiking trails.

History

In the early 1970s a group of interested persons began looking for land for a Mennonite camp in southeast Iowa. None became available and the idea was shelved until 1979 when several Mennonite businessmen bought a parcel of land along the banks of Crooked Creek with the idea of forming a camp. The Southeast Iowa Mennonite Camp Association was formed in 1980; more land was acquired and the first summer camps were held in 1981 in the great out-of-doors! Cabins and a building with meeting space, kitchen, and restrooms were built in 1984. A motel-style building was added in 1994, providing varied accommodations for all types of groups.

Mission Statement

Crooked Creek Christian Camp provides a natural setting for persons of all ages to enjoy creation and meet God the Creator. Nurturing Christian faith, building wholesome relationships, and studying the Scriptures shall be central to the programs offered by the camp. May all who come here find rest, renewal, and the peace of our Lord Jesus Christ.

Stories

Hearing Her [Sobering] Story Made My Work Worthwhile

By Mary Lou Farmer, Director

Each fall Women Living Sober (AA Women) hold a retreat at Crooked Creek Christian Camp. The ladies who come have been sober anywhere from a few days to many years. It is always good to have them at camp and inspiring to hear the stories of how lives have been changed. It was especially poignant in 2004. Here's Dorothy's story; names have been changed.

In the fall of 2004, Sylvia (one of camp cooks) told me one of the ladies looked familiar but she couldn't place her. During the weekend Sylvia had a chance to talk to the lady and discovered it was Dorothy, whose daughter, Jane, dated Sylvia's son, Bob, while they were in high school. Sylvia enjoyed Jane but had concerns about the relationship since Jane's home life was far different from the Christian home that Bob grew up in. She spent much time in prayer for Jane and the relationship. Bob and Jane did not continue a long-term relationship.

2830 Coppock Road
Washington, Iowa 52353-9317
Phone/Fax: (319) 653-3611
E-mail: ccccamp@lisco.com
Website: www.crookedcreekcamp.org
Administrator: Mary Lou Farmer
Sponsoring Organization: Southeast Iowa Mennonite Camp Association.

Now, years later, in talking with Dorothy at the retreat, Sylvia discovered that Dorothy is a Christian, has stopped drinking, and has made positive changes in her life. Dorothy commented that she remembered Bob and his family and how she noticed their Christian lives. It was a hope and inspiration to Dorothy. While Dorothy's life didn't change immediately, Bob's Christian commitment and lifestyle had an impact on her and her family.

With tears in her eyes Sylvia commented, "Hearing Dorothy's story made it worth my time to work this weekend."

Others notice our Christian lives. Sometimes we know that. Sometimes it is years before we learn how that happened. Other times we won't know at all. But living the Christian life does have an impact on others.

Camp Deerpark

Description

Camp Deerpark is located in the lower Catskills, eighty-five miles northwest of New York City. It supports the ministries of seventeen New York City Mennonite churches, with rental facilities for other Christian churches, individuals, and families. Year-round lodging available for seventy; summer facilities for 100.

Our summer program includes 10-day "sleep-away camps" for inner-city children and youth. Christian education and nurture are integrated with activities that include hiking, swimming, snow tubing, basketball, handball, volleyball, campfires, and hayrides. More of a camp than a retreat center.

History

The efforts of Pennsylvania Mennonites doing mission work in New York City in the 1940s resulted in eight Mennonite churches by the mid-1960s with numerous active youth ministries. In the fall of 1968, NYC church leaders purchased the Old Homestead Farm Resort for $85,000. A place with the essentials of a tractor and barn, dishes in the cupboard and blankets on the beds, it still looks much as it did at its beginning in 1969, with the same tables and chairs in the dining room, and even like it did for many years before that under its former owner. In 1989 Camp Deerpark was incorporated as a not-for-profit organization.

Mission Statement

"Empowering youth to serve Christ in the city"

The purpose of Camp Deerpark shall be:

· To share the gospel of Jesus Christ within the community.

· To provide church-related programs in Christian nurture, training, camping, religious seminars, and retreats.

· To collaborate with the Mennonite Church, with special emphasis on the ministry of the New York City Mennonite Churches.

Stories

The following poem is written by a former Camp Deerpark camper. This poem was collected as part of a camp program that was designed to help young people address the issues of peace and justice in their communities from a Christian perspective. The perspective represented is a direct result of the ministry of Camp Deerpark on this young woman's life. Camp also served as a facility to encourage this kind of reflection and helped to give confidence and a voice to her poetry.

"The Way" By Devonne Lilla Mc Morris, camper at Deerpark

I am homeless,
Please help me,
My stomach's at war.
I am filthy,
I am smelly,

200 Brandt Road, P.O. Box 394
Westbrookville, New York 12785-0394
Phone: (845) 754-8669
Fax: (845) 754-8217
E-mail: Info@campdeerpark.org
Website: www.campdeerpark.org
Director: Ken Bontrager
Sponsoring Organization: Mennonite Action Program of the New York City Council of Mennonite Churches
Memberships: MCA, Christian Camp and Conference Association

Can't you see I'm poor?
I hold out to you a cup,
A cup for you to throw in change.
But yet you ignore me,

And give me a look of disgust in exchange.
Yes, I do live on the trains,
But this wasn't my dream.
My dreams fell down the drain.
You think I like bothering
And begging for change?
No, not at all.
I wish I had a job with a check to wait on.
I wish I was a lawyer with a case to debate on.
But I don't and more than likely won't.
I'm unhealthy and malnourished.
To me everything looks delicious.
My teeth are rotten
What little I have.
Only God can remember when I last took a bath.
In the winter I'm cold
Due to the shortness of clothes.
But I survive as I strive
To get by, day by day.
This is my living
My lifestyle called the way.

Drift Creek Camp

Description

Incorporated in 1960, Mennonite Camp Association of Oregon, Inc. is a nonprofit corporation and as representative agency of its membership owns Drift Creek Camp. DCC relates to the Pacific Northwest Mennonite Conference of the Mennonite Church USA.

DCC is located in the Coast Range Mountains providing a secluded setting for conferences, outdoor schools and retreats just twelve miles from beautiful Pacific Ocean. Located on twenty-eight acres of land, it is completely surround by "The Loop" of Drift Creek, a pristine mountain stream which in fall and winter is resident to migrating giant salmon and steelhead fish.

Recreation includes hiking, swimming/inner tubing in the creek, fishing, softball, volleyball, shuffleboard, horseshoes, a climbing wall, plus overnight backpacking.

DCC is a conference and retreat center, rents to various church, family, school, and community groups, has handicapped accessible lodging. The summer youth camp was the beginning focus and continues to be so. The summer occupancy is 180; fall and winter, 117.

History

DCC was founded on a grassroots interest in Christian camp programs for youth in a natural environment. With the primary functions of DCC as a location for youth summer camps and a rental facility for retreats and reunions remaining true through the present, the major changes at camp have been the steady improvements and additions to facilities.

Mission Statement

Sharing God's love in harmony with creation

The unique setting of DCC in an old growth, temperate rain forest allows campers and guests to experience the majesty of God's handiwork. Preservation of this ancient forest is foundational to the camp's perpetuity and purpose. DCC is located on Siuslaw National Forest land by special use permit which allows camp staff the opportunity to witness God's love to people from a broad range of faith backgrounds.

Stories

Datum

By Jonathan Heppner, former youth camper

In thinking about the role which Drift Creek Camp has played in my life I think of the datum; a consistent post against which I can accurately measure my physical and spiritual growth.

P.O. Box 1110 Lincoln City, Oregon 97367
Phone: (541) 996-3978
Fax: (541) 764-5115
E-mail: driftcreek@harborside.com
Website: www.driftcreek.org
Administrators: Jerry and Amy Markus
Sponsoring Organization: Mennonite Camp Association of Oregon, Inc.
Membership: MCA, Christian Camp and Conference Association

Within the forest of blustery firs, through which planes of sunlight were lucky to penetrate, a sanctuary from the ever-present world of telephones, strip malls and televisions existed. In this sanctuary I learned that slugs, when rubbed on a nettle wound, can soothe the penetrating sting. And I observed how they can effortlessly glide over the sharp edge of a razor unharmed. I was able to shoot a bow and arrow, an arcane practice within my family. I was able to feel comfortable discussing more serious issues with my fellow-pilgrims, not because I knew them, but because we were in a safe place together.

As the years have gone by, Drift Creek Camp has changed significantly as all things do. The road seems to be more sparsely forested, the playing fields have a new building on them, the mysterious third floor, once a haven for avid "mattress jumpers," has been turned into a "cabin," and the belching drone of the generator has been reduced significantly.

Yet, all these being noted, Drift Creek Camp still remains the sacred sanctuary in the forest by which I can measure myself and the world around me.

"I knew the grounds would look the same, the air would smell as sweet, the damp breeze would hit my nose, and the birds would be singing the same songs they were fifteen years before." —*Anna Heppner, former camper and counselor*

Camp Elim

Description

Located on the shores of Lac Pelletier within the grasslands of southwest Saskatchewan, our primary purpose includes a summer camp program during July and August. The facilities, featuring sixty beds and a trailer court, are available to church and family groups for retreats year-round except when summer camps are in session. Activities include canoeing, kayaking, waterskiing, swimming, beach volleyball, and hiking. Buildings include a large hall, campground, nature centre, and ten cabins (4 winterized).

History

Camp Elim was purchased in 1945 as a place to do evangelical outreach. The dance hall on a beach resort on the shores of a small lake ("an oasis on the prairies") was converted into "the tabernacle" where people could meet God. Speakers came from afar and children's camps were held. Later camps included teens, and became more nature oriented. Now summer camps for all ages are held and rentals are available yearround. School groups are welcome for outdoor education, and there is a small nature center. Evangelism is still important but it is done in a different way, relating it to God's world.

78 - 6th Avenue NE
Swift Current, Saskatchewan S9H 2L7
Phone: (306) 627-3339
E-mail: camp@campelim.ca
Website: www.campelim.ca
Executive Director: Kalyn Wiebe
Contact: Ben Dyck, Board Chairperson
Sponsoring Organization: Mennonite Church Saskatchewan
Memberships: Saskatchewan Camping Association, MCA

Mission Statement

· To provide an opportunity for spiritual retreat.
· To develop Christian community, living together and meeting new people.
· To teach and learn Scripture and human relationships from an Anabaptist perspective.
· To offer children the opportunity to make commitments appropriate for their age and maturity, as well as to challenge teens and adults to make adult commitments.
· To relate to nature and waterfront ecology in an effort to promote stewardship towards all creation.
· To have fun positively.

Stories

Shaped by Camp, the Camp Elim Influence

By Amy Peters, a former camper and recent staffer of Camp Elim

I have attended camp since I was about seven-years old and have worked at camp for the past five years. My experiences have been a very influential part of my life. I find I can experience God in a way that I could not any other place. I feel completely surrounded by God's love at Camp Elim.

Being in nature makes me more aware of God's presence. Every moment I spend at camp I feel totally in awe that God could create such beautiful things. God has put so much detail into everything surrounding us. I am amazed to think that the God who created this world is the same God who loves each of us so much.

Working with children has also been an important part of my life. I have learned a lot about God's love through them. Their enthusiasm for life inspires enthusiasm in me about what I am doing.

My relationship with God has been strengthened through working at camp. I have learned the importance of relying on God in times of trouble. I have also learned a great deal about what I believe through working with children. They often want to know what I believe and talking about my faith has strengthened it a whole lot.

Reflecting on my time at camp, I am thankful for all the relationships God has put into my life. I am thankful for relationships with campers, staff members, and especially thankful for my friendship with God. I feel fortunate to have had the experience of being a camper and a staff member at Camp Elim.

Camp Friedenswald

Description

Camp Friedenswald began as a diverse year-round camp/retreat center on 350 acres of woodland and lakefront. Facilities are 56-person and 24-person lodges, cabins, and motel-style rooms with bed space for up to 300. Activities include swimming, boating, volleyball, a ropes challenge program, and a nature center, with winter activities of cross-country skiing and tubing. Youth, adult, family, and outdoor education programming is available. Camp Friedenswald is twenty minutes north of Elkhart, Indiana. It is handicapped accessible and rents to other groups.

History

In 1950 land was purchased on Lake Shavehead in southern Michigan as a place for youth of the Middle and Central Districts of the General Conference Mennonite churches to gather. It was to serve as an evangelistic arm of the church. An early leader stated, "There are more than twice as many hours of opportunity for Christian education in a week of camp than a whole year of Sunday school." It had become apparent that the meetings of their youth in other established camps indicated the need for their own place.

The mission remains the same but the size and scope have increased significantly. Now Friedenswald activities include summer and winter youth camp, adult and senior retreats, conference groups, church retreats, family retreats, and more recently outdoor education, and in cooperation with nearby Amigo Centre, has provided a model for the larger church. (Amigo and Friedenswald co-direct programs, as well as intentionally set schedules to offer more opportunities for programming.)

Mission Statement

Camp Friedenswald seeks to provide people of all ages the opportunity to gain a better understanding and love for God and Christ, self, others, and nature.

In support of this mission statement, our summer and winter youth programs remain strong. Countless memories of faith experiences at camp lead youth into long-term relationships with Christ and the church. In addition, our fall adult retreats (women's, men's, and senior) provide opportunities for continued spiritual renewal, fellowship, and growth beyond childhood years. Our retreat center offers unique opportunities for churches, families, and other groups to meet in God's creation.

15406 Watercress Drive Cassopolis, Michigan 49031
Phone: (269) 476-9744
Fax: (269) 476-9745
E-mail: info@friedenswald.org
Website: www.friedenswald.org
Executive Director: Todd Kirkton
Sponsoring Organization: Central District Conference, Mennonite Church USA
Membership: MCA

Stories

It Grows on You, This Place of Caring
By Dave, a summer staffer

The mission of the camp is to change lives using God's love, nature, and mentors that matter. They all come together at camp. My life changed early on, at about eight or nine-years old, and the camp's influence modified my life again this summer. The kids come in their age groups to experience the wonders of nature in the peaceful woods with their peers, led by a summer staff of college students and a permanent staff of caring Christians.

A Love Letter to Camp Friedenswald
By Rebecca, a fourth-grade camper

Dear Camp Friedenswald,

I had a real fun time at your camp. I loved the Bible stories and how they actually got acted out. My favorite was Zacchaeus because it was funny how he asked people to pay their taxes, but I also liked the lesson that Jesus loves everybody no matter what they do.

I loved the songs and their motions. They were great. I had fun with the games and the people, too. The food was excellent. I liked your camp and I think other people would like it, too.

Thanks for all you've done and thanks for the privilege of letting me come. I also thank Jesus for keeping the camp in order and the plants beautiful and nicely growing.

Harman Mt. Farm Campground

Description

We are located in the scenic mountains of West Virginia. We offer family camping – some sites with water and electric hookups, a small playground with mini-golf, slide, swings, basketball, volleyball and horseshoes, a pavilion with electric range and refrigerator, and hot showers. Open mid-May through October.

History

Harman Mt. Farm, about 120 acres, was purchased by Virginia Conference's Mission Board in the mid-1940s as a "mission property" in the mountains of West Virginia. It was bought to provide a living for a Virginia Conference pastor who was asked to serve in this area.

The pastor farmed and pastored, as did a number of subsequent pastors, until the mid-1980s when the property was rented to a local farmer. Within the past several years, Virginia Mennonite Board of Missions has transferred ownership of Harman Mt. Farm to Central District of Virginia Mennonite Conference and it is now governed by a board of directors. The farmhouse still provides housing for the pastor of Riverside Mennonite Church.

In the early 1970s, Central District Overseer, Glendon Blosser, was instrumental in developing a vision for a small campground on one corner of the property to provide a place for church and youth groups from the Shenandoah Valley of Virginia to use for campouts and retreats. He, along with others began to develop what became known as Harman Mt. Farm Campground. Over the years, the campground was used less and less by the Valley churches and has become a place for travelers passing through our scenic area to camp.

The campground started as a very rustic facility but over the years has had many improvements. The first of these was a bath house with hot showers. Then came a pavilion, a ten-hole mini-golf course based on the Old Testament life of Israel, shuffleboard courts, a paved basketball court, and more recently three small cabins (sleeping only) with a combined capacity of twenty-two bunks. We have ten camping spots with water and electric hookups and a lot of "open field" camping for tents.

Harman Mt. Farm Campground continues to operate on a small budget with no paid staff and depends on volunteer groups and donations to fund any improvements.

HC 70, Box 67-A Harman, West Virginia 26270
Phone: (304) 227-3647
E-mail: rolowenger@juno.com
Directors: Robert and Lois Wenger
Sponsoring Organization: Central District of Virginia
Mennonite Conference,
Mennonite Church USA
Membership: MCA

Mission Statement

"Camping in a Christian environment"

We endeavor to provide a relaxing, friendly place for families to enjoy a quiet setting and the natural beauty of our local area. We hope in the next few years to be in a position to offer some limited camping experiences for local children.

Camp Hebron

Description

Camp Hebron is a Christ-centered conference and retreat center with a capacity of 250 to 300 in winter and 350 to 400 hundred in summer where people experience growth and renewal through recreation, teaching, and fellowship in God's creation.

Programs include weekend and week-long events for all ages, including family camps and camps for adults with developmental or physical disabilities. Over seventy programs are hosted each year with a variety of ages and interests. Facilities (campsites, shelters, cabins, or motel-style rooms) are available for rental by Christian groups. Some are handicapped accessible. We strive to be a special place.

Camps for youth include creative arts (drama, art, nature, worship dance, guitar). Six weeks of summer camp are devoted to entire families or to Moms and Tots (children 6 and under) with more events for women. We have a strong horsemanship program that includes summer camps, trail rides, horse-drawn wagon rides, and riding lessons. We also host youth retreats and focused banquets to teach, encourage, and edify believers and introduce Christ to nonbelievers. Finally, we are available year-round to groups and individuals as a conference and retreat center.

History

From its beginning in 1956-1957, Camp Hebron was envisioned as a place youth workers in the cities of Harrisburg, Reading, and Lancaster could use to get children and youth out of the urban environment and into nature where it would be easier to communicate God's love for them. The ministry expanded to include churches and families when the retreat center was built in 1972. Over the years the city churches used it less and the focus shifted more to building up the church body. In 2004 we are placing a heavy emphasis on family-oriented ministry.

Mission Statement

Camp Hebron—where people connect with God, nature, and each other.

A Christ-centered sanctuary where people find renewal and growth through recreation, teaching, and fellowship in God's creation.

Stories

Up Close and Personal

By Lanny Millette, executive director

In 1995 the weekly curriculum theme at Camp Hebron was the life of Jesus. Our staff went to great lengths to develop realistic re-creations of different aspects of Jesus life. On Sunday we took a hike to the outdoor chapel and found Mary and Joseph and a young baby in a manger snuggled into the woodshed next to the fire circle. We walked to Mountainview Lake and witnessed his baptism and two days later sat on the hillside there as a box lunch miraculously appeared during Jesus' lengthy prayer over a small basket of bread and fish (during which

957 Camp Hebron Road
Halifax, Pennsylvania 17032-9520
Phone: (717) 896-3441
Toll Free: (800) 864-7747
Fax: (717) 896-3391
E-mail: hebron@camphebron.org
Website: www.camphebron.org
Executive Director: Lanny Millette
Sponsoring Organizations: Camp Hebron Association;
fraternal organization with Lancaster Mennonite Conference.
Memberships: Christian Camp and Conference
Association, CHA (horses), MCA

we all had our eyes closed). I did not count the leftovers but there were indeed twelve baskets. We climbed Peter's Mountain and watched as Satan tempted Christ on a rock ledge. All of the campers had a ring side seat and clear view of the vast valley below them as Jesus was offered all of the kingdoms he could see (including the city of Harrisburg) and then was invited to jump into the arms of waiting angels. The campers cheered when Satan was rebuked. Throughout the week we witnessed several miracles around camp and had a wonderful triumphant procession using the camps horses. One could believe that the rocks and trees were capable of crying out in that pristine setting.

We put down the legs of the tables and ate supper while sitting on the floor and enjoyed communion and foot washing together. Later we went to a clearing and witnessed Jesus' impassioned prayer for his disciples and his task. We also had a quiet moment on the last night of camp as we went to bed with our Jesus crucified and buried. Like the disciples we did not have the end of the story that night. But the next morning we triumphantly celebrated Easter and the opportunity to experience new life in Christ. (The campers even got breakfast in bed that day!) I was privileged to walk through the curriculum eight times that summer and observe many persons come to a new and deeper understanding of Jesus and the wonderful sacrifice he made for them. The most profound thought came from an eight-year old who remarked to his friend, "You know I've heard a lot about Jesus, but this is the first time I've met him face to face." Camp gives us poignant opportunities to help children and families meet Jesus, up close and personal, and to grow in their relationship with him. What a privilege to be here.

Hidden Acres Mennonite Camp and Retreat Centre

Description

Nestled among the rolling hills of Perth County in southwestern Ontario. Programs include co-ed camps for children ages 8 to 15, single moms' camps, retreat programs, and school programs. Facilities feature a retreat centre, heated and rustic cabins, picnic shelters, a spring-fed pond for swimming, nature trails, climbing wall, basketball, tennis, and beach volleyball courts.

History

Hidden Acres began as a summer camp program for children from low-income families under the umbrella of the Western Ontario Mennonite Conference. There was an old stone farm house on the property. During the first years of summer camp, small tents and later army Tee-Pee tents were erected on wooden platforms. Later cabins were built as well as additions and renovations to the Stone House; accommodations for use by youth groups, and church retreats.

In 1974 special needs children were integrated into the regular camping program. In 1982 a week of camp for single moms and their children was added. It is now two weeks.

In the summer of 2000 a basketball camp was started and run by Mana Watsa who loves to teach the game of basketball and develop positive attitudes in children with a Christian emphasis.

Mission Statement

· To provide a setting in nature for all groups to experience a meaningful encounter with God through times of recreation, reflection, worship, and service.

· To offer camp programs which take into account the spiritual, physical, social, emotional, and educational needs of children, adults, and families.

· To promote retreats nurturing Christian discipleship and personal growth.

· To promote respect for the natural environment through modeling, and training for appropriate lifestyle decisions.

· To offer individuals and groups within the Mennonite church various opportunities for service.

Stories

A little boy who was attending the Grandparent/ Grandchild day in the warm spring was waiting for his bowl of ice cream so he could top it off with the provided sprinkles and sauces. Looking up at his grandpa with a big smile and wide eyes, he exclaimed, "Life doesn't get much better than this."

1921 Line 37 New Hamburg, Ontario N3A 4B5
Phone: (519) 625-8602
Fax: (519) 625-8606
E-mail: info@hiddenacres.ca
Website: www.hiddenacres.ca
Director: Campbell Nisbet
Sponsoring Organization: Hidden Acres
Mennonite Camp Association
Membership: MCA

How Hidden Acres Camp Prepared Me for Christian Peacemaker Teams

By Scott Albrecht

This fall I spent two months in Colombia serving with Christian Peacemaker Teams (CPT). With the team, I was a presence in civilian communities threatened by one of three or more armed groups, and attempted to witness to Christ's way of peace within that civil war. During my time there I missed two Hidden Acres board meetings, so Campbell Nisbet asked me write this article to make up for that!

I spent three summers as a counselor here at Hidden Acres Camp, which were formative to my faith development. Although I was exploring baptism at my church beforehand, my first summer was a powerful experience of getting to know Jesus as Savior and Lord, and working within a Christian community. This led me to accept baptism at the end of that summer. That led me to desiring to act out my faith in God.

At Hidden Acres I learned about service by doing it. Here I practiced leadership, dealing with physical and emotional problems, and caring for the spiritual health of campers and coworkers. All of these were helpful in CPT work. (Camping skills were even used, although I was stringing up mosquito nets instead of lean-tos.) Dealing with some problem campers may be harder than dealing with heavily-armed paramilitary soldiers. And remembering that each person, whether a difficult camper, annoying coworker or a guerilla, has spiritual needs and is loved by God, is important in any context.

Highland Retreat

Description

Highland Retreat is located on 168 acres twenty-eight miles northwest of Harrisonburg, Va. A strong summer youth camp program is offered.

Facilities include a fifteen-room retreat center, a year-round youth center for sixty, two winterized cabins, and two camping areas with thirty-two campsites, including sites with full and partial utilities. Also ten rustic cabins with twelve bunks each, three pavilions, and bathhouses. Total housing capacity is 230 people. Recreation includes a 25-meter swimming pool, hiking trails, a ropes course, playing fields, volleyball, basketball, and horseshoes.

History

Highland Retreat was established in 1958 by the Highland Churches of the Northern District of the Virginia Mennonite Conference to provide a place for groups from these churches to gather. In the early years, the primary activity was summer youth camps. In 1977, thirty acres were added to the original eighty-two allowing expanded activities, particularly the family campgrounds, a popular option. Today Highland Retreat owns 168 acres. In 1983 a retreat center was constructed to provide a new dimension to Highland's ministry and to make it a year-round facility. In 2000, a new youth facility, Red Oak Lodge, was built to provide a place for youth and family groups to gather yearround for inspiration, teaching, nurture, and wholesome recreation, expanding the ministry to a broader population.

To extend the use of the facilities and to expand the program beyond the Northern District, Highland Retreat was incorporated as an association in 1965 and membership was extended to others.

Mission Statement

To provide an outdoor retreat setting for wholesome recreation and spiritual enrichment.

Stories

Rustic Setting Nurtures Spiritual Growth at Highland Retreat

By Lindsay Deel, summer program director, 2003

The sky breaks open with the first slivers of pink and lavender. The outline of the pine trees and mountains gradually becomes clearer, and soft clouds of mist hanging over the mountains form a brilliant shade of gray contrasting sharply with the bright green of the pines. Shortly after sunrise, the summer staff members of Highland Retreat begin to gather on the basketball courts one by one and form a circle on the warm concrete. Some wear sweaters and carry mugs of coffee or tea. They use this time in the early morning to share a brief devotion and to pray for their day, their week, and their summer. Golden Nugget,

14783 Upper Highland Drive
Bergton, Virginia 22811-9712
Phone: (540) 852-3226
Fax: (540) 852-9272
E-mail: info@highlandretreat.org
Website: www.highlandretreat.org
Administrator: Paul Beiler
Sponsoring Organization: Highland Retreat of the
Mennonite Church Association, Inc.,
a membership corporation
Memberships: Christian Camp and Conference
Association, MCA

as it is called, is a valued time each day where staff can find renewal and support.

Highland's mission in programming seeks "to provide personal group experiences that encourage meaningful spiritual growth, focusing on young people and youth-related constituencies, and capitalizing on the rustic setting."

From early-morning prayer time to Wednesday hikes to evening recreation, the staff are obviously dedicated to their campers and to providing a place that encourages "meaningful spiritual growth."

Many parents send positive feedback about the fulfillment of this mission. One parent wrote, "Thank you so much for providing such a neat summer camp for children. My son recently attended wilderness camp and had a great time. I believe the camp had a significant spiritual impact on him as well, which is becoming increasingly evident by his changed behavior. Since coming home, he has consistently been more considerate, more respectful, and more obedient. He is looking forward to coming back next year."

Highland Retreat also has a great impact in the spiritual life and growth of the staff who participate in the program each summer. Many are prepared for leadership in other areas of the church. They have opportunities to share testimonies, Bible studies, and firesides with campers and each other.

Staff, campers, parents, and churches have continually provided support to Highland through their prayers, volunteering, and other contributions. Together they have kept the mission of Highland Retreat alive and well.

Camp Keola

Description

Camp Keola is located on the shores of beautiful Huntington Lake, California, surrounded by thousands of acres of Sierra National Forest. Camp Keola's programs are designed to provide a meaningful Christian experience through utilization of its natural setting.

Activities include campfires, hiking, nature studies, crafts, softball, volleyball, and other group games. Campers also enjoy sailing, swimming, canoeing, paddle and row boating. Facilities are suitable for groups of up to 140, and include rustic cabins, a lodge, and dining hall.

History

Camp Keola was acquired by the Mennonites in 1967 and turned into a summer youth camp. Before that the camp had been used by California State University at Fresno as a summer school for teachers. At one time the United States military used the camp for mountain and survival training under the name of Camp Black Fox. Before that the camp was used to house workers building the four dams that "created" Huntington Lake.

Mission Statement

To develop, promote, and facilitate excellent, wholesome retreat programs that draw people closer to Jesus Christ and to each other."

"Jesus said . . . , 'I am . . . the life'" (John 14:6). Camp Keola's primary purpose for existing is to strive to exemplify Jesus to all its campers.

Keola campers today are living the easy life compared to those of the 1960s and 1970s. In those days, campers stayed in canvas tents and slept on steel-springed army beds. The last tent platform was pulled apart in the 1980s. Now campers stay in rustic cabins with doors, windows and electric lights. Early campers who needed discipline got hard labor, digging trenches for water or electric lines. Today they get off easy, sweeping the large dining hall. Campers of old ate outside. The lake front used to be dirt hillsides and an earthen dam leading to the water. Now a wooden boardwalk surrounds the waterfront and the boats are accessed from floating docks.

Stories

"The Life, the Name"

The name Camp Keola was given to the camp by a previous proprietor. One story is that the camp was named after the proprietor's daughter, Keola. Keola is a Hawaiian name. It means and directly translates as The (Ke) Life (ola). Leola Beamer, a Hawaiian musician, says Keola means "life from heaven."

Both translations are appropriate. For many youth, their week at Camp Keola is their first true encounter with God;

P.O. Box 25925
Fresno, California 93729-5925
Phone: (559) 661-4422
Fax: (559) 661-4422
E-mail: info@campkeola.org
Website: www.campkeola.org
Executive Director: George E. Harper
Sponsoring Organization: Pacific Southwest Mennonite Retreat Ministries.

experience in nature, starry intense nights, an intimate community of faith, and words of teaching and mentoring from caring adult leaders. The fun and thrill of camp life is "the life." And the experience of God, however manifested, is truly light from heaven.

"The Life According to Artie"

By George Harper, executive director

Over the years since 1967, many people have contributed to the development of Camp Keola facilities and programs. One person in particular deserves to be mentioned.

Every summer since 1967, Art Froese has come to Camp Keola to be the summer-staff lifeguard and waterfront director. Art, a tireless worker (a farm boy from Shafter, California), has devoted thirty-five summers to transforming the waterfront and garden areas of Camp Keola into beautiful and beloved places. Nearly every camp dock, building, bench, fence, plant, and camper bears the imprimatur of Artie.

In thirty-five summers of ministry, Art has mentored three generations of summer campers and staffers, teaching us how to work, to play, to live, to whistle the "Artie" whistle, and how to worship God. It can fairly be said that Art Froese is living the life.

Lakewood Retreat

Description

Lakewood, a year-round facility which serves primarily church and family groups, is located thirty-five miles north of Tampa, Florida, on 114 woodsy and rolling acres with frontage on a 500-acre lake with canoeing and good fishing.

There are overnight accommodations for 230, a recreational campground with over fifty sites, six meeting rooms (the largest seats more than 200), and recreation facilities including tennis, shuffleboard, miniature golf, swimming, horseshoes, ball fields, human Foosball, volleyball, Ping-Pong, and carpet ball.

History and Mission are included in "The Lakewood Retreat Story."

Condensed from "The Lakewood Retreat Story" published by the Southern Mennonite Camp Association, Inc., for its 25th Anniversary 1965-1990. Compiled by Jean Pfeiffer.

Church Leaders with a Vision

Prior to 1965 "The Lakewood Retreat Story" started with the rental of Camp Gilead, Polk City, Florida, and other years at Camp Florida at a YMCA camp. All of these were rented.

Since people of color could not yet attend the regular camp because of racial tension, the Ida Street, Ybor City, and College Hill Mennonite Churches decided to camp together. It was an integrated camp. The last night of that first week of integrated camping, when everyone was in bed, shotgun blasts were heard. Those who got up to investigate saw the familiar symbol of Ku Klux Klan disapproval – a burning cross. Later a note was found with verbal hatred. The owners felt that it would be a good idea for us to find other accommodations for the next year, and the camp planners also agreed.

In Search of a Permanent Site

One morning in summer 1966, Arthur Wise (board member) left home after praying, "Lord, show me the land we are to buy today." His wife describes his return: "Late that evening, exhausted, Arthur returned ecstatic with excitement as he told about the beautiful rolling land he had discovered for a camp."

A few days later, five members of the board went to see the land. After seeing the property and praying together, all five directors voted to purchase the land.

First Summer Camp

That first summer camp of 1969 at Lakewood was a real milestone in SMCA history. Five weeks of camping were planned, with three age groups: 9 to 11, 12 and 13, and older teens. The staff alternated jobs, sometimes taking kitchen detail one week and counseling the next, or lifeguard one week and camp store the next.

25458 Dan Brown Hill Road
Brooksville, Florida 34602
Phone: (352) 796-4097
Fax: (352) 796-7577
E-mail: info@lakewoodretreat.org
Website: www.lakewoodretreat.org
Executive Director: Steve Wilson
Sponsoring Organization: Southern Mennonite Camp Association.
Membership: MCA

Vision for the Future

Lakewood attracts Mennonites from all over North America. A goal might be for Lakewood to network with other Mennonite camps with Lakewood's emphasis being on the elderly in the winter while "snowbirds" are here.

An Extension of Congregational Life

Every time a car pulls onto the grounds at Lakewood, there are persons in the vehicle who have a need. It may be to relax, lead a retreat, find relief from the hustle and bustle of work and life, get away from the phone, spend time with the family, to join with others in fellowship, and commune with God.

Purpose and Statement of Faith

The purpose of Lakewood Retreat, as with the larger Mennonite church, is to represent Jesus Christ to the world. We are here to enable all people to find purpose and fulfillment in Jesus Christ and to provide opportunities for all to experience training in leadership development, Christian discipleship, inspiration, and worship.

Lakewood Retreat and its programs seek to nurture body, mind, and spirit.

Laurelville Mennonite Church Center

Description

A conference and retreat center on 200 acres along rhododendron-lined Jacob's Creek in the Laurel Highlands, forty-five miles southeast of Pittsburgh, near the Pennsylvania Turnpike. With 350 beds, you may choose from camping to gracious hotel-style accommodations, including a few handicapped accessible. Enjoy full services for meals and banquets.

Year-round programs include workshops, retreats and specialized ministries, and summertime youth camps. Or, rent the facilities for your group and enjoy genuine hospitality. Near ski resorts, white-water rafting, Fallingwater (Wright home). Comfortable for groups up to 275.

History

"The Ground That Nurtured Seeds for Mennonite Camps" Edited excerpts from a talk by Alice M. Roth at the celebration of the Sixtieth year of Laurelville Mennonite Church Center ministries, October 2003

Laurelville Mennonite Camp was an outgrowth of the changes that came to the Mennonite Church (OM) during and after World War II. Many young men across the church, but in especially in Southwestern Mennonite Conference (now Allegheny) had entered the armed services instead of Civilian Public Service. Other changes put increased pressure on the nonconformity stance of Mennonites.

Some in the western Pennsylvania mountain area were passionate about their conviction that the church needed to provide a wholesome camp setting where the new phenomenon of leisure time could be profitably utilized for Christian fellowship and teaching. Church leader Orie O. Miller wrote in 1934, "Our young people are in need of help and in most communities are not getting it. They need help in meeting perplexing problems and temptations of the modern world."

The idea of young people's institutes was introduced across the country. From 1935 to 1945 many large institutes met on our college campuses. The first church conference to sponsor a YPI was Southwestern, at Mennonite Church of Scottdale. An institute was held annually at Arbutus Park in Johnstown. The search was on for a permanent Mennonite home for such activity. So the decision was made sixty years ago to purchase the Methodist campground which became Laurelville Mennonite Camp. At the dedication service, A.J. Metzler's dedicatory prayer included "every cup on the kitchen shelves and the highest leaf on the tallest tree."

Route 5, Box 145
Mount Pleasant, Pennsylvania 15666-8908
Phone: (724) 423-2056
Fax: (724) 423-2096
Email: info@laurelville.org
Website: www.laurelville.org
Executive Director: Jerry Troyer
Sponsoring Organization: Laurelville Mennonite Church Center Association
Memberships: Christian Camp and Conference Association, MCA

Is it surprising that a few Mennonites were passionate about their conviction that the church needed to provide a wholesome camp setting where the new phenomenon of leisure time could be profitably utilized for Christian fellowship and teaching?

Looking back sixty years, we remember a country at war, rapid social and economic change, Mennonites struggling to discern a faithful response to these challenges. Does that sound familiar to us in 2003? How will the vision of sixty years ago carry us into the decades ahead?

Stories

"Farming and Earth Care as a Spiritual Issue"

By Ron Meyer, a sustainable agriculturist from Fresno, Ohio

On Sunday afternoon, February 29, 2004, I felt both exhausted and exhilarated. The "Farming with Values That Last" conference had just wrapped up at Laurelville Mennonite Church Center. As a member of the planning group and moderator for the weekend, I was physically and mentally drained. But I was also emotionally charged by the energy and enthusiasm I'd experienced.

The conference was everything we planners had hoped for and more. Bringing together people keenly interested in sustainable agriculture with nationally known leaders in the movement, and keeping a Christian faith perspective at

continued

the forefront, this meeting set an attendance record for a first-time conference at Laurelville. A retired pastor, veteran of countless church meetings, announced to the group that it was the best conference he had ever attended. On their evaluation forms, participants called for a follow-up conference in 2005.

How did Laurelville come to host this historic meeting? Three years earlier, at a conference on sustainable agriculture held at Denison University, I had been struck by the careful thinking, support, and goodwill on the part of participants and speakers. It was obvious that farming in a way that treated the earth gently was a deeply spiritual issue. Why, I wondered, couldn't there be a conference that explored the same issues from a Christian faith perspective for Mennonites?

I shared these thoughts with Greg Bowman, a friend from college years and another Mennonite, at the Denison meeting. An editor of Rodale Publishing's *newfarm.org*, Greg had wide contacts in the sustainable farming community, lots of ideas, and unquenchable enthusiasm. We agreed the time was ripe for a Mennonite sustainable farming conference.

Several months later I met Jerry Troyer, new executive director of Laurelville. I knew Laurelville had hosted "faith and farm" conferences in the 1980s and often sponsored conferences on cutting-edge issues. It occurred to me that Laurelville might be just the group to help sponsor the meeting.

I raised the issue with Jerry and he showed immediate interest. He brought then-program director Robert Kanagy into the discussion. Over a period of months we worked out a tentative format for a conference, based loosely on other meetings Laurelville had sponsored. Greg and I put together a planning group that met with Robert at the Center in April 2003. In that day-long meeting we planned the schedule for the weekend, put together a tentative workshop list, and came up with names of potential speakers.

Planning group members contacted speakers and workshop leaders, while Laurelville provided administrative support. We secured speakers of national and international renown in the sustainable farming community: John Ikerd, a clear-thinking agricultural economist in demand around the world as a speaker and consultant; David Kline, an Amish bishop, organic dairy farmer, and writer; and a host of expert farmers and others who relate to the land in ecologically viable ways.

We mailed brochures and sent out news releases. Planners contacted friends. Then we waited and wondered. Would we have enough registrants? Our goal was at least 50 registrations by one month prior to the conference, or we would cancel.

Registrations trickled in at first, but came in a flood in the last six weeks. The conference was on! As I greeted participants in the Laurelville office on Friday afternoon, I was thrilled. Here were market gardeners, organic dairy farmers, conventional farmers considering transition to organic, ecologists, environmentalists, farmers' market promoters, organic grain farmers, college students, extension agents, people who simply cared about how their food was produced, all drawn together by a common interest in the careful use of God's creation.

The weekend was filled with meaningful worship, dynamic and thought-provoking speakers, overflowing workshops, and plenty of time to talk to each other. The Laurelville staff supported us with enthusiasm. Taking a step of faith, the kitchen crew helped put together a Saturday evening meal of sustainably produced food; participants received mugs to cut down on disposables; administrative and maintenance staff constantly worked at details.

It was a memorable, inspiring meeting, made possible by Jerry Troyer and the Laurelville staff. May this effort encourage and equip those who grow food sustainably (and those who eat it).

Little Eden Camp

Description

Little Eden Camp, a conference and retreat center located on Portage Lake in northwestern Michigan, 1.5 miles west of Onekama, provides thirteen weeks of summer program camps. The rest of the year it offers a lodge and several winterized cabins for family or other group retreats, including rentals. Bed capacity is 200 in summer and eighty-five in winter, including handicapped housing, plus room on the floor for sleeping bags. It is a place to relax, play, and worship together.

History

Little Eden Camp began in 1944 when five Mennonite men from northwest Ohio learned of some property for sale on Portage Lake in Onekama, Michigan. After looking at the camp and praying about it, they completed the purchase and financed it by selling stock. The men saw a need to create a camp for family and youth with a Mennonite Christian atmosphere. In the mid-1970s the original stockholders donated the camp to Little Eden Camp Association, a member association.

Mission Statement

Little Eden Camp, a member of Mennonite Camping Association, offers families and friends an affordable place where they may gather as brothers and sisters in Christ to be inspired, to share and to grow, while relaxing among the beautiful nature created by God.

Little Eden has concentrated on keeping the camp affordable for families. Volunteerism has been at the heart of Little Eden Camp from its origins and is a continuing core value today. Little Eden reflects God's presence in its natural setting of beautiful northern Michigan. During summer months, Little Eden provides a resource person who gives the Sunday message, and has two chapel periods a day. Most resource persons are from Mennonite churches supporting Little Eden's Mennonite focus. *Hymnal: A Worship Book*, as well as earlier Mennonite publications, is used in worship and the weekly hymn sings.

Little Eden has also continued its focus on being a Mennonite Christian camp in other areas. Approximately two-thirds of the winter retreat groups come from Mennonite churches and about ninety percent of the staff hired are Mennonite. The "Mennonite Game" is played frequently! Little Eden is also known for its good food, which has its roots in Mennonite cooking.

3721 Portage Point Drive
Onekama, Michigan 49675-9751
Phone/fax: (231) 889-4294
E-mail: littleeden@jackpine.com
Website: www.littleedencamp.org
Contact: Wendell Beck
Sponsoring Organization: Little Eden Camp Association
Membership: MCA

Stories

"My Special Place"

By Erin Stuckey, an age 13 camper

Most people have a certain hideout, or a special place they've always loved going to in their lifetime. Somewhere where life is simple and good. Somewhere that always feels like home no matter what. That's kind of what Little Eden is like to me.

Every day is different, but every day is also so much alike. I wake up about 9:00 a.m. Even though I grew out of it, I used to spend the morning making necklaces or painting carved wood at the craft shop. I then walked into the famous lodge and stood in line with my friends awaiting the aroma of warm roast beef and mashed potatoes and gravy. The food quickly rested in my stomach and then I made plans with Josh (my friend) to go swimming in the lake. I sprinted out of the lodge with my hair flying wild, anxious to put on my bathing suit and splash into the tempting waters. The hard, cold floor in the cabin was speckled with particles of sand that pinched my feet, and I was off to make an adventure out of my day.

Little Eden has a place in my heart and shows me how it is to lead a simple yet good life.

Camp Luz

Description

"Another place God is." Attractive fifty-acre camp nestled in the gently rolling hills of Wayne County, fifty miles south of Cleveland. Seasonal activities include swimming, boating, skating, sledding, fishing, and a variety of other recreational activities.

The camp is named after the place where Jacob met God as found in Genesis 28:19. We offer summer resident camps for ages 7 to 18; camp-sponsored retreats for youth, adults, and families; and rental facilities for church group retreats, reunions and meetings, housing 145 persons in cabins and lodges.

History

Camp Luz is a nonprofit Christian organization operated by the Ohio Mennonite Camping Association. OMCA members are a vital key to the work of Camp Luz through prayer support, financial donations, and voluntary service.

Mission Statement

Our mission is to promote the ministry of the church by providing a camp setting that exalts Jesus Christ. It is a place where people can gather to exercise body, mind, and spirit for personal growth in the beauty of God's creation through recreation, outdoor learning experiences, fellowship, nurture, and worship of our Lord Jesus Christ.

Stories

Homeless at Camp Luz

From an article by Celia Gehman, *MCA Newsletter*, Fall, 1991

When the seventy-two high school campers at Camp Luz, Kidron, Ohio, went to eat supper in the dining hall, they found the doors closed. "No food," they were told. Disgruntled stomachs growled after a strenuous afternoon of activity. After minutes passed, an announcement came of a "soup kitchen" open under a nearby tree. Lines quickly formed for a bowl of soup, two half sandwiches, crackers, and an apple half. This was the first phase of a plan to give the campers an unexpected firsthand experience of how it feels to be without the comforts and necessities of life—to be homeless.

Following their meager meal, they watched a videotape, *Shelter Boy,* and learned that two million Americans, including 100,000 children, live without a roof over their heads. After seeing the family in the film lose their home to a tornado, the campers found homelessness could happen to anyone. It happened to them. Program Director Eileen Krabill announced, "You have been evicted. You have seven minutes to get anything from your cabin."

152 Kidron Road Orrville, Ohio 44667-9699
Phone: (330) 683-1246
E-mail: camp.luz@juno.com
Website: www.campluz.mennonite.net
Camp Director: Deb Horst
Sponsoring Organization: Ohio Mennonite
Camp Association, Inc.
Membership: MCA

Each person was forced to decide what items to take. Those who opted to take their sleeping bags were fortunate; because after seven minutes, cabins were locked. Campers would be sleeping under the stars.

Each group and a counselor chose a spot to spend the night, any place where they could have some protection in case of rain. The counselors discussed how it feels to be evicted, the emotions of homeless people. For bedtime snacks, the campers scrounged through the "city" dump, a large cardboard box with bags of snacks to share as a group. Cabin groups varied in their reactions, counselors said. "I had a really good group of girls," Kathleen Shank reported. 'They encouraged each other and had ideas how one could help others. It unified us."

When dawn finally arrived, no breakfast was served in the dining hall, and the cabins remained locked. One camper said, "I really feel grubby. I always take a shower first thing each morning, and I'm not sure I like this." Each camper had to cook his or her own breakfast of eggs and toast over a "buddy burner," a small stove made of two tin cans filled with some paraffin.

Youths who thought camp would be a routine and predictable experience found this week an exception. The Camp Luz staff hopes the experience will help the campers appreciate the comforts and necessities of life and better understand the plight of the homeless.

Menno Haven Camp and Retreat Center

Description

Located in north central Illinois, Menno Haven offers year-round retreat facilities as well as summer and winter camps for youth on 231 acres of rolling hills and timber with a small lake, outdoor swimming pool and new Activity Center (spring of 2003).

History

The ideas for youth camping for Illinois Mennonite Youth took form on June 21, 1959, when Menno Haven was dedicated. From 1960-1962, cabins and bath houses were built. Long-range planning in 1964 led to the main lodge dedication in 1968 and the first year-round staff person. In 1976 the campground, Oak Lodge and Hickory House were completed. After the final payment of the debt in 1983 a campground pavilion was built in 1992, the main lodge made handicapped-accessible in 1993, and an adventure course was added in 1997. Hotel rooms were revitalized in 1999 along with lake renovation, Faith in Action in 2001, and an activity center completed in 2003.

9301 1575 East Street Tiskilwa, Illinois 61368
Phone: (815) 646-4344
Fax: (815) 646-4301
E-mail: camp@mennohaven.com
Website: www.mennohaven.com
Executive Director: David Horst
Sponsoring Organization: Illinois Mennonite
Camp Association Membership: MCA

Mission Statement

To invite all to experience God's world and Christ's kingdom in a camp and retreat setting through opportunities for worship, fellowship, recreation, growth, and renewal.

Stories

Seven Grade School Boys and a Roll of Duct Tape

Adapted from an article by Karen Bachman Nafziger

The setting was the Annual Illinois Mennonite Camping Association Retreat held at Menno Haven Camp and Retreat Center, Tiskilwa, Illinois, November 16-18, 2001. Participants were instructed to divide into smaller groups to create a display of "What Menno Haven Means to Us." "One boy was seen proudly carrying a roll of duct tape. "Oh no, young boys and duct tape – this should be interesting," observed one adult member.

When the time came to share, the group of seven boys asked to go first. The mother of one of the boys watched as he was bound with duct tape around his wrists and ankles, with a piece of tape dangling from a corner of his mouth.

"Ben! What are you doing?" she asked, slightly embarrassed.

"I'm part of the display, Mom!" explained the boy, to which the mother rolled her eyes while other parents suppressed knowing smiles.

The boys had carefully laid out physical and emotional aspects of Menno Haven. A cabin was constructed of interlocking wood blocks, and miniature pine trees surrounded the display depicting the nature aspects of Menno Haven. Other noted details consisted of a replica of the lake complete with the island bird haven. A red rose made of silk represented the concept of love. The adults applauded the cleverly designed model and began to proceed to the next display.

"We're not done yet!" exclaimed the boys, as they brought the since forgotten duct-taped boy to the forefront.

In addition to his wrist and ankle restraints, the boy now sported a facial blindfold made of cloth, netting and … duct tape! The other boys gathered around the restrained boy to unwind lengths of duct tape and remove the other items that prohibited the boy from seeing, speaking, or moving. As the boy was released from his sticky mode of confinement, he exuberantly exclaimed with outstretched arms, "And the best thing about Menno Haven is you learn about Jesus, who sets you free!"

A moment of silence filled the air as the adults marveled at the profound message expressed by the seven young boys. They applauded loud and long with admiration at the insight of the youth. Participants then moved to four displays created by the groups of adults, as the ministry of Menno Haven was explained through the venues of mustard seeds, crosses made of sticks, and craft foam hearts. Concepts of teamwork, rest and rejuvenation, spiritual growth and reflection, and the gospel story were exhibited in a variety of ways. The displays were creative and thought provoking, but no model quite measured up to the carefully thought out presentation of seven grade school boys and a roll of duct tape.

Camp Mennoscah

Description

Located on the South Fork of the Ninnescah River, thirty miles west of Wichita, Kans., Camp Mennoscah sponsors a nine-week summer camping program for children grades 4 to 12, work and play camp for senior citizens, camps for developmentally disabled, grandchildren, families, and others.

Activities include swimming, river play, fishing, outdoor activities, crafts, nature studies, and organized games. Facilities in addition to a retreat center are campsites, primitive cabins, a modern dormitory-style winterized building, a modern building with individual sleeping rooms, all together providing 220 beds, and a large dining hall/kitchen. It is handicapped-friendly. They rent to other groups.

History

Camp Mennoscah began in 1948 when the Western District Young People's Union purchased a camping site where young people could get away, be in nature, and learn more about God's out-of-doors. In the first camping years, beginning in 1949, the only kinds of shelter were tents. Each additional building, including the most recent one, the Retreat Center completed in 2002, has changed the way we run our camp.

Although the camp was bought by the Young People's Union, years later they found out that they could not legally own property. Therefore, in 1960 the camp was donated to the Western District Conference of the General Conference Mennonite Church.

Mission Statement

In accordance with the vision of the Western District Conference, Camp Mennoscah aspires to:

· Encourage staff and campers to follow Jesus Christ more faithfully by enriching their prayer, worship, and study of the Scriptures.

· Encourage the growth of community by calling and nurturing congregational and lay leaders for ministry in the unique outdoor setting that Camp Mennoscah provides.

· Encourage the growth of a community by practicing love, forgiveness, and hospitality that affirms diversity and heals brokenness.

· Encourage campers and staff to live as a people of healing and hope that invites others to faith in Jesus Christ.

· Encourage campers and staff to seek God's peace in their homes, work, neighborhoods, and the world at large.

· Encourage campers and staff to know God in a new way by experiencing the beauty of God's creation in Camp Mennoscah's outdoor setting.

P.O. Box 65
Murdock, Kansas 67111-0065
Phone: (620) 297-3290
E-mail: campmno@mennowdc.org
Website: www.mennowdc.org/campmenno.htm
Director: Joyce Pankratz
Sponsoring Organization: Western District Conference, Mennonite Church USA
Membership: MCA

Camp Mennoscah emphasizes our youth programs with nine weeks of summer camp including about 600 youth. We help train people to be leaders as we pair up junior counselors with older more experienced counselors. Our program directors model leadership to the counselors. The codirectors lead Bible studies for the staff and conduct training weekends for the counselors, staff, and program directors.

Camp Men-O-Lan

Description

Located in historic Bucks County, forty-five miles northeast of Philadelphia, on 160 wooded acres, Camp Men-O-Lan offers youth and adult retreats, outdoor classes, family gatherings. The June-to-August summer camping program features six weeks of overnight camp (grades 4 to 12); 4 weeks of day camp (grades 2 to 3), and four weeks of day camp for special needs youth.

Available lodging includes cabins, dormitory rooms, and four semiprivate rooms: summer 230, winter 165. The facilities are available for mission-compatible rentals, September to June. The camp has a confidence course, high ropes, climbing tower, obstacle course, large gym, sand volleyball court, swimming pool, ball fields, environmentally planned trail system, tennis court, street hockey, basketball, small lake with boating and, fishing, and campfire sites. Throughout the year our facilities are used by 250-some church, parachurch, school, business, and family groups, and almost 12,000 people—predominantly youth but including persons of all ages.

History

In 1937, a long-standing dream of persons in the Eastern District Conference of having camp property for conference youth/young adult activities and retreats took shape when J. Walter Landis, a member of East Swamp Mennonite Church, donated part of his property for such a purpose. Lame since age four with a leg injury, Landis was known for his cheerfulness and congeniality. His offer was accepted, and the following year planning and development work was begun. The camp has traditionally dated its beginning to the arrival of the first campers in the summer of 1941. We believe we are the oldest continuously operating Mennonite camp in North America.

The original twenty-three acres, a few buildings, volunteer staff, and summer camp have grown to almost 174 acres, thirty-five buildings, an eleven-member staff, and a year-round operation serving 250 plus groups and 12,000 persons.

Mission Statement

As a Christian camp, our mission is to use the unique qualities of an outdoor setting for developing Christian commitment, character, leadership, and service, and to provide a place for retreat, worship, study, fellowship, recreation, and personal development for individuals, families, and groups.

1415 Doerr Road
Quakertown, Pennsylvania 18951-2042
Phone: (215) 679-5144
Fax: (215) 679-0226
E-mail: info@menolan.org
Website: www.menolan.org
Executive Director: Clyde H. Smoll
Sponsoring Organization: Eastern District Conference, Mennonite Church USA
Memberships: Christian Camp and Conference Association, MCA

Stories

Beginning with just a dream and twenty-three acres over sixty-four years ago, could J. Walter Landis and the other early founders and developers of the camp have imagined the impact this camp would have on many people?

The most important story of the camp is what has happened to people here—the adventures, memories, friendships, some leading to marriage, and particularly the beginning or renewing of personal Christian commitment, renewed vows, first hearing or reconfirming the call to pastoral ministry and a variety of Christian service positions and roles, spiritual growth for untold numbers year after year, and helping produce generations of Christian leaders serving local congregations in many denominations, here and around the world, and the unknown ripple effects of all that on untold others. Could J. Walter and friends have imagined that? How does one fully grasp and tell that story?

It's a big story that keeps getting bigger. For example, given our mission, as reflected in the camp verse from Philippians 3:10 (KJV), "That I may know him," how many Christian commitments and rededications have occurred at Camp Men-O-Lan throughout its history? We don't know. However, if recent percentages are reflective of the ten decades of the camp, just from our own sponsored summer camps and retreats alone, the number would be over 10,000. In addition would be all those from the thousands of other groups and persons who have used our facilities over the years. Praise the Lord.

Merry Lea Environmental Learning Center

Description

We are a 1,150-acre natural area and day-use facility that provides for: (1) the protection, restoration, and management of native plant and animal habitats; (2) environmental science education and research experiences for all ages; and (3) appropriate recreational experiences.

History

Merry Lea represents one of the largest privately owned natural areas in Indiana. Presently Goshen College owns about half of the acreage and the remainder is leased from Mary Jane Rieth who, with her late husband Lee A. Rieth, established Merry Lea in the mid-1960s. In 1980 the Rieths began a gradual transfer of ownership to Goshen College with the assistance of The Nature Conservancy.

Mission Statement

The resources of land and people at the Merry Lea Environmental Learning Center of Goshen College are dedicated to:

· Providing a natural sanctuary for northern Indiana's plants and animals.

· Providing environmental education for people of all ages.

· Providing a setting for re-creating opportunities that benefit the human body and spirit while not exploiting the land or excessively disturbing its ecosystems.

The Merry Lea Story

Merry Lea is the responsibility of Goshen College and The Nature Conservancy. The Nature Conservancy preserves natural diversity by acquiring lands that contain the best examples of natural diversity. Goshen College is a four-year undergraduate institution where students study liberal arts in a setting that has the teachings of Jesus as a central focus. Goshen College at Merry Lea is committed to development of a multifaceted environmental program that teaches about Christian stewardship of natural and human resources.

Merry Lea's Natural Features

The Merry Lea State Nature Preserve, part of Indiana's system of dedicated state nature preserves, features oak hickory forests on the gravel ridge tops, soft maple forests in the lowlands, and a buttonbush swamp. Geological formations include a gravel esker, a marl pit, and extensive peat deposits. Upland forest areas are recovering from use as woodland pasture and timber harvest. Wetland systems present at Merry Lea include permanent wetlands, bogs, temporary ponds, lakes, temporary flowing streams and maintained drainage ditches. The interplay of geological features, past disturbance, and available seed sources has provided Merry Lea with many of the plant communities present in northern Indiana. Soils present at Merry Lea range from sand to silty clay, calcareous clay muck, and peat. Merry Lea's diverse habitats support a wide range of

P.O. Box 263
Wolf Lake, Indiana 46796
Phone: (260) 799-5869
Fax: (260) 799-5875
E-mail: lukeag@goshen.edu
Website: www.goshen.edu/merrylea
Director: Luke A. Gascho
Sponsoring Organization: Goshen College
Membership: MCA

plant, animal, and bird species. Lists of species observed at Merry Lea have been compiled although they are not exhaustive and further work is needed.

And It Is Unique

As an environmental educational center, Merry Lea Environmental Learning Center adds breadth and uniqueness to the Mennonite Camping Association. And to that it brings features that make it unique among environmental education centers such as:

It is a natural sanctuary within thirty-five miles of nearly three-quarters of a million people.

Management of the center is guided by a Christian theology of earth keeping.

Most of the habitats found in northeastern Indiana are present on Merry Lea (short-grass prairie, buttonbush swamp, cattail marsh, swamp maple forest, oak-hickory forest, old field, peat bog, open meadow). Unique geological features such as peat bogs, a marl pit, and glacial gravel formations are present.

Observable management practices include preservation, walnut culture, no-till farming, conventional farming, wildlife habitat improvement, wildlife food plantings, wetland maintenance, orchard management, specialty crops (sorghum and sunflowers).

A vigorous educational program interprets the significant biological and geological features. The director and program coordinator are faculty members of Goshen College and many of the teaching volunteers are college graduates.

Pine Lake Fellowship Camp

Description

Pine Lake Fellowship Camp is a conference and retreat center on ninety-four acres, five miles northwest of Meridian. The main camp facility for our summer youth program is a three-season facility with rustic bunk space for fifty-two. The dining hall will accommodate eighty with meeting space for 120. Pine Lake also features a duplex that is fully winterized for 8 to 10 people.

Our newest facility is a six-bedroom, hotel-style lodge with a meeting room, kitchen, heating, and air-conditioning. Accommodations are available for year-round rental, as the summer program allows. Recreation at Pine Lake includes boating, swimming, and fishing on a seven-acre lake, hiking, softball, volleyball, low-element ropes course, and zip-line.

Mission Statement

The mission of Pine Lake Fellowship Camp is to provide an environment that draws people of all ages and diverse backgrounds into renewal of spirit, soul, and body and into reconciliation with God, God's creation, and each other.

Stories

"Overcoming Barriers"

By Rhoda Byler Yoder, camp board secretary

Pine Lake lies misty and peaceful in the pine forest of Mississippi. Clumps of lily pads lace its edges and cluster in its backwaters. Pine trees tower around its banks. Two arching bridges stitch its island to the main land.

For over twenty-five years PLFC has been a retreat for Mennonites and their friends in the Deep South. Founded during the turbulent racial tension of the 1960s, PLFC was largely the vision of Nevin Bender and his son, Titus Bender. Nevin's church planting among the Choctaw Indians was severely tested when their church building was bombed three times in three years. The camp originated as a much-needed haven for Mennonites working for racial harmony and a place where diverse groups could come together for fellowship. Reconciliation was a key part of the initial mission and is and remains central to the current mission.

Today the camp is an important unifying factor for the Gulf States Mennonite Fellowship, a widely scattered conference of eleven churches whose membership includes Native Americans, African Americans, Hispanic Americans, Cajun Americans, and Caucasian Americans. Several of the churches are primarily first-generation Mennonites.

10371 Pine Lake Road
Meridian, Mississippi 39307
Phone: (601) 483-2267
E-mail: pinelakecamp@juno.com
Website: www.pinelakefelcamp.mennonite.net
Directors: Jeffrey and Cheryl Landis
Sponsoring Organizations: Gulf States Mennonite Conference, Mennonite Church USA
Memberships: Mississippi Camping Association, MCA, and Christian Camp and Conference Association

Conference people meet and mingle at PLFC in summer camp, youth retreat, women's retreat, family camp weekend, and the annual conference gathering. Some church groups regularly travel six hours to participate in conference activities held at the camp. Being together in this relaxed setting is a natural way to overcome barriers which most of society finds insurmountable.

Although PLFC probably has the smallest support base of any Mennonite camp, it has built itself into a sturdy, well-maintained site with a quality program. In the early days, campers took cold showers under suspended forty-gallon drums, slept on the ground in tents, and found fresh beaver construction in the lake every morning. Gradually, the camp added facilities: a kitchen and screened pavilion, cement slabs for the tents, then screened cabins on the slabs, bathhouses, and shelter for large gatherings.

Mennonites in the Deep South are scattered and diverse with an extra opportunity to show God's way of reconciliation to the society around them. Pine Lake Camp draws them together with its pine trees, quiet waters, and abundant peace.

Rocky Mountain Mennonite Camp

Description

Rocky Mountain Mennonite Camp enjoys 110 acres surrounded by breathtaking views of Pike National Forest located on the west slope of Pikes Peak. Programs for all ages are offered year-round. These include winter snow camps, men's and women's retreats, summer youth camps, wilderness camps, family camps, and fall church retreats. Facilities are also available for church groups, family reunions, families, and individual guests. Handicapped housing is limited.

We offer campsites, rustic cabins, chalets, ridge cabins, and a retreat center. Up to 225 guests in the summer and 125 guests in the winter can be served by the camp. Summer activities include hiking, backpacking, rock climbing, rappelling, basketball, sand volleyball, wilderness camping, horseback riding, mountain biking, rafting, and a recreation field. Winter activities feature tubing, ice skating, snow-shoeing and cross-country skiing.

History

Mennonite camping in the Rocky Mountain area began in the summer of 1934. A youth retreat was held at the Mennonite church in Manitou Springs. In 1945 Colorado Mennonite churches renewed enthusiasm for camping.

In November of 1951 a group of individuals purchased the property that became Rocky Mountain Mennonite Camp. The first camp sessions were held on the property during the summer of 1952.

Rocky Mountain Mennonite Camp is developed around the fundamental belief that spiritual growth is the "rudder" that guides the programming and the physical development of camp facilities. The "wind in our sails" comes from the evidence of God's work among us. Rocky Mountain Mennonite Camp has been blessed by campers, staff, generous support from donations, and board members who share a passion for the ministry of the church and camp.

Our facilities are available to some non-Mennonite groups. One of the significant groups to be our guests are the people from Colorado State University and the Conservation Camp they conduct. Their participation and counsel guides our soil conservation, forestry, and wildlife issues.

Rocky Mountain Mennonite Camp conducted a goal-setting process in 1992 to guide us to our fiftieth anniversary celebration in 2002. In conjunction with this anniversary observance we defined a vision and strategic plan for this decade. This process has served us well and our constituents undergird the camp in this endeavor.

Mission Statement

Rocky Mountain Mennonite Camp is a ministry of the Rocky Mountain and South Central (Kansas District)

709 County Road 62
Divide, Colorado 80814
Phone: (719) 687-9506
Fax: (719) 687-2582
E-mail: info@rmmcamp.org
Website: www.rmmcamp.org
Executive Director: Corbin Graber
Sponsoring Organization: An independent association with membership from Rocky Mountain Mennonite Conference, and Kansas District of South Central Mennonite Conference, Mennonite Church USA
Memberships: Christian Camp and Conference Association, MCA

Mennonite Conferences to facilitate the program of the Mennonite Church by providing a place of retreat which encourages wholistic Christian growth by fostering the spiritual, social, physical, and intellectual growth of each participant. Various programs are offered throughout the year for everyone.

Stories

"Unobstructed View"

By Mary Yoder, permanent staff person

Unobstructed view of the sky
Stars reaching out through the blanket of night
Far-reaching tree-covered hills
Reach out to capture my heart.

A ribbon of trickling clear water
Song of the stream through the night
Vast acres of wide open spaces
Reach out to capture my heart.

Morning sun glinting on frost-covered hills
Warm afternoons that drift into night
Scents of autumn in the air
Reach out to capture my heart.

Wildflowers and double rainbows
Icicles glittering in sunlight
Seasons and feelings of peacefulness
Have reached out and captured my heart.

Shekinah Retreat Centre

Description

Shekinah Retreat Centre is located in central Saskatchewan on the banks of the North Saskatchewan River, and is comprised of 287 acres of semi-developed river hills and flats with over four miles of developed hiking and skiing trails.

Facilities include Timber Lodge which sleeps approximately 100 and is used for conferences, retreats, weddings, and family reunions; chalet, summer tent cabins, two winterized cabins, and a hermitage for year-round use. Year-round programming is available for various organizations and individuals, such as school groups, with full-summer camping programs for children and youth operating during July and August.

History

Shekinah, started in January 1979, is a summer camp and year-round retreat center owned and operated by Mennonite Church Saskatchewan. The Word *Shekinah* is Hebrew in origin and means "the abiding presence of God." It is the radiance, glory, and presence of God dwelling in the midst of God's people.

Mission Statement

Shekinah is a setting where everyone who comes will experience the presence and glory of God.

Principles and Values Statement

Shekinah Retreat Centre is dedicated to glorify and honor God. It provides a place for inspiration, relaxation, and recreation. It encourages commitment to Christ through biblical teaching from an Anabaptist perspective. It provides Christian nurture and growth, to develop faith, and to expand human relationships. It enhances the understanding of God as Creator, to gain knowledge of nature and to develop environmental responsibility. It encourages Christian stewardship of all resources in developing and expanding the utilization of Shekinah.

Stories

A Growing Up Experience

By Hillary Fast

Six years ago I had just turned six. That year I rode in the Shekinah bike-a-thon on a little red, one speed bike. My mom rode beside me all the way. Even though she said I could quit any time, I didn't want to. The hills on the gravel road made me really mad, but I had biked that far and I was determined to make it to the end.

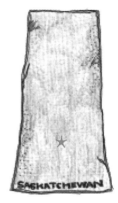

P.O. Box 490 Waldheim, Saskatchewan S0K 4R0
Phone: (306) 945-4929
Fax: (306) 945-5506
E-mail: office@shekinahretreatcentre.org;
retreat@sasktel.net
Website: www.shekinahretreatcentre.org
Executive Director: Lill Friesen
Sponsoring Organization: Mennonite Church Saskatchewan
Memberships: Saskatchewan Camping Association, MCA

The next three years I rode a slightly bigger, one-speed bike. Some years the weather wasn't good. There's been rain, wind, and hot sun. I never gave up. I've gone from riding with my mom and dad, to riding with my sister and by myself. The fastest time I've ever ridden was on the one-speed bike. It took me three hours and twenty-five minutes (that was the year I rode with my dad and he didn't want to go any slower). The last two years I've ridden on a mountain bike which makes it a little easier climbing the hills and riding on the gravel.

The best part of the bike-a-thon is going down the big hill that goes into Shekinah. Sometimes when I'm riding along, I ask myself, "Why am I doing this?" I answer myself by saying, "I am doing this because I love Shekinah." One year, I even missed a soccer game to ride in the bike-a-thon. In total, I've ridden the whole seventy kilometers six times.

I only missed the first bike-a-thon in 1998. I guess my mom thought I was too little. I could have shown her! I really like it!

Silver Lake Mennonite Camp

Description

Silver Lake Mennonite Camp provides primarily a children's summer camp program for ages 6 to 17. Activities range from on-site canoeing, sailing, swimming, crafts, quest, nature, low ropes, and initiatives, to off-site canoe trips. Silver Lake is situated on 150 acres of bush, meadows, and wetland that border two lakes.

A large dining hall and cabin accommodate campers and staff. There is a counselor-in-leadership training program for ages 15 to 17. Children with developmental challenges are integrated into the regular camp program. The number of campers per week is approximately eighty-two. During the off-season, the entire facilities are available for rent.

History

In the 1940s and 1950s, a variety of Mennonite youth retreats were organized in Ontario. Attendees had the vision to begin a camping program at Silver Lake. In the late 1950s the Ontario Youth Organization (OYO) held annual summer youth retreats at Chesley Lake, annual one-week boys camps began in 1959, and in 1960 one-week girls camps. That was the year the Silver Lake property was purchased for $15,000. In 1961 the OYO set up a provisional board of directors for the camp, and the first delegate meeting was held in Waterloo.

Mission Statement

As a Christian denomination, the Mennonite church shares the beliefs of the wider Christian church. Over the years, Mennonites have chosen to emphasize certain Christian values, such as being a disciple of Christ, community, fellowship, peace and justice, believer's baptism, and responsibility for one's actions, one's faith, and one's fellow human beings. These values are not exclusive to Mennonites, but they have become very important to the Anabaptist/Mennonite understanding of Christianity.

At Silver Lake, we try to integrate these values into our life and work together to become a deep Christian community: a place where campers, staff, and volunteers develop a sense of belonging, roots, and friendships. We intend to be at peace with each other and our environment; to be forgiving people; to try to stand together with our neighbors including those who are weak, oppressed, or victimized; and to work as healers in the world.

Stories

Through the Eyes of a Child

By Jim Penner, from *MCA Newsletter*, Fall, 1996

During the years my children grew up at camp, Silver Lake operated a special needs program, integrating those with special needs into the regular camp program. While at the time I thought of this program as important to the

Route 1 Hepworth, Ontario N0H 1P0
Phone: (519) 422-1401
Off-Season
33 Kent Avenue
Kitchener, Ontario N2G 3R2
Phone: (519) 747-0627
E-mail: silverlake@sympatico.ca
Website: www.slmc.on.ca
Director: Reynold Friesen
Sponsoring Organization: Mennonite Conference of Eastern Canada
Membership: MCA

campers, both "special needs" and "regular," I didn't fully fathom the impact of this program on my own children.

This summer my wife Julie and I assisted some friends of ours who were running a retreat weekend for developmentally challenged young adults. We brought our children with us, not giving a thought to how they would react.

When we arrived, Julie asked me if I had told our kids who would be at this retreat. I said I hadn't thought of it. It hadn't crossed her mind either. Before we were able to process this any further, the campers and other staff surrounded our car and began to unload it. (*Yes*, we were late!) By the time we caught up with our kids they were busy exploring their new environment.

Over the course of the retreat I watched my children. They enjoyed themselves completely. As they grow up, they won't identify people by the challenges they face, but rather by the unique people that they are. In Christ here is no east or west, nor mentally retarded (to use an archaic term). The proof is in the eyes of a child.

Spruce Lake Retreat

Description

Spruce Lake Retreat enjoys a secluded setting in the Pocono Mountains of northeast Pennsylvania in a 320-acre wooded mountain setting. Planned programs as well as facilities are available for groups. Activities include adult retreats, youth camps, wilderness expeditions, outdoor school, and family campground.

Accommodations range from tent sites, bunkhouses, dormitories, to private rooms. The camp can handle groups as large as 300 (or more). Recreation includes hiking, swimming, tennis, basketball, volleyball, cross-country skiing, skating, tubing, miniature golf, and a ropes course. Operates yearround.

History

A nonprofit organization formed in 1961 by a group of Christians from Franconia Conference of the Mennonite Church envisioned Spruce Lake Retreat as a place of nurture and outreach in the church and community.

FMCA upholds the articles of faith of the Mennonite Church as the basis for all programming for children, youth, and adults. More than 900 persons are already FMCA members, helping to sponsor the camping and retreat ministries of Spruce Lake Retreat.

Mission Statement

Christ-centered discoveries in the out-of-doors!

Spruce Lake Camp is a Christian camp and retreat center developed within the Franconia Conference of the Mennonite Church. Its purpose is to provide Christian nurture, fellowship, and recreation in an informal, natural, setting for children, youth, and adults.

The mission and purpose are carried out with 20,000 children, youth, and adults involved in the areas of ministry of:

· Adult and family programming.

· Wilderness camp for children and youth.

· Outdoor school for schools and homeschoolers.

· Adventure trips and challenge initiatives.

· Guest groups from a great variety of Christian churches and organizations.

· Personal retreats for friends and families.

Stories

Mom, You Can't Climb; You Can't See!

In 1983, a degenerative eye disease called *retinitis pigmentosa* consumed most of Elaine Eng's sight at age 29. She could no longer see the eager faces of her two young children or continue her medical practice in ob-gyn. On New Year's Day, 2000, Elaine sat in Lakeview Program Center at Spruce Lake Retreat participating vicariously in the climbing wall with friends from Chinese Evangel

Route 1, Box 605
Canadensis, Pennsylvania 18325-9749
Phone: (570) 595-7505
Fax: (570) 595-0328
E-mail: info@sprucelake.org
Website: sprucelake.org
Executive Director: Mark Swartley
Sponsoring Organization: Franconia Mennonite Camp Association, Inc. (FMCA)
Membership: MCA

Mission Church of Queens. Her lithe, energetic body ached to climb . . . but without sight, how could she?

"Mom," one of her children informed her, "you *can't* climb the wall because you can't see the pegs."

Complaints against such predictions would've clashed with Elaine's warm and gracious character. But she certainly felt pulled in opposite directions, desire and disappointment.

Suddenly she overheard coach Dave Kallatch explaining how he had guided someone up the wall blindfolded. *Maybe I could do it, too!* Elaine thought.

And so, starting out by feel, and then following Dave's calm, clear instructions, Elaine made her way up the thirty-foot wall to the very top, banging the bell that signaled her amazing accomplishment to everyone below Elaine gained a new understanding of Philippians 3:13-14 that day, the part about straining toward the goal.

"Faith is blind, too!" she said. "We're trusting God, yet can't see how God will work things out. I draw strength from God even though I can't see."

"God has been gracious to me," she went on, "allowing me to see things through the eyes of faith." She has come to view her blindness as an asset, especially in her second profession as a Christian psychiatrist, having switched medical fields when blindness settled in.

She is better able to "see" into a person with the "eyes" of her heart, and is far less tempted to take spiritual and emotional pain lightly.

Elaine Eng has spoken and written widely on mental health issues from a Christian perspective, especially as they relate to women.

Camp Squeah

Description

In addition to offering children's summer camp programming and midweek outdoor education for public and private schools, Camp Squeah offers facilities for conferences, retreats, and outdoor education.

Accommodations include 200 beds (three handicapped accessible), a full catering or self-catering option, three large conference areas, cabin and main lodge options, RV hookup, and tenting sites. Leadership is available for canoeing, climbing wall, archery, orienteering, backpack trips, forestry/ecology education, and much more.

History

In 1961, Camp Squeah began operating by the BC Mennonite Youth Organization as a place where "children could learn about God in a natural setting."

Mission Statement

In response to God who loves and calls us, Camp Squeah provides a "Place of Refuge" in a natural setting where people of all ages can build relationships, grow, and be nurtured.

Stories

This is the story of a life of a little girl who was forever changed because she went to camp.

This girl grew up with a strong Christian mother and a somewhat heathen father. Her upbringing included church and Sunday school, Bible stories at home, and a sense of God's dominion over all things. But it wasn't until she went to camp as an eight-year-old that she realized that there was a relationship involved; a relationship with God.

Her counselor modeled for her an enthusiastic, passionate relationship with God that was personal. Other staff members did the same. This was the first time that the little girl had seen young people living the daily life of a Christian. She decided that she wanted the same and one night on her bunk, she began her journey with God.

For the next twenty years, this girl had a summer camp experience of one kind or another. First as a camper, where each year she grew in her faith. Then as a counselor-in-training where she began to develop her leadership skills. Then as a counselor, a crafts instructor, a drama instructor, a music leader, a counselor-in-training director, camp committee member, a curriculum writer. She met her husband there and together they worked in leadership at Camp Squeah for six years. She went on to be a youth pastor and now works for two Christian organizations, the Canadian Mennonite and MCC. She has been part of the Camp Squeah committee and continues to write curriculum for their summer program. She and her husband have one child who is now old enough to be a camper – a new generation of camp experience. When this little girl, this now grown woman, thinks back about the significant influences in her personal life, the first thing that comes to mind is camp. This little girl, the grown woman, is me.

#4 - 27915 Trans Canada Highway
Hope, British Columbia V0X 1L3
Phone: (604) 869-5353
Toll-free in British Columbia: (800) 380-2267
Fax: (604) 869-5364
E-mail: info@campsqueah.bc.ca
Website: www.campsqueah.bc.ca
Executive Director: Rudy Koehler
Sponsoring Organization: Mennonite Church of British Columbia
Memberships: British Columbia Camping Association, Christian Camp and Conference Association, MCA

A couple of years ago, at their annual retreat, the camp committee was asked to describe what Camp Squeah meant to them. These are some of the phrases they used: "a holy place," "my Bethel," "a place of fun and laughter," "a life-changing place," "simplicity," "community," "relationships," "family," "restores my soul," "a place to meet God." Notice that no one said "a piece of land with buildings on it located between Hope and Hell's Gate!"

Squeah is for many a "place of refuge." Refuge is defined as a "shelter, protection, retreat, sanctuary." It is a safe place for people to come and meet God, who is also a refuge. It is a place of beginning, of journeying, and even of ending. This is what camp is all about and it's not just about summer camp; Squeah is a place of refuge for young and old. A retreat and sanctuary where one can come to be removed from the world of television, radio, newspapers, schedules, day-timers, and cell phones. Its geography is itself a metaphor for journeying with God: we go up the mountain to meet God, we come down with shining faces.

I currently work with two organizations whose missions and purpose I firmly believe in. But no ministry stirs passion within me like camp. And the reason for that is simple. Camp changed my life, both as a child and as an adult. I am a better person because I went to camp. And if that is true for me, it can be true for anyone.

Micah 4:2 Come let us go up to the mountain of the Lord . . . He will teach us his ways so that we may walk in his paths.

Angelika Dawson—May, 2004

Swan Lake Christian Camp

Description

This camping facility in southeast South Dakota appeals both to youth and adults. Year-round rental facilities are available. One hundred acres of campground border a 180-acre lake. Activities include swimming, canoeing, sailing, volleyball, an adventure course, ice skating, and tobogganing. Summer capacity is 150; winter capacity is 100.

History

Swan Lake's youth camps have been the major thrust of the organization since it first began, and are the reason it began. It provided a place for the youth of the conference to gather. Although it still is providing that today, it has reached far beyond conference lines, mostly because the youth have invited their friends.

Mission Statement

Be still and know that I am God.
Rest, fellowship, and grow.

Stories

A Little Oasis Set Apart for God's Purpose

By Judi Kroeker, Codirector beginning 1997

Camp has been a time of getting away and taking a break from the everyday things of life. It is a special time to be still and get to know God. Nightly campfires are one of the ways that youth are impacted the most. Being still in the day of technology and business is something many people don't often do and campfire provides that atmosphere. That is when growth happens; they can reflect on life and hear what Jesus can do for them.

One camper wrote, "I first accepted Christ here four years ago and every year my relationship grows stronger. I want you to know that this camp is mainly the reason I'm a Christian!" That is what Swan Lake Christian Camp aims to do—provide a place to meet God. The fellowship happens as youth make new friends whom they come back to see year after year.

As Swan Lake Christian Camp has expanded to include retreat facilities, we hear people comment, "What a beautiful place. I didn't know this was out here." Being located in rural farm country of South Dakota, many people are surprised by the little oasis set aside for God's purposes.

45474 288th Street
Viborg, South Dakota 57070-6437
Phone: (605) 326-5690
Fax: (605) 326-5563
E-mail: slcc@hcinet.net
Website: www.myslcc.com
Codirectors: Jerry and Judi Kroeker
Sponsoring Organization: Swan Lake Christian Camp Association, affiliated with Central Plains Mennonite Conference, Mennonite Church USA
Membership: MCA

Adults also have found through their retreats here a place to rest and be still; to listen to the birds and the quiet that many of those who come from the city don't ever hear. And in the quiet, away from the hustle and bustle, they stay up late and get to know each other better.

I think also about not only the individuals that have been impacted by Swan Lake Christian Camp, but whole families. Married couples have met here. Parents who went to camp here are now sending their children and grandchildren to camp. It just seems to get into the blood of some families. Four out of the five children in my own family served here on summer staff. There are many other families like mine. What a great way to build family relationships and spiritual relationships at the same time!

There are so many other people through many years; they all have their story to tell. But one theme predominates. They all took time to "Be still and know that God is God."

Camp Valaqua

Description

Located in the foothills of the Rocky Mountains among spruce forests and rivers, Camp Valaqua provides an ideal place to experience God in creation. Summer programs for children, teenagers, and families. Activities include climbing wall, swimming, canoeing, archery, nature, camp skills, chapels, and campfires.

Mountain biking and horseback riding are offered, during teen camps, as well as canoe, bike, and backpack trips. Trails cross through much of our 250 acres for hiking, skiing, and biking. Camp Valaqua also serves as a ministry outreach to the larger community by inviting others to participate in the use of its facilities and Christian ministry. The lodge, recreation hall, and cabins are available for off-season rental.

History

In 1956 a Bible camp for the children of Mennonite churches was held at Menno Bible Institute. Increasing interest in camping resulted in the decision to find a suitable wilderness site that would offer a varied camping program. Efforts were aimed at involving the churches in the development of a camp program to complement congregational Christian education and to raise funds for purchase and development. Thus the vision for Camp Valaqua was born – to provide a Christian experience in a wilderness setting for all camp participants.

In 1960 Alberta Mennonite Youth Organization and Mennonite Church Alberta joined to own and administer the camp. Dedicated in 1961, Camp Valaqua became one of the major on-going projects of the Alberta Conference. The facilities and site have constantly been upgraded and modernized since its establishment, but the core values supporting the camp vision have not changed. In summary they are:

· to keep a wilderness camp rather than a commercial resort.

· to retain a strong Christian emphasis through hiring committed Christian staff.

· to keep close ties to the church through use of pastors as chaplains and other volunteers

· to find ways to enjoy and make use of the camp year-round.

Mission Statement

Camp Valaqua is dedicated to proclaiming the good news that God is the Creator, we are God's people, and the earth is placed in our hands as a gift and a trust.

P.O. Box 339 Water Valley, Alberta T0M 2E0
Phone: (403) 637-2510
Fax: (403) 637-2183
E-mail: valaqua@telusplanet.net
Website: www.campvalaqua.com
Directors: Don and Tanya Dyck Steinmann
Sponsoring Organization: Mennonite Church Alberta
Memberships: Alberta Camping Association, Christian Camp and Conference Association, MCA

We give campers the opportunity to develop a personal relationship with Jesus Christ, to be with others in a Christian community, to learn how to care for God's creation, and to have a lot of fun. Our mission is to provide a place where campers can experience God through worship, recreation, and interaction with others in a beautiful natural setting through a wholistic Christian ministry centered on the teachings of Jesus Christ.

Summer children's camp is the central program focus for Camp Valaqua. By encouraging a wholistic Christian community, campers, staff, and adult volunteers are all part of the overall camp ministry. Morning chapel, evening campfire, and cabin devotions are central to the camp program, with an emphasis on teaching the Christian message through singing, sharing, storytelling, and biblical teaching. Camper activities promote fun and cooperation, while challenging campers to grow in all aspects of their lives. Summer staff and training positions offer youth and young adults an opportunity to serve and minister to others as well as grow in faith and leadership development.

Wilderness Wind

Description

Wilderness Wind conducts 4 to 7 day canoe tips and some backpacking trips in the wilderness of Boundary Waters Canoe Area Wilderness and Canadian Quetico, for individuals and groups regardless of skill level and experience, including people in wheelchairs on overnight canoe trips.

A trained guide teaches the required skills, promotes wilderness discovery, and leads daily devotional discussions. We can accommodate thirty canoeing campers and sixteen people in cabins on waterfront property for people interested in day trips. Many of our trips include (or are exclusively for) youth and their youth directors/ pastors. All our bath houses are wheelchair accessible.

History

Wilderness Wind was started in 1986 by Paula and Tim Lehman. They were interested in designing a wilderness program that included at least two facets: a quality wilderness experience and a spiritual encounter with creation. Tim and Paula involved persons from the St. Paul and Minneapolis region, and staff and board from other camps to see how these communities might be involved. In addition to three new buildings at base-camp, we acquired the lakeside property in 1994 to extend the season and as a place for personal retreats for non-canoers. It has definitely been an asset to all who come through Wilderness Wind.

Mission Statement

To nurture relationships with God and creation through wilderness living which promotes spirituality, cooperation, and environmental sustainability.

In support of this mission, we observe daily twenty minutes of silence preceded by an inspirational reading. At the end of each day we discuss the theme for the day and observations from the day's experience. At the end of each trip there is a closing ritual with opportunity for reflection on the meaning of the day for the campers.

Quotes and a journal in the cabins invite people to take note of their surroundings and listen to the voice of God moving in the wilderness.

Stories

Challenges Achieve Changes in Receptive Hearts and Lives

A few years ago, a 13-year-old camper came on a Wilderness Wind canoe trip with his family. It was as usual a good week of paddling, portaging, and learning new skills and new things about himself. During the week, he

2945 Highway 169 Ely, Minnesota 55731
Phone: (218) 365-5873
Email: wildernesswind@juno.com
Website: Wildernesswind.org
Director: Kathy Landis
Off-Season (October-April)
511 West 11th Street
Newton, Kansas 67114
Phone: (316) 283-5132
Sponsoring Organization: Wilderness Wind Board of Directors
Membership: MCA

was keenly aware of the many miles of waterways that distinguish the Boundary Waters from many other canoe routes. The water was clean, vast, and full of life.

Back home, he developed a plan for a two-year project for school. He would begin something and invest in it for two years while he assessed the resulting developments and changes. The strip-mined area in which he lived had little fertile top soil, and a small creek that ran through his back yard had few signs of life in it. He decided to put his school project and his Wilderness Wind experience together.

He studied wetlands in his region and did a water quality study in the stream to see what types of life were present. A nearby farmer and his dirt-moving equipment changed his backyard into two ponds. He planted native grasses along the edges and pond plants that were native to the area.

Two years after his canoe trip, I visited his house. He had done another water quality study that confirmed the changes he achieved in his backyard environment. He was also able to share with me and other visitors the numbers and types of waterfowl that visited his backyard ponds.

Williamsburg Christian Retreat Center

Description

In a beautiful wooded setting in southeast Virginia near historical sites including Colonial Williamsburg, Laurel Cottage accommodates thirty-six people in four bunkhouse-style bedrooms, with a kitchen, lounge, and meeting area and two bathrooms. Holly Cottage has twenty-two beds in six motel-style rooms, one handicapped accessible, a kitchen, lounge, meeting area, and deck overlooking the woods. Oakwood Lodge features a twenty-four-room (two handicapped accessible) motel-style building for ninety-two people with two conference rooms with capacity of fifty each. A welcome center has a dining area for 130. Recreation facilities include swimming pool, hiking trails, a ropes course, playgrounds, basketball, tennis, and softball. We offer year-round youth programs.

The RV campground area has full hookups along with a pavilion and bathhouse. A primitive camping area with 14-foot x 16-foot canvas tents has twelve sites for group camping.

Future plans include a youth camp facility with four duplex-style cabins for eighty people and a multipurpose-building with meeting, eating, and bathhouse areas.

Most of our clients are rental groups, but we also plan retreats and events throughout the year and a summer camp for children and youth.

History

The Williamsburg Christian Retreat Association was formed in 1984 by pastors and overseers in southeast Virginia desiring a place for young people to make decisions for Christ. With fewer church-related activities such as literary societies or revival meetings, they recognized that youth were making that decision at camps. However, as plans for the camp was being developed and other Mennonite camps were visited, it was suggested they build a retreat center first along with camping facilities to ensure financial success.

WCRC is a Virginia Mennonite Conference Related Ministry with an independent board. Two board members are selected from Virginia Conference Commissions.

Mission Statement

The mission of WCRC is to provide Christ-centered retreat facilities, services, and programs to encourage fellowship, growth, and renewal.

9275 Barnes Road
Toano, Virginia 23168
Phone: (757) 566-2256
Fax: (757) 566-4875
E-mail: wcrc@wcrc.info
Website: www.wcrc.info
Executive Director: Herb Lantz
Sponsoring Organization: Williamsburg Christian Retreat Association
Memberships: Christian Camp and Conference Association, MCA

Stories

Imprinted by God and Others, It Happens at Camp

By Emily Beasley, summer program director

Before attempting to describe my summer, I wish to begin with a verse that articulates the feelings of my experiences at WCRC: "And we know that in all things God works for the good of those who love [God], who have been called according to [God's] purpose" (Romans 8:28, NIV).

This summer was nothing short of amazing. I know I am more equipped to serve the Lord than ever. For the first time in my life, I am beginning to understand what it means truly to love the Lord, and how God intends to use God's children. Each child left camp this summer, not only changed, but has helped a staff person to be changed as well. The memory of each camper is imprinted on someone's heart. Each week of camp, we have found ourselves faced with new personal challenges. With the Lord's help, we have grown into more efficient servants for God.

As I prepare to leave and return to school, I am excited to reenter my old environment a new, wiser, changed woman of God, and I can only pray that my learning doesn't stop there. I pray that as our campers changed us, we too can change the lives of others and further spread the good news. I am so thankful and so blessed to have had God direct me back here to WCRC again for another wonderful summer, and I look forward to following wherever God desires me to serve in the future.

Willowgrove Farm

Description

Willowgrove Farm is the owner of the following two camps, Fraser Lake and Glenbrook Day Camp. The histories of their separate beginnings and eventual combination into Willowgrove Farm are given below.

Fraser Lake Camp

Route 4 Bancroft, Ontario K0K 1P0
Phone: (905) 642-2964
Fax: (905) 640-5263
E-mail: info@fraserlakecamp.com
Website: www.fraserlakecamp.com
Camp Director: Naomi Weir
Sponsoring Organization: Willowgrove, a nonprofit organization of Toronto-area Mennonite churches
Membership: MCA

Description

Fraser Lake Camp is located on a 270-acre waterfront site in the Kawartha region of Ontario. Specialties include instruction in swimming, canoeing, kayaking, climbing tower, mountain biking, guitar, and a water trampoline.

Mission Statement

The mission of Fraser is to provide a camping experience for children and youth which focuses on promoting their personal and spiritual growth within a Christian and Mennonite context

Glenbrook Day Camp

11737 McCowan Road Stouffville, Ontario L4A 7X5
Phone: (905) 640-2127
Fax: (905) 640-5263
E-mail: info@glenbrookdaycamp.com
Camp Director: Sarah Dougald
Sponsoring Organization: Willowgrove, a nonprofit organization of Toronto-area Mennonite churches
Membership: MCA

Description

Glenbrook Day Camp is the summer program of Willowgrove Farm. The 92-acre site allows a diverse program for children ages 4 to 15. Activities include pony rides, singing, beach volleyball, hiking, a climbing gym, outdoor playground, hayloft play, baseball, basketball, soccer, arts and crafts, canoeing, swimming, and archery.

Mission Statement

Our mission is to provide a setting to help individuals, families and groups develop a sense of personal worth, community spirit, service to people, and appreciation of the natural world.

11737 McCowan Road Stouffville, Ontario L4A 7X5
Phone: (905) 640-2127
Fax: (905) 640-5263
Website: www.glenbrookdaycamp.com
E-mail: info@glenbrookdaycamp.com
Executive Director: Kyle Barber
Sponsoring Organization: Willowgrove Farm
(see Fraser Lake, and Glenbrook)
Membership: MCA

History

Fraser Lake Camp (1955) was pioneered by three Mennonite pastors. Development occurred because of the sincere dedication of people who gave of their time, skills, and money. In 1960, Fraser Lake started a second camp named Frontier Forest Camp.

Frontier Forest Camp was designed for inner-city boys who were troubled. This camp was sponsored by the welfare board but closed in 1970 because of difficulty in finding enough qualified staff members. Fraser Lake camp continued to grow and provided good experiences through the 1980s and into the 1990s.

In the mid-1960s, Emerson McDowell, (one of the three pioneer pastors of Fraser Lake Camp) had a new vision to start a new "day" camp close to Toronto. His vision was not shared by the other Fraser Lake colleagues so Emerson pioneered a new organization—Willowgrove (1968).

Willow grove began as a day camp (Glenbrook) and as a group home for troubled youth. The day camp continued to grow and still exists today, while the group home closed in 1982 because of tightening legislation. Gradually, other programs were added because of community need including the centre rental program in 1975, the outdoor education program in 1976, and the Willowgrove primary school in 1994.

Meanwhile, Fraser Lake Camp had begun to falter in the mid-1990s because of a sagging economy and

continued

shortcomings in staff structure. By 1997, Fraser Lake Camp was near financial collapse. Through an amalgamation process, Fraser Lake Camp was transferred to Willowgrove ownership. Fraser Lake Camp continues to operate as a program of Willowgrove and has fit nicely into the menu of programs that Willowgrove now offers.

Mission Statement

Willowgrove is a Christian organization that seeks to nurture the spiritual, social, emotional, and physical growth of children and youth through a variety of programs in a natural setting. Willowgrove is committed to:

· Serving a diverse community.
· Peacemaking and nonviolence.
· Caring for the land that God has entrusted to us.

Stories

Anatomy of an Amalgamation

By Kyle Barber, executive director of Willowgrove in *MCA Newletter*, Winter, 2000

When amalgamation is mentioned, most minds jump to large-scale business such as banks, insurance companies, or AOL and Time-Warner. The amalgamation trend is certainly alive and well and has been a significant theme over the past five years as businesses jostle for market share and overhead efficiency.

Amalgamation, though, is not only for the large, profit sector. It has now occurred within the Mennonite Camping Association. This is how it happened.

Fraser Lake Camp, a residential camp in the Kawartha region of Ontario began in 1955 and had a long history of providing Christian summer camping for children. A private Mennonite association camp based in York region, Fraser was plagued by low registrations through the 1990s and had serious financial shortfalls over a seven-year period. Programs and facilities suffered as the camp struggled to stay afloat. Something needed to be done or the 257-acre, well-equipped facility would be lost.

In December, 1997, Fraser Lake Camp approached Willowgrove, Inc., to seek a relationship that would allow Fraser Lake to continue. Willowgrove, a private Christian, not-for-profit charity is located in Markham, Ontario and is a Mennonite association. Willowgrove runs diverse year-round educational programs (a primary school, an outdoor education program, and an agricultural education program) and Glenbrook Day Camp— the only Mennonite day camp in the MCA!

It was clear after initial discussions that a relationship was imminent and specifics would be addressed by a combined panel of board members from the two organizations.

A process would be put in place that would address the short-term needs of managing camp but also the long-term goal of transferring camp ownership to Willowgrove.

The first step was for the Fraser board to allow Willowgrove entire control over the camp operation while remaining financially liable. It was agreed that the Fraser board would serve as a program committee that was available for consultation but that the Willowgrove board would have final authority. Based on the trusting and prayerful nature of these two partners, legal contracts were not written.

With a management agreement in place, the combined panel then focused on legally joining the organizations. This process would need to be communicated clearly to both associations and sensitive feedback was welcomed at regular intervals. It was crucial to amalgamate the associations as well as the operations. The goal was to have all members, supporters, and alumni from Fraser become part of Willowgrove. The panel also had to consider the legal processes of establishing bylaws and conforming to provincial law. These things take time!

In December, 1999, both memberships voted unanimously in favor of the amalgamation and the papers have been filed under the Corporations Act. It is the first amalgamation of non-share corporations that our experienced law firm has ever processed.

On the program front, the management contract gave Fraser Lake a new lease on life. Fraser & Glenbrook were blessed with exceptional summers in 1998 and 1999. The year-round management team of Willowgrove has allowed for a more complete and specialized approach to marketing, program planning, volunteer recruitment, and maintenance while reducing the significant overhead costs of staffing. Cross marketing, central purchasing, public relation considerations and synchronized staff recruitment/hiring are other strengths of this new company. The complete service of operating a day camp as a feeder system to a residential camp is a unique combination—sort of a camping "farrow to finish." Christian seed planting at Glenbrook is leading to a more direct ministry at Fraser and allows for a more significant impact on those who attend both camps. Willowgrove with Fraser is far less regional and welcomes the interest of a wider participation.

Many have commented that the process has resulted in an excellent marriage. Some have joked that it is an excellent marriage because the camps lived together for two years. Anyway, we are thankful for God's leading through this process and are excited by the new opportunities with which we have been entrusted.

Woodcrest Retreat

Description

Woodcrest Retreat, located on over 100 acres of beautiful woodlands in Lancaster County, Pa., is a place where youth and adults alike can enjoy the natural beauty of God's creation. Woodcrest offers summer camps for youth (both day and resident), challenge courses, and family activities such as canoe trips and weekend camping getaways. There are forty campsites with water/electric hookup, nearby bathhouse, cabins and pavilions. Participants enjoy hiking, 225-foot. waterslide, and an obstacle course.

History

Founded in 1959 as a non-profit Christian camp, the summer camp program has grown rapidly in the last decade from seventy campers in 1993 to more than 900.

Mission Statement

Sharing Christ's love

The mission of Woodcrest Retreat is to provide programs and facilities in a natural setting for guests to enjoy spiritual nurture, physical refreshment, meaningful fellowship, and wholesome recreation—sharing Christ's love, drawing persons to a personal relationship with Christ, and to encouraging Christian growth.

Objectives

- To provide programming and facilities for a summer camping program.
- To provide a campground for Christian families and church groups.
- To provide year-round rental facilities for church groups, youth groups, and other Christian groups.
- To provide programming that encourages spiritual growth and Christian fellowship.
- To provide a variety of recreation to promote physical health and wellness.
- To provide opportunities and resources to explore and learn about God's creation.

Stories

225 Woodcrest Drive Ephrata, Pennsylvania 17522
Phone: (717) 738-2233
Fax: (717) 738-3128
E-mail: info@WoodcrestRetreat.org
Website: www.WoodcrestRetreat.org
Administrator: Clifford Martin
Sponsoring Organization: Woodcrest Retreat Association.
Membership: MCA

Hi! My name is Kate Hurst and I was the office assistant at Woodcrest Retreat. It was a summer that I will never forget! I learned so much about God's love and plan for my life.

My typical day included spending most of the morning in the office answering phones, registering campers, and other office-related tasks. In the afternoon I took pictures and videotaped campers in their activities, which was a highlight for me.

Throughout the summer I was challenged and encouraged by the other staff. Fellow office workers, counselors, and support staff surrounded me with big smiles and cheery hellos no matter how hot and long the day was. We continuously encouraged each other and the campers to give them the best camp experience possible! Seeds were planted in the campers' lives by God working through our staff! The summer was awesome and God's presence was definitely felt here!

Youth Farm Bible Camp

Description

In the months of July and August Youth Farm Bible Camp is bustling with children ages 6 to 13, or special needs adults. We offer three weeks of children's camp and four camps for special needs adults.

Another attraction of the camp is teen trail rides. We have three weeks when youth come to our camp to ride horses on a trail. The trail ride usually lasts 3 to 5 days.

History

YFBC began in 1943 when the Saskatchewan Mennonite Youth Organization purchased it to begin a camping program to reach children for the Lord, an idea envisioned by Henry Friesen. Also some local Mennonites were interested in having a children's camp near water as at Camp Elim and Pike Lake. In 1965 the board of directors for the Youth Farm gave the Rosthern Mennonite Church permission to start a children's camping program. From 1968 to 1974 eight cabins and a 60 foot x 100-foot multi-purpose Quonset were built. The latter is used as a kitchen, dining hall, chapel, and auditorium for the summer camping program.

Begun in the 1980s, there is a four-week program for adults with mental disabilities with an average of 120 adults attending each year. In 1984 the camp house, including three suites for leadership staff and a staff lounge in the basement, was built.

In 1990, a horse-riding program began and remains a prominent part of the program. A wrangler is hired for the months of June to August with the sole responsibility of working with the horses and petting zoo. Since 1991, a teen trail ride has grown from 3 to 4 youth signing up for the five-day horse camp to three weeks of teen trail rides with an average of thirty youth attending each year.

In 1997, the YFBC board decided to build new cabins to replace the ones on the west side of the camp. There have been many changes to the camp over the years, but one thing remains. The ministry is with the campers that come each year.

Mission Statement

YFBC is dedicated to providing a camp setting where campers learn the importance of Christian daily living and grow in their relationship to God. This is done through chapels, campfires, devotionals, cabin groups, and the daily interaction with others.

Our camp directly reflects an Anabaptist/Mennonite theology of Christ's peace and love as central to the gospel.

P.O. Box 636 Rosthern, Saskatchewan S0K 3R0
Phone: (306) 232-5133
Fax: (306) 232-5167
E-mail: info@yfbc.ca
Website: www.yfbc.ca
Contact: Mark Wurtz
Sponsoring Organization: Mennonite Church Saskatchewan
Membership: MCA

Stories

Head Wrangler

By Ruth Isaac

This year I came from Canadian Mennonite University to camp. Often I wonder what purpose there is in working at camp. Why am I here? It is definitely not for the money, but is for the chance to minister to kids and to touch their lives in a little way.

I began the summer as head wrangler (I work with horses) and was set back by the fact that eleven of our saddles were stolen. However, God has been showing me that God's power is more than I know. The summer has progressed smoothly and we have been blessed with donations of saddles. Also, each of our three teen trail rides was packed to overflowing. This is great, since for many years the trail ride numbers have been declining.

God moves in ways beyond my understanding. So, as I contemplate camp I feel small in the grand scheme of things. I am here at camp, working for God, and allowing my love to touch others. Praise be to God!

Chapter 7

For the Love of Camping and Retreating

Chapters 7 and 8 are a potpourri of various essays and poems, many of which appeared in the MCA Newsletter over about twenty years from the late 1980s to the present. Additional ones are from other publications or were contributed by camps or individuals. The first chapter features encounters with creation, personal accounts of how camping and the camping program have given opportunity for personal expression, and anecdotes of individuals and unique programs.

The second chapter is about people who have been involved in specific aspects of Mennonite and other camping settings, of particular camps and programs, and some important teaching pieces about program and theology. The first essay by Bob Wiebe will help those of us who are given the task of writing our camp's history with ideas for doing that well.

Little attempt has been made to arrange the two chapters topically. Edited lightly for this book, the parts are loosely chronological. You may read all of them in order, or skip those of less interest and go on to something more intriguing. But don't shortchange yourself with too much skipping. You could miss some of the best parts!

Whether in a cabin high in the mountains in the West, along a bubbling stream or lake in the Midwest, in rhododendron-adorned woods in the East, or in a canoe in the waters of the northern wilderness, a camp setting is unlike any other to create an awareness of our connectedness to our Creator and the wonder of it all. In the following pages, persons express from their experiences with God in nature what it has meant for them to go to that special place apart, waiting for God's still small voice.

The stories will come in great variety—in some cases personal encounters like our leadoff story by Jim Penner, longtime MCA Newsletter editor. Others tell of special events, of places of retreat, relaxation, refreshment, and reflection, of persons who by their presence and sharing helped many of us experience closeness to God and each other in God's awesome universe.

You are invited to get comfortable and enjoy what is about to be shared with you!

I Sing the Mighty Power of God
By Isaac Watts in Divine Songs for Children, 1715

Lord, how thy wonders are displayed, where're I turn my eye, if I survey the ground I tread, or gaze upon the sky!

There's not a plant or flow'r below, but makes thy glories known, and clouds arise and tempests blow, by order from thy throne.

While all that borrows life from thee is ever in thy care, there's not a place where we can flee but God is present there.

Dancing in the Lights

By Jim Penner, editor, the MCA Newsletter, Winter, 1998

I left the dining hall and wandered across the field toward the lake.

Far from the city, with the air clear and free of pollutants, this is the perfect place for stargazing. Clouds begin to form. Like fingers reaching across the night sky, these wisps of bright cloud will soon obscure my old friend Orion.

I am almost ready to go in out of the cold (it's minus 25). The fingers begin to shimmer and wave as though they are blown by some invisible wind in the heavens. They wrap around themselves and now hang like curtains...a veil of light in the prairie sky. I watch the northern lights as they twist and turn in a mysterious dance to a song I do not know.

I have often been mesmerized by the northern lights. Why, I do not know. Perhaps my father, who grew up in Northern Ontario, inspired the love for things of the North in me as a small child.

I remember as a teenager, my brother came home after a date and woke the family up. When his girlfriend dropped him off he had seen the northern lights (no jokes here, it's way too easy). Anyway, there we were, my whole family, standing on the lawn gazing up at the sky as my future sister-in-law, clearly unimpressed, debated whether she wanted to get involved with this kooky family, "oohing and aahing" at lights in the sky.

"He once told me that if I could do a loon call, and do it well, I could call the northern lights down to the ground and they would dance around me."

I remember flying to Calgary and staring out the window for most of the flight as the northern lights put on their show. I remember canoe trips when I was able to lie on my back and watch the curtains of light ripple across the heavens.

There are explanations for this phenomenon: light particles from storms on the sun come flying through space and smash into terrestrial atoms trapped at the poles...

But there is something more mysterious about these lights. As I stand beneath them a voice echoes in my head, it is Helen Reusser: "Be still and know that I am God." There it is.

I came to Manitoba feeling somewhat detached, seeking re-creation. Having gone through many changes this year, and not knowing what the future held, I felt an uncertainty in my life.

"Be still and know that I am God." I hear the voice again.

I calm myself and rest my thoughts. Anxieties and concerns abate. A forgotten peace enters my life. I watch God finger-paint a message of beauty and love.

On the shores of Lake Winnipeg, I commune with God and creation. I feel connected again. This is how it should feel.

I remember the words of a native friend of mine. He once told me that if I could do a loon call, and do it well, I could call the northern lights down to the ground and they would dance around me. I cup my hands and blow. A feeble, mournful sound fills the air. But the northern lights continue their dance overhead, teasing as if they will join me, and then pulling coyly away to remain in their place in the heavens.

In the distance, a dog howls. I wonder if it's answering my call, or even if it can hear me. Perhaps it's just that he too wants to dance with the northern lights.

I Danced with Mother Earth Under the Trees

By David Helmuth, Goshen, Indiana, 2004

What draws me into the wilderness? During the past 20 years I have often spent a week canoeing and fishing in the pristine Boundary Waters of northern Minnesota near Ely. Our group at times included Virgil Brenneman and six to eight others including family members.

'What has drawn me into the wilderness these many times?" There is no question about it. I feel a mystical attraction and connectedness to the earth on which I stand and walk, especially when there are not the usual distractions of my daily routines.

Late one afternoon during a week on the Boundary Waters, as the group began preparations for our evening meal, a severe storm with strong wind and heavy rain enveloped us. We took refuge under the tarpaulin which was fastened securely to the surrounding trees.

As the wind intensified and the treetops above us were swaying and bending back and forth, the ground on which we were standing also heaved and fell. The heavy rain was hitting the lake before us with intensity and beauty and my friends and I were being lifted up and down gently and rhythmically.

"There is no question about it. I feel a mystical attraction and connectedness to the earth on which I stand and walk, especially when there are not the usual distractions of my daily routines."

With some fear, but also exhilaration, I felt I was dancing. Deeply within myself, a growing sense of solidarity and connectedness with the biomass on which I stood entered my being, and I danced in rhythm with the forceful work of the wind pushing the treetops and lifting the roots of the trees on which my friends and I stood.

After several hours the storm passed, sunlight broke through, and the lake glistened before us. Like after storms of life, peace returned.

A similar experience occurred several years later while crossing one of the larger lakes in the Boundary Waters at midday. It was sunny and slightly breezy along the shore. Three canoes containing some of my cousins and I with our leader from Wilderness Wind Outfitting Camp, started across Lake Three. Nearing the deep water mid-lake, we realized that the wind and waves were becoming intensely strong. In our canoes we struggled with what in the excitement of the moment seemed like five-to-six-foot waves! In actuality, the fact that we are here to tell about it likely indicated that they were considerably less than that. Nevertheless, they presented a challenge equal to the adrenalin surge that energized our straining muscles.

My cousin Harlan was my canoe partner, he in the stern and I in the bow. With all our combined energy, Harlan kept the canoe pointing into the waves as they came rushing toward us and I paddled hard to propel us forward as we zigzagged our way to the other shore. Even with good life jackets, I, a nonswimmer, felt near panic.

What a sense of relief when we finally scraped onto the shore! Our guide and another cousin were ahead of us but the third canoe was forced by the wind to go back to the beginning shore from which they took a longer but safer route around the lake margins. Again I felt like dancing with Mother Earth, the biomass of which I am an integral part and of which I am physically made.

Reflecting on this experience, I remembered that in some Native American cultures, the older people when no longer feeling useful, wander off into the wilderness, find a river, and stepping into its flow are carried forward into the next life. They find oneness with the

water of which theirs and our bodies mostly consist, and return to ultimate unity with Mother Nature and God.

Life is a dance! A dance with danger but also at times with pure joy and exhilaration. That is what draws me into the wilderness....and a time to be alone and also a time to spend in community with fellow-travelers.

Here is one of those special places where poetry expresses what we feel!

Little Eden
By Vincent Beck, 1984

> *Standing on Portage Point, watching the setting sun.*
> *A picture that no artist can portray.*
> *Graceful swans are swimmin', close to Little Eden*
> *I hear a sea gull cryin' overhead.*
> *Sweet peas are bloomin', cool water everywhere,*
> *And the dunes of sand are all around.*
> *I tell you folks, it's heaven to be at Little Eden*
> *When the summer sun goes down!*

At Drift Creek Camp in Oregon, the "water event" is a twenty-minute float on inner tubes in Drift Creek, a rushing mountain stream with mild rapids and deep, slower-flowing holes. Beginning on one side of the camp property, the creek flows around a large oval, nearly meeting itself as it journeys through the mountains on its way to the Pacific Ocean.

Beware! Counseling may not be "a picnic." Gina Hansen's account, "Some Days Are Bad-Hair Days" in **Spirit Roots**, *the Drift Creek Camp forty-year anniversary book, 2000*

During high school week, a camper from my cabin was the lifeguard. She was good, but very nervous. I agreed to go with her as one of two counselors that accompanied the group. One camper was reluctant. I tried to be patient, but she kept trying to back out.

"Up until this point I had the image of 'service' in my head. People 'in service' were supposed to be saintly and rather perfect. They never lost their tempers or looked like drowned rats."

She didn't seem frightened; she just didn't want to get wet. I finally got her into the creek. I was the counselor who brought up the rear of the group. This girl kept lagging farther and farther behind until the others were far ahead. She had already told me she couldn't swim.

However it was a warm year and the water level was low. There was only one spot where the water would be over her head, and it was a very calm area. Just about the time we got to that spot, the rest of the group were far enough ahead that they had entered the next rapids and couldn't slow down to wait. About then she saw a spider on the log on the bank, screamed and threw herself off the inner tube into the water.

She really couldn't swim and started to sink. I hopped off my tube and swam back to her, dragging the inner tube with me, pulled her onto it, and swam after hers. When we got to the shallow water, we got out and walked to the lodge. The other counselors and lifeguard were looking for us, and very worried. They were very impressed with how I had "saved" the girl. I just wanted a shower.

Up until this point I had the image of "service" in my head. People "in service" were supposed to be saintly and rather perfect. They never lost their tempers or looked like drowned rats. They helped others willingly, with joy. I did not feel joy when I fished out that girl. I felt irritated and cold and tired. Service is a great thing, but regular people serve God, not perfect saints who never get angry or mess up their hair.

This lesson has been important in my life. In early childhood education, you spend all your time serving, and often doing unpleasant things, like changing diapers, cleaning toys, and dealing with angry parents. I get frustrated and depressed, angry and tired. Yet I know all those emotions are part of serving God, just as much as positive feelings of joy, excitement, caring, and tenderness. As a counselor I learned the basics of serving others.

Seeking the Wilderness: A Spiritual Journey
From the book Seeking the Wilderness: A Spiritual Journey

By Tim Lehman, then MCA president-elect, from the author's preface as written in the MCA Newsletter, Fall, 1993

We find ourselves at a critical juncture. Much of life seems confusing and hollow. Do we save the whales or just save souls? Should we hug a tree or build another house? Do we sing the praises of a future world or strive to save the one God has already made?

"Do we save the whales or just save souls? Should we hug a tree or build another house?"

These questions seem endless and they seem to exist without answers that satisfy. Perhaps the questions themselves only serve to polarize the problem and preserve it. What if we did not ask such questions, but rather nurtured a relationship with the world about us as if it really were God's.

Wilderness, as discovered and explored within the pages of this book, remains as much a part of the heart and soul as it does the natural environment. I invite you to enter this wilderness with me. Let us together look inward and outward for God's Spirit to guide us. The biblical theme of wilderness represents a person's need to be apart and be with God. The Bible stories about people of faith seeking God chronicle the dramatic effect of the wilderness experience. People of faith are changed into faithful people full of God's love and passion for life. Today we may still seek God by seeking the wilderness.

Above are excerpts from the preface of **Seeking the Wilderness: A Spiritual Journey.** As the writer of this book, one of my hopes is that Mennonite camping people will read it and find encouragement and challenge. I hope that we as leaders and educators will see our way clear to aid the Mennonite Church toward a more full and rich experience of God through experiences in creation.

If we are to do this, I believe we will need experiences of our own that nurture us spiritually and link us relationally to the earth. We will also need help to combat the constant intrusions of society and culture which tell us in a myriad ways that creation is not a spiritual concern.

I have written this book as a spiritual catalyst, and not a summation of thought on the subject. I hope too that it will bring us into further dialogue and serious study of our place within God's universe. May Mennonite Camping Association always be a place where we wrestle honestly with these issues.

* * *

In A Vision and a Legacy *(Faith and Life Press, 1984), Jess Kauffman stated, "The story of Mennonite camping would not be complete without recognition of the important role women played in its formative years." This has become much more apparent in the last two decades as evidenced in various parts of this book with contributions from or allusions to such women as Gayle Gerber Koontz, Lily Lowen, Helen Reusser, Marlene Kropf, Eleanor Snyder, Mary Jane Eby, and others too numerous to mention. Through their input at binational and regional conventions,*

serving on the MCA board, teaching and writing, and giving of themselves as camp directors and board members, women have had a great deal to do with shaping our various camps over the years.

Following are two articles in the MCA Newsletter, Winter, 1994, by two women sharing their experiences in assuming roles that in former times were allotted to men. The benefit of their courage and struggles has made the Mennonite camping scene a better place.

A Place of Freedom
By Roxie Ramseyer, program director at Camp Luz in Kidron, Ohio

As God's children, whether male or female, we are called to a life of service; we are called to live like Jesus. The church camping ministry, and my role as program director at Camp Luz, need to be shaped by that vision. It is exciting to be a part of a ministry where this is so strongly emphasized.

Part of the reason I enjoy this ministry is because I believe it so strongly parallels the ministry of Christ while on this earth. Think about it. Jesus did much of his teaching in the outdoors, using nature numerous times in his stories and examples. He primarily spent his time teaching his small band of followers, his twelve disciples (a large cabin group) as well as often teaching the entire camp.

"Camp provides, by its very nature, a place of freedom to relate to one another much differently than is often possible within the organization of the local church."

Jesus lived with his disciples; he ate with them and slept with them. They sang together and they had disagreements among one another. The lives of the disciples were never the same. I believe the same is true of those who attend our church camps, no matter what their age.

In the past, I have experienced numerous disappointments in pursuing a ministry position as a woman. Christian camping, however, is one place where I have found an acceptance closely reflecting the camping ministry. I have experienced nothing but respect for who I am and the gifts I possess. I have found a place here where I feel I belong, doing ministry I enjoy and feel called to.

Camp provides, by its very nature, a place of freedom to relate to one another much differently than is often possible within the organization of the local church. The day-to-day living together in community and attempting to live out Christ's example gives a greater openness to appreciate each individual for who God made them to be.

As more women are called to some sort of ministry within the church and church agencies, it is exciting to think about the possibilities that wait within the church camping field. Keep up the good work, MCA, in welcoming individuals to join in the leadership ministries of Christ's kingdom.

Stepping from the Shadows
By Mary Jane Eby, president-elect in the MCA Newsletter, Winter, 1994

My soul-sisters are the friends who have known me: my interests, my concerns, and my beliefs. They are women of various ages whose lives have met mine, who have cared, empathized, and supported our common struggle to be catalysts for change, especially in the church.

Patterns of church leadership are changing, eliminating some of the obstacles to women's full participation in the ministry of the church, including camp ministry. Women, however, continue to experience conflicting feelings over their desire to offer the church their God-given gifts as ministering persons. A part of the nurturing of women in the church has been a tradition that names self-denial and self-sacrifice a virtue; defining the appropriate places for women and men in the church.

In my role as a staff person in the Ohio Mennonite Conference, I began to realize the disappointment and the reality of the lesser value placed on women as they interviewed for youth ministry roles in the church. The unspoken assumption of greater strength, more knowledge, and more competence assigned to men continues to prevail.

The story of Mennonite camping is a history of a male institution in areas of administration and leadership, with a reluctance to include women in these significant roles. In *A Vision and a Legacy: The Story of Mennonite Camping, 1920-1980 by Jesse Kauffman*, two pages give tribute to the important role of women in the camping ministry (pp. 115-116). As I look through the recent MCA directory, the church has basically called male administrators to give vision and direction to camp ministry. Does the directory listing tell the whole story? Women are the nurturers, and caregivers in every camp, ministering to hundreds of campers, and conference participants.

Much of our thinking and living regarding men's and women's roles in the church has been patterned after our culture. Male domination and female subordination are images tightly woven into western culture and religion. Jesus dared to speak out against the culture of his day, by relating to women in revolutionary ways. As followers of Jesus, how can we do less? Our message of bringing wholeness to everyone must include women in leadership ministries, using inclusive language and a new holistic interpretation of the Bible as the way of Shalom.

Stepping from the shadows is a natural unfolding of who I am, but I more often think of it as circuitous, indirect, and rather surprising. In 1985, I was asked to be licensed for pastoral ministry as I ministered to the many youth coordinators in the churches of the Ohio Mennonite Conference.

I found myself in a place I never expected to be . . . but I realized I was in this place by listening to what was within me and allowing something deeply rooted in me to move out into expression, being aware of God's presence and gifts given to me. Ten years later, I am in my fourth year as a camp director, in another state and working with a new church conference.

"...a soul-sister, gave me a special gift, a cup with a message that read, 'Some leaders are born women.'"

There have been affirmations and expressions of support from both men and women. At the time of my licensing, an older woman, a soul-sister, gave me a special gift, a cup with a message that read, "Some leaders are born women." That is the message of the equality that God intended for humankind; we are all made in God's image. Stepping from the shadows for many women is a path that leads into healing and wholeness.

Women as gifted leaders in camping ministry are not a passing phenomenon. Today women form a chorus that bears a powerful message of a new creation, of an outpouring of an all-inclusive love, of a gospel call to be part of the body of Christ. In partnership, women and men are called and challenged to mutually minister and encourage all persons to utilize their gifts for the building of the church.

Some of the Pharisees in the crowd said to [Jesus], "Teacher, order your disciples to stop." He answered, "I tell you, if these were silent, the stones would shout out." Luke 19:39-40, NRSV

Margaret Yoder, head cook, Rocky Mountain Mennonite Camp is the voice for such a rock in the MCA Newsletter, Fall, 1995.

From My Vantage Point...Monkey Rock

I've been able to watch Rocky Mountain Mennonite Camp (RMMC) in its development over the years. One of the highest points of RMMC, I'm known as Monkey Rock. I like to think of myself as a sort of sentinel, standing guard over the camp.

In the 1950s a dream was born, a flickering fire in the hearts of early camp developers. It's been exciting for me to observe the many people who have come to this place over the years, each one bringing with them a part of the dream, and carrying away with them a spark from the fire.

"From my perch on this hill I watch the sun set, then wait for darkness to surround me. One-by-one little twinkling lights appear, until suddenly the sky is full of stars. The moon, suspended just an arm's reach beyond me, casts a soft mellowing light."

The people who come are truly the lifeblood of RMMC, from the youngest campers to the very oldest family campers, or those coming as part of reunion groups. Many special relationships develop between campers and staff members alike, resulting in life-long friendships.

The camp's physical attractions continue to include hiking trails, leading to mountain-top experiences; clear singing streams; towering pines, whispering in the winds; aspens, changing with the seasons; chipmunks and ground squirrels, fighting for attention; humming birds, tiny but very aggressive at the feeders; columbines and wildflowers consuming summer hillsides.

*My favorite of RMMC's natural beauty is the night sky. From my perch on this hill I watch the sun set, then wait for darkness to surround me. One-by-one little twinkling lights appear, until suddenly the sky is full of stars. The moon, suspended just an arm's reach beyond me, casts a soft mellowing light.

Cabin lights are turned off one-by-one, until finally everyone is quiet, sleeping. The camp sleeps, gaining energy for tomorrow, energy for another busy day of camp experiences, or for some, energy to return to homes and work, refreshed as a result of the time spent here in this peaceful and restful setting.

As the camp sleeps, I continue my watch. Like the warm blanket carefully drawn over the shoulders of sleeping campers, the special glow of Christ's love spreads over Rocky Mountain Mennonite Camp.

* * *

Many of our Mennonite camps, especially in the earlier years as they were perhaps struggling to get by financially, were recipients of lots of pre-used gifts. Some of these ended up not being of real usefulness but what some well-meaning person thought could be used. But in many cases the alertness of a director, board member, or friend made a huge difference in improving the quality or scope of what a camp could offer within their budget.

When Mary Jane and Larry were administrators of Drift Creek Camp in the mid-1990s, a friend of the camp was aware that at Oregon State University one of the dormitories was purchasing new beds. The old ones were still very serviceable and could be purchased for a nominal fee plus transportation. It was a day of great joy when these "new" beds arrived and we could recycle old metal nursing home beds that had been the mainstay in most of our rooms for the first thirty years.

So we will share with you how Crooked Creek Christian Camp in Iowa received something "new" in a similar way.

As told by Jim Penner in the MCA Newsletter, Fall, 1997.

We Have New Cabins

Earlier this year eight motel units were lifted off their foundations, hauled to Crooked Creek, and then set onto new foundations to begin a new life. The story of how they came to Crooked Creek is lifted from their newsletter.

Sometimes it pays to read the newspaper.

Last fall an alert Camp Partner sent us an article from the Iowa City Press Citizen which told of the imminent closing of the Blue Top Motel cabin units in Coralville as the land had been purchased for development of a medical plaza. Accompanying the article was a handwritten note: "Do you think the camp could use these?"

We began making some contacts as we were running out of cabin space during some of the larger children's camp rental groups. One thing led to another and eventually an agreement was reached with plaza owner, Dr. Ian Charles Skaugstad, for the units to be donated to Crooked Creek if the camp would bear the expense for moving them. After three donations were promised to the camp to cover moving costs, the board voted to accept the units. They are now here at camp.

We are grateful for this quick way to expand our cabin space and provide other housing options for smaller families. We have also received a lot of positive publicity. We have heard that as many as twenty other parties may have been interested in acquiring these units.

Dr. Skaugstad tells us that he hopes to visit soon to see the units but wants to come when our food services are in operation! We take that as a compliment and give him our thanks.

"I wonder how many other innovative ways there are to allow people to donate to your camp and its programs."

Very clever! Hats off to Crooked Creek! This article sparked a memory for me. I visited a camp in Ontario several years ago that had received a similar donation of pizza ovens from a restaurant that was closing. They knocked a wall out of their kitchen, expanding their facilities to accommodate the new pizza centre.

I wonder how many other innovative ways there are to allow people to donate to your camp and its programs. All it takes is a little creativity, a certain amount of desire, and at least one person who reads a newspaper!

* * *

Another Jim Penner story in the MCA Newsletter, *Spring, 1997, with Trisha Shepley's excerpt from* United Mennonite Educational Institute School News *tells of a person for whom the camp experience at an unidentified Mennonite camp sowed seeds which opened windows for a camp to a world far beyond the geographical setting of her camp and home.*

Sow Seeds, Trust the Promise, Face-to-Face with God

"As a child I was an active member of a Mennonite camp. I spent summer after summer camping, learning, meeting new friends and getting reacquainted with old ones," writes Trisha.

"It wasn't until my fifth consecutive year at camp that I learned of Mennonite Central Committee (MCC). The camp director was doing an all-camp devotional one night at campfire. His devotional was one that I will never forget. He spoke of all the starving children in Africa and told us of the horrifying numbers of deaths per day.

"I was astonished. That was the first time I'd heard of poverty in such detail. Sure, we prayed about it in Sunday school and before meals but it never seemed like reality until that night.

"After his devotional, I was so upset, that I talked to one of my counselors and asked what I could do. She told me about Mennonite Central Committee (MCC). From that day on I had the dream to one day join the MCC team. I learned more about MCC through UMEI (United Mennonite Educational Institute).

"Every year UMEI gave us the opportunity to participate in service projects during our March break, so for my grade 11 and 12 years, I spent my break in Toronto working with inner city children at Warden Woods. These projects gave me a good feel for what I wanted to do. And I'm grateful that I was able to do it through SALT (Serving and Learning Together). I returned in July from serving a one-year term with MCC in Brazil."

* * *

The above excerpt from the UMEI School News *(United Mennonite Educational Institute) is important, not because it tells us anything new, but because it reminds us of what has always been and will always be true about our camping programs.*

One of our roles within the church is to be seed planters. Camps have three things going for them in this regard.

1. Setting. When people are surrounded by God's creation, day and night, week after week, one cannot escape God, the Creator. Just as the aroma of fresh bread permeates everything in the house when bread is baking, so too the Spirit of God permeates the woods and meadows in which God walks. It is true that God also walks through cities and towns, but there we have built walls and signs and barriers to hide God from us, or to hide ourselves from God.

2. People. The point was made by Helen Reusser at the '96 Biennial at Lakewood Retreat Center, that all you need for a camp experience is a counselor and a group of campers. At camps we also add into the mix various resource staff, administrative staff, kitchen staff, maintenance staff, board members, and volunteers. All of these people have become involved in camps for various reasons and are usually willing to share their stories, in part because of the intimate settings that camps provide.

3. The church. More important than anything we do at camp is the fact that when we have done what we do, the participants return to the larger church community to put their newfound experiences and feelings into context. Congregations, families, and church schools can see things to fruition that we cannot because of the short time we spend together.

"We don't know which story, which song, or which cloudless night will bring someone face-to-face with God."

As we prepare for summer and the season of planting, may God guide our planning and keep us focused on the goal. We don't know which camper or staff member is being prepared now for an epiphany this summer. We don't know which story, which song, or which cloudless night will bring someone face-to-face with God. With this in mind, let every choice we make be one that allows for God's Spirit to work through us.

For some the first wilderness experience can be habit forming. That's what happened to Larry Penner as written in The Mennonite, *July 21, 1998.*

Wilderness Lessons

To the sick the doctors wisely recommend a change of air and scenery. — Thoreau in Walden

When several college friends and I planned a reunion canoe trip in northern Minnesota several years ago, I had no idea I would return to the Boundary Waters annually or that summer vacations would take on spiritual significance. I expected to enjoy the beauty of God's creation, but the world I found was so different from home that the experience was more like a cross-cultural encounter. In the years since, I have learned more about God and my place in God's creation with each return trip to the wilderness.

My first trips into the Boundary Waters, a network of thousands of lakes in wilderness set aside for canoe travel only, were like entering another culture. I had little wilderness-living experience, and I was in a world I did not understand. The things I took for granted—meals, a soft bed, shelter—took planning and effort. Distances I would measure in minutes in my car took days in a canoe. Every small act, from preparing food to using the bathroom (or accommodating the lack thereof), required effort and taught me lessons about my misconceptions of time, priorities, and my place in my environment.

The irony, of course, was that this foreign, awkward lifestyle was more natural than the artificial ways of living that had become second nature to me over the years. We live with this irony every day. We spend our lives in an artificial, human-constructed environment of office buildings and housing developments.

Where I live in Lancaster, Pa., paved streets, manicured lawns, and mini-marts have become so much the norm that an isolated plot of park or farmland can seem unnatural, as if someone intentionally inserted a bit of nature into the otherwise natural order of concrete.

When we find ourselves for the first time in undisturbed wilderness, in the world as God created it, we feel disoriented. Unless we are within reach of some safety blanket, a telephone or car, anxiety accompanies the overwhelming beauty of the place. The natural world is completely unnatural to us. On the first day into a canoe trip I am reminded how far my daily life is from the immediacy of God's presence I feel in the wilderness. The wilds remind me that God, after all, did create this world. Entering the undisturbed wilderness is like entering God's house.

"Every small act, from preparing food to using the bathroom (or accommodating the lack thereof), required effort and taught me lessons about my misconceptions of time, priorities, and my place in my environment."

Humility. One of the first spiritual lessons the wilderness teaches is humility. Our human-made environments nurture our false sense that we control our lives. I can't start out on a trail without accepting my weakness and my dependence on God. Once the first lake is crossed, the social position I have created for myself at home with all of its attendant control and security is gone. Civilized society gives us a distorted, self-important view of ourselves that we cannot perceive until we leave it. In the wilderness I am not defined by memberships, affiliations, or career. At the same time I am surrounded by a world that does not revolve around humans. I am a small part of the balance of life.

Another reminder of humility is the sense of my place in the lifetime of the woods. At home I am hard pressed to find elements of my environment that are more than perhaps 100 years old. In the North Woods (the vast forest of which the Boundary Waters are a part), campers sleep on the granite roots of mountains that stood hundreds of millions of years ago. About 12,000 years ago (give or take a millennium) glaciers carved the lakes that allow canoes to navigate the wilderness. The oldest trees in the Boundary Waters are over

113

400 years old, and pictographs left scattered through the park by Native American cultures likely predate these.

As I enter this grand-scale timeline, hours and minutes lose their significance. In the woods I feel a small step closer to experiencing God's time. For the duration of any trip, there will be no appointments to keep, no clock metering my activities. Wilderness Wind, the Mennonite outfitter that has given me and many other Mennonites our first experience of canoe travel and wilderness living, insists that campers leave their watches behind. While the requirement strikes some campers as ridiculous (I've even seen it make some outright hostile), I have been on trips where first-time campers said giving up the watch was one of the most significant parts of their trip. Sunrise, sunset, and the rumblings of your stomach regulate the day. Living without a clock shows us how artificial our dependence on it is and takes us closer to understanding a God that does not measure time in hours and minutes, a God for whom 1,000 years is as a day.

Culture Shock. Just as the wilderness refocuses my sense of time, it resets my understanding of necessities. Development workers often return from overseas and talk about culture shock readjusting to the luxuries of North American life. Returning from the woods has the same effect. Fitting all necessities for living a week or more, including food and shelter, into one backpack can be a spiritual discipline. Campers learn to redefine what is really necessary to live. The physical exertions of a day's paddling make simple meals of dried fruits, peanut butter and jelly, and fresh lake water more satisfying than a dinner at an expensive restaurant. The woods teach gratefulness for what God has given rather than the constant dissatisfaction I've learned to feel at home.

"On the first day into a canoe trip I am reminded how far my daily life is from the immediacy of God's presence I feel in the wilderness."

These lessons in simplicity have made me keenly aware of an increasingly pervasive, ironic twist to the relationship between consumerism and the simplicity of living outdoors. The wilderness has become a selling tool. Outdoor companies market their fashions as if they were selling a wilderness experience, as if purchasing a Polartec jacket could bring you closer to the kind of spiritual experience the woods offers. The skyrocketing sales of sport utility vehicles and environmental license plates (as if you are saving the environment by driving your car) symbolize to me both the pervasiveness of the commercialism virus and the spiritual desire our country has for the simplicity the wilderness offers. If only we could learn that our consumerism is exactly what stands in our way.

Another gift of renewal the wilderness gives is the redefinition of work and play. A wilderness trip erases the artificial distinction between the two. In the woods, tasks like crossing a lake, building a fire, or preparing a meal become pleasures. Vacation is not an escape from responsibility but a lesson in taking pleasure in responsibility. The dangers of a canoe trip, from a bear threatening your food to a thunderhead approaching as you cross a lake, require heightened responsibility. But with the responsibility comes freedom as canoers experience independence and the ability to become truly self-reliant. Satisfaction comes as one's ability to care for oneself in the woods grows—as one becomes more at home in God's house.

There is no end to the spiritual lessons of the outdoors. And with each trip I learn more. As I watch a beaver or chipmunk, I wonder whether God watches me this way, taking delight in the beauty of my life while I go about my daily tasks. Rounding a bend to find a moose grazing is a gift, as if God has stepped into my path. The silence of a lakeside morning can be a form of prayer, when every smell, sight, sound, and touch seems full of God's presence. In stepping out of my domesticated world into a world raw with God's

handiwork, I find a more honest understanding of self and of creation. It is a work I hope to continue throughout my life.

Valerie Ford, volunteer at Camp Hebron and spouse of program director Mike Ford, shares MCA conference experiences in the MCA Newsletter, *April, 1999*

Connecting in the Spirit
(report of the Eastern Regional MCA conference)

I don't routinely have the opportunity to accompany my husband to a camping conference; two small children complicate that notion. But I was privileged to attend this year's Eastern Regional MCA Conference at Kenbrook Bible Camp in Lebanon, Pa. It was a significant treat to meet my husband's colleagues and join in the fellowship and dialogue with people involved in similar ministries, struggles, and triumphs.

The theme of the conference was "Connecting in the Spirit." The speaker for our main sessions, Warren Hoffman (moderator of the Brethren in Christ Church), beautifully addressed this theme through his gentle manner of convicting and encouraging. He exhorted us to pursue the Holy Spirit with passion; to thirst after the Spirit as one who thirsts for water in a dry and parched land (Psalm 63:1). It is good to realize that some who have been followers of Jesus Christ for years may have never asked the Holy Spirit to infiltrate their lives.

Warren shared his own testimony of the baptism of the Holy Spirit (John 3:1-8) and the subtle, but distinct transformation in his life since then. That was a personal encouragement to me since it was just two weeks earlier that I prayed for a spiritual renewal. I have been a Christian for over a decade, but having gone through a dry and frustrating period, was uncertain of the Spirit's hand in my life. Since my prayer for spiritual awakening, I have continued on believing in faith that I am, as promised (Luke 11:9-13), filled with the Holy Spirit. I have been humbled to see God's faithfulness in my life as God allows the Spirit to work in me and through me. I look forward with joy and anticipation to God's further good work in me. During the conference I was blessed to hear others share with me their testimonies of the workings of the Spirit in their lives.

"Fellowship was savored while overeating in the dining hall, singing around an indoor illuminary campfire, playing Wally ball, tree climbing, zip-lining, or sitting in on a roundtable discussion."

Warren's second exhortation was to seek out and be faithful in our connections with other believers (whether they be in camping circles or not). We benefit so much from intentional relationships that provide accountability and encouragement. Proverbs 27:17 tells us that as iron sharpens iron, so one person sharpens another. Often the Lord will use other Christians to refresh us when we are dragging, encourage us when we are discouraged, and convict us when we are misled. We can miss out on so much the Lord has for us if we are not connecting with other dear ones in the Spirit.

The three days at Kenbrook were just one way to foster connections. Fellowship was savored while overeating in the dining hall, singing around an indoor illuminary campfire, playing Wally ball, tree climbing, zip-lining, or sitting in on a roundtable discussion. A final highlight was our closing communion celebration where we offered blessings of encouragement to one another while we praised our God from whom all good things flow. I am so pleased to have been able to "connect in the Spirit" with other happy MCA campers.

* * *

*The former director of Camp Valaqua, Alberta, Tim Wiebe-Neufeld shares the awe of his personal encounter with a creature of wildness in the **MCA Newsletter**, July, 1999.*

Tree Tales and River Raves: Seeking God's Face in Creation

The Great Gray Owl is the largest owl in North America. It wouldn't take much to convince my brother of that fact. The Great Gray was definitely the biggest owl he had ever seen. Of course, everything looks bigger when you stare into its face less than a metre away!

We hadn't meant to get that close. When we had spotted the owl landing in the tall grass of the field, our only thought had been to get a good picture. I have a photo record showing the owl growing larger and larger as I took shots thinking that each one was the closest we were possibly going to get.

Suddenly, we realized that I was standing barely two metres away, and my brother was so close he would not have had to extend his arm to reach out and touch the magnificent creature. When the owl turned its head and looked him straight in the eye, for an instant his life flashed before his eyes.

Fear wasn't the only thing my brother felt as he stared into the face of such a magnificent part of God's creation. He also experienced a mix of awe and wonder. In that curled beak and piercing eyes there was a glimpse of the Creator. In those brief seconds before the owl finally turned and took flight, each of us felt the hand of God at work here in the world. The owl had allowed both of us a rare glimpse at the untamed beauty of God's handiwork, and as the owl floated over the trees in the distance we too took our leave with spirits lifted and hearts renewed.

"The societies we have constructed for ourselves paint over the forests in asphalt and the stars with streetlights. We have worked hard to separate ourselves from the rest of God's creation."

Seeing the hand of God in creation is not something new. Throughout the history of humanity people have marveled at the work of God in creation. Nearly 3,000 years ago, King David proclaimed, "The heavens are telling the glory of God; and the firmament proclaims [God's] handiwork" (Psalm 19:1, NRSV). The words are just as meaningful today as when they were written. Who wouldn't feel their spirit touched by the sight of a lofty mountaintop view, the vast expanse of stars, or staring into the face of a Great Gray Owl?

Yet, even though the evidence is here to see, we have done our best to mask God's hand in the world. The societies we have constructed for ourselves paint over the forests in asphalt and the stars with streetlights. We have worked hard to separate ourselves from the rest of God's creation.

Our world is a constant stream of heating and air-conditioning as we move from the climate control of our homes through garages to vehicles that whisk us away to office parkades and indoor shopping malls. We make our homes in neighborhoods of dead asphalt and a mono-culture lawn, sloped for easy drainage and void of wildlife. Even our food comes not from the land but from the grocery store, nicely prepackaged and displayed. We seldom get the chance to experience the beauty and wildness of God's creation in our daily lives. That's what makes camping ministry so important. Camps offer us a place where people can find healing and hope by seeking God's face in creation.

Through camping ministry, people experience God through the Word, through others around them, and through God's creation. It's the one place that brings together these three important relationships that offer a witness of God to the human spirit. That's why we have camps by forests, lakes, and rivers instead of in parking lots and shopping malls. People yearn to be reconnected to the Creator in all their relationships, including their relationship with the rest of creation itself. Camps offer us a chance for even a temporary reconnection with God's world. They give us the opportunity to stare face-to-face with creation, and in that meeting catch a glimpse of God.

* * *

Shekinah Retreat Centre at Waldheim, Saskatchewan, shared the following two inspiring pieces:

One of the parents who accompanied a group of students to Shekinah for an outdoor education excursion wrote the following poem:

> In the Valley of Shekinah
> Like the first morning ray that briefly caresses the tree-
> top before spilling into the valley,
> Shekinah, you warm me.
> From the cool stream that flows surely past the dock
> then widens into a rushing river,
> Shekinah, you quench my thirst.
> When I am alone to hear the soft whisper of a leaf floating gently to the earth,
> Shekinah, you soothe me.
> As the rain mists softly all-around only to gather
> and then disperse once more,
> Shekinah, you sustain me.
> Before the Moon dances across the dark night sky
> embraced by a thousand sparkling jewels,
> Shekinah, you lay claim to me.
> By going to camp, you might end up on national TV!!!

* * *

The following article appeared in the Canadian Mennonite *(February 10, 2003)*

Ever wonder what could happen by coming to Shekinah for summer camp?

Ask recent CBC [Canadian Broadcasting Corporation] television contest winner Stephanie Siemens. Stephanie, a 13-year-old from Warman and yearly summer camper at Shekinah, designed a poster showing all the things she loves about Shekinah and sent it to CBC television. And then she got a phone call asking if she could co-host some TV segments from Shekinah because her poster won the contest!

On December 13, a five-person film crew arrived at Shekinah, along with about sixty junior high students from two local towns, Martensville and Waldheim. Joining Stephanie as host was Anthony McLean, host of InfomatriX, the kids program that sponsored the contest.

The show had received over 1,000 entries to the contest. A panel of judges picked the best entry from each province. The final thirteen were presented on the show and kids were asked to vote for their favorite.

The crew spent the day filming various winter activities which included skating, tubing, and the popular "Flying Fox." They had a wiener roast for lunch, with the high-energy Anthony sitting by the fire for awhile so that the excited kids could have their photo taken with him. "Each scene was shot up to five times," said Stephanie. "It was a bit exhausting, but a great experience. I learned a lot of great stuff." The best part of the day, she said, was talking to Anthony off camera and watching the television crew go on the Flying Fox. The segments aired on InfomatriX on January 8 and 9, 2003.

When through the woods,
and forest glades I wander
And hear the birds
sing sweetly in the trees;
When I look down
from lofty mountain grandeur
And hear the brook
and feel the gentle breeze;
Then sings my soul,
my Savior God to thee;
How great Thou art!

Words by Carl Boberg,
tr. by Stuart K. Hine,

copyright 1955 by Manna Music, Inc.

*This first of the two stories about Kelli Beechy that follow is from **Spirit Roots, the Drift Creek Camp** history. A unique camper, deaf from infancy, Kelli had much to teach both campers and staff. Note especially how the senses of feel and sight made up for the quiet world in which she has spent her entire life.*

The second story, from the Portland Oregonian, *is not directly camp-related, but those of us connecting with Kelli observed a camper take satisfaction at her continued experiences in her silent world.*

Special People Come to Camp
By Larry Eby, coauthor of In Harmony with Nature

We were in the middle of registration for third- and fourth-grade camp in 1992, when a non-preregistered camper arrived with her parents. The camper was Kelli Beechy. Her parents had been on the way to take her to a special camp for hearing-impaired children when Kelli signed, "I don't want to go to this camp. I want to go to Drift Creek Camp with my friends."

For several summers at Drift Creek Camp we enjoyed Kelli's enthusiastic participation. She entered energetically into the activities, even though she was not always able to understand perfectly what was being said.

"I also remember waking up in the morning and seeing the sunlight shine through the big trees and enjoying the shape of the cabins... It felt good to hike there, and it feels good to know the trail now in my memory."

The first summer, she actually was there without a person to interpret for her. Other years, various persons would come for the week—one time a woman who herself had a hearing-impaired child who also participated in the camp activities. Another year Kelli's sister Tiffany accompanied her. It was interesting to see Kelli lip-reading the speaker rather than watching Tiffany.

It was a good experience for all to have Kelli as a part of the summer camps. Some of the counselors became very interested in signing, and one, Art LaVaque, subsequently majored in sign language in college.

We asked Kelli to contribute something about her experiences. She sent the following. Note how the senses of sight and other sensations made up for the quietness in her camp experiences:

My first memory of Drift Creek Camp is playing Capture the Flag. That was the most fun activity for me. I also remember waking up in the morning and seeing the sunlight shine through the big trees and enjoying the shape of the cabins. Hiking to The Rock is another good memory. It felt good to hike there, and it feels good to know the trail now in my memory.

"When I was younger, playing with the kids was fun, but being deaf meant that the camp was lonelier as I got older. I remember Beth Stutzman especially because she would sign with me all of the time."

Kelli, now a young adult in the winter of 2005 when this is being written, is a member of the USA Soccer Team for the 2005 Summer Deaf Olympics in Australia.

Put Your Hands Together for an Athlete Named Kelli Beechy
By Brian Meehan, Staff Writer, in the Portland Oregonian, *December 5, 2004*

Kelli Beechy has an adventurous soul. She roams hiking trails in the [Oregon] Cascades and carves wide turns on Mount Bachelor.

On a clear winter day, she stands on her snowboard atop a ski hill in the Sierras and gazes down in wonder at the rich blue of Lake Tahoe. It is her favorite spot in the world.

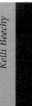

Kelli Beechy

When you meet her, you quickly see she is one of those people who seize the moment, whether on a soccer field, a basketball court, or as a deaf person in a hearing world. Whatever you do, don't feel sorry for her. She sure doesn't.

"Deaf people are just the same, except we can't hear," Beechy said. She talks to me in American Sign Language, her words translated by Jane Mulholland, director of Oregon School for the Deaf.

At age 23, Beechy is poised for her great adventure. Next month, she will compete in the twentieth Summer Deaf Olympics Games in Melbourne, Australia. She is a mid-fielder on the U. S. women's soccer team. It is the first time the games have had women's soccer. Beechy intends to use her speed and her strong left foot to run down a gold medal and a piece of history.

But the games are more than an international competition. Deaf people don't see themselves as disabled but rather as a cultural minority complete with their own language. And the Deaf Olympics are a time to celebrate that culture.

"I enjoy being deaf and I enjoy the life I have as a deaf person," Beechy said.

That life has been lived at full speed. Beechy was born deaf; the doctors never could tell her why. Her parents, John and Claudia, and her older sister, Tiffany, can hear.

Her father began enrolling the active little girl in soccer, basketball, and volleyball teams in Salem, Oregon. Beechy loved being part of a team and played the games with gusto.

"Sports has taught me to be well-disciplined, to have fun and to take care of myself," she said. "Sports was also my way of meeting new people. It makes me feel good about myself; it is part of who I am."

She went to Salem public schools into her freshman year at Sprague High School. Then Beechy transferred to Oregon School for the Deaf. The change in school had a profound impact on Beechy.

"I was very shy at first," she said, "but I was in awe of the way everyone could sign so well. It really helped me to prepare for Gaudelet." At OSD, classes were taught in sign. Student discussions in class and social banter in the halls were conducted in sign. Beechy, like so many deaf kids, felt more plugged in.

She excelled in sports, breaking the scoring record for girls' basketball and playing volleyball. She put her other love, soccer, on hold because the school didn't field a team. But she began playing again at Gallaudet, the university for the deaf in Washington, D.C. Now she is among twenty women who are working to forge a team to bring home a gold medal.

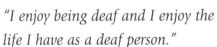

"I enjoy being deaf and I enjoy the life I have as a deaf person."

How Disabled Toni Impacted Our Entire Summer

By Cliff Derksen, former executive director of Camps with Meaning

"I'll be back in a minute. Why don't you take the three-minute tour while you wait?"

I was standing in the middle of Toni's college living quarters. All I needed to do for the tour was stand in one spot and look around. What I saw was certainly a strange mixture of student clutter. Yes, there was the mandatory ghetto blaster, the textbooks, files, and a bulletin board covered with memos, schedules, pictures, and a host of cards from a recent birthday celebration.

What was unusual was the technology. There was a large-screen computer, while next to it stood a contraption that looked like an overhead projector but much larger. Obviously these were special aids for this handicapped college student.

Camps with Meaning is an organization of three camps jointly owned and operated by the Conference of Mennonites in Manitoba. We have accepted and integrated handicapped campers into our camping program since 1977. But this was different. I was here to interview Toni, a prospective male staffer, for Bible instructor at one of our camps.

Toni had experienced a brain tumor plus a severe car accident resulting in serious head injuries. These incidents had left this former athlete with poor coordination, short-term memory difficulties, speech problems, and the need for life-support medication.

"He put his Bible down and with perfect timing, gestures, and articulation, he quoted the rest of the passage for us."

As Toni showed off his equipment, I began to appreciate his determination and desire to enter a meaningful summer ministry. He had come to accept his limitations and was able to explain matter-of-factly the domestic and medical requirements for his stay at camp.

We offered him the job. At staff orientation, we began to discover and appreciate Toni's personality and gifts. It was obvious the athletic resolve and competitive spirit were still very much a part of Toni. There seemed to be few limits to his participation in camping activities. At the end of staff orientation he agreed on short notice to read scripture and have a prayer at our staff commissioning service. The roomful of staff, parents, and friends hushed into an embarrassed silence as he began haltingly, finding it difficult to read.

Suddenly, a few verses into the passage he came across a portion he had memorized earlier. He put his Bible down and with perfect timing, gestures, and articulation, he quoted the rest of the passage for us. What an exciting send-off into the summer!

"We are talking with Toni trying to persuade him to stay longer!" explained my summer program director later over the phone. "He communicates beautifully with the children. He is creative and a tremendous influence on the staff. No one can really complain about their little problems when they see what Toni has to cope with. He's an encouragement to everyone."

Toni's faith story, his attitude, his Bible instruction, and his presence touched everyone. The campers, disabled or not, staff, and leaders will not soon forget the many lessons taught both formally and informally by one Bible instructor who, regardless of disability, used his gifts to the fullest.

Thanks, Toni!

From Beaver Camp

By K.J., August, 2002

Dear Beaver Camp,

Thank you for giving me a good and fun week. Before I came to camp, I didn't believe in God, but now I do. I also hated camping, but now I can stand it a little. I would go back, but I would go to Outpost again.

Before we went to The Rock, I hated canoeing and boats. I liked it until the storm came when we were on Beaver River. We went to an island and, thanks to God and Lydia, we made it even though we were cold and scared. I didn't like water that much, but now I will go out in the woods after dark.

I had a great time and hope to come back next summer. I hope I see Lydia again. The thing I was amazed at was the food. It was good and I liked the fact that Outpost could cut to the front of the line.

Thanks, again, for a great time and I hope to go back to Beaver Camp soon

Solstice

By Larry Eby, written in Anchorage, Alaska, December, 2003

A bichromal world emerges upon us
as the first sunrise of winter reveals
last night's snow, inches upon inches
of puffy whiteness. Dry snow even though
made of water, its lightness piling onto
boughs of bare birch branches.

The world looks small, this gray day;
just us with a few houses and trees.
The visible horizon; the tree-bordered far lakeshore
where yesterday's moose, two of them,
a mother and yearling, browsed
their way, doing nature's pruning of boughs,
surviving the long, frigid arctic nights.

It's a grim world; cold, spare, a tough place to survive
on one's own. Yet the place of moose and wolf,
of mouse and owl, bear and salmon, bobcat and hare,
musk oxen and Alaska Native.
Interdependent on this orb.

Once again the solstice season calls
for the sun's return.
As long as the earth stands.

Chapter 8

Foresight and Faithful Stewardship

"The story of the camping movement is not the story of an easy road. There were trails to blaze. Those who blaze trails often travel alone. It can be lonesome and frightening, with a future that is uncertain and unknown. It required men and women of faith and courage who forged ahead in spite of the obstacles. But God's timing was good. The church would be needing this outdoor ministry in the days ahead. We have blazed trails. We have labored in the valleys and reached the summits. Ahead are more peaks to climb, more valleys to cross." —Jess Kauffman in **A Vision and a Legacy***, Faith and Life Press, 1984, p. ix.*

What are the trails blazed, the summits reached, the valleys crossed in the thirty-two years since Jess Kauffman penned those words? In the following writings, some persons closely related to the Mennonite Camping Association organization will share some "how-to" advice, the importance of Mennonite identity and connections, some of the thoughts regarding the MCA organization, and challenging ideas on program development.

Adding to the saga are accounts of what some member camps have done and are doing in special programs and projects, the joys of volunteers, a shocking experience of losing a barn full of horses in a fire, what makes a good menu, and the sadness of tragic death impacting our MCA family twice in these years. Also mentioned are the celebration of a couple who served long and well at one of our member camps. And near the end of the chapter, two reports appear of a very exciting Goshen College Inquiry Program (CIP) for students to discover their potential in camping ministry. Some items are lightly edited for this book.

Are you interested in writing a history of your camp or retreat center but don't know how to begin or what may be important? Useful ideas are given by Bob Wiebe, MCA President in the MCA Newsletter, 1998...

"Who Has Your History?"

Archives and camps—what's the connection? What does a dusty set of historical records have to do with living, breathing persons involved in outdoor ministry?

This is not a question that comes to mind every day for persons involved in camping ministry. Nevertheless, when camps come to significant milestones, such as fiftieth anniversaries, they often find themselves reflecting on God's faithfulness over the years. At such times, historical records are priceless. These "dusty documents" are in fact the very story of living and breathing persons involved in outdoor ministry.

MCA president Mary Jane Eby became aware of historical materials housed at the MCA office in Elkhart, Indiana. She was concerned that they be preserved, especially in light of any changes which take place as a result of denominational integration. Her efforts to find these documents a home resulted not only in their safe deposit at an archive in Goshen, but in a vision for encouraging all camps to take steps to deposit their minutes and other historical records with an appropriate institution. Mary Jane contacted all the Mennonite archives in North America and invited them to share a list of the camp records in their care. Most of them replied, and revealed a wealth of historical holdings, as well as a willingness to help camps collect their histories in an orderly way.

Dennis Stoesz, archivist at Mennonite Church USA Archives—Goshen, encourages several steps in the process of preserving history. One is for a camp to designate an official repository for its documents. A second is to assign a person within the camping

organization to be responsible for forwarding records. A third step is to canvas past directors and board members for older resources which they may have in their files. The actual records which archives are looking for include minutes, reports, correspondence, financial statements, newsletters, files from conferences, membership lists, photographs and tapes, and artifacts. Perhaps this article will be a prompt for someone in your camp to don the historian's hat.

If you need further information about how to get in touch with the archives in Canada and the United States, feel free to contact Dennis.

* * *

Rudy Kehler, director of Camp Squeah, Hope, British Columbia, was not sure of the practical value of being a member camp of Mennonite Camping Association. Attending a biennial meeting gave him fresh insight...

What Exactly Makes My/Your Camp Distinctly Mennonite?

I must say that I arrived at Camp Arnes a skeptic. Circumstances made it possible for me to be in Manitoba at the time of the convention and so I attended, albeit with some reservations.

I am the director of Camp Squeah, a General Conference Mennonite camp in British Columbia. About eight years ago or so I discontinued our camp's membership with MCA because I failed, at the time, to see the value of being associated with so far-flung a group which provided no recognizable benefit for our camp. "What exactly is it that makes my/your camp distinctly Mennonite? Why belong to Christian Camping International and MCA? Does the MCA really represent Mennonite camping in North America or only a selection of camps that can justify the membership cost?

When we discontinued our membership years ago, it was a simple economic decision and life moved on. I began to think about this again, however, when this year's membership mailing arrived.

As all of us who are appointed stewards of someone else's resources do, I evaluated the value of re-joining MCA from an economic as well as a "soft" benefits perspective. My rationale sounded something like this: "There's a convention every two years, usually very far away. There's a directory. Who gets the directory and why would it be useful to a prospective guest group? Aren't most retreat destination decisions made regionally? There's a newsletter...

With a membership budget of just over $1,000 why would we consider spending one-fourth of it on MCA?" I apologize for my tone but these were my thoughts. Admittedly, I'm a reactionary thinker. To a certain extent I guess we all are. I am trying, however, to be a "part of the solution" kind of guy. I hope that I can be that in some way here.

I truly enjoyed the conference. The workshops were good. They weren't necessarily distinctly Mennonite, but they were good. The relational stuff was the biggest challenge, but also the biggest benefit for me. As with every conference I attend (and there are heaps of them), I picked up ideas and contacts that will be helpful in my work.

I have decided to commit myself to being involved in MCA again for a few years in order to make a fair assessment of our camp's long-term participation. How have I committed myself to being involved? I've signed up with MennoLink to ask questions about Anabaptist camping and to hear what others have to say. I'm also working with Carl Wiens (Shekinah Retreat Center, Saskatchewan) and Tim Wiebe-Neufeld (Camp Valaqua, Alberta) to plan the first Western Regional Conference here at Camp Squeah in 1999. I will also

continue to ask the question: "What makes our camp Mennonite?" I hope you continue to ask it as well. Let me know what you come up with.

* * *

In this 2000 account, Bob Wiebe, MCA president, tell us of the...

Planks and Toothpicks Used to Build the Structure We Know as Mennonite Camping Association...

Jesus warned that we should detect the log in our own eye before pointing out the speck in the eye of our neighbor. The MCA board at its November 2000 meetings exercised discernment relating to somewhat similar images, those of "planks" and "toothpicks," in charting a course for the next several years.

The MCA continues to sail ahead on a raft of two sturdy planks. These planks are (1) the encouragement of pastoral fellowship among members, and (2) the pursuit of the vision statement adopted in 1998. To these planks the board has added some "toothpicks," projects that relate to one or the other plank

Three toothpicks have been added to the plank of pastoral fellowship:

· The board set aside $2,000 as a grant available upon application to the newly emerging Western Region. The purpose is to encourage attendance at that region's convention.

· A second toothpick was the decision to send one board member to the Western Region Convention as an indication of MCA's encouragement of the pastoral fellowship which takes place at these gatherings.

· A third toothpick on the plank of pastoral fellowship is the decision to pursue the creation of a resource which will address in part the needs of camp staff whose responsibilities prevent them from regular participation in congregational worship. This resource might also serve to alert congregations and pastors of ways they can minister to the unique needs of camp staff.

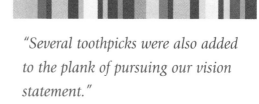

"Several toothpicks were also added to the plank of pursuing our vision statement."

· Several toothpicks were also added to the plank of pursuing our vision statement. The board feels that the MCA should be recognized by the newly emerging Canadian and U.S. Mennonite Churches. The next step is to be given a place, and possibly some staffing or funding, in these new structures. A list of priorities for the deployment of any available resources has been prepared.

Other toothpicks on the plank of pursuing our mission are still in the discussion stages. These include:

· increasing general Mennonite public awareness of the MCA. This could involve ads and media releases.

· raising the MCA profile with students in camping-related fields of study. As part of this toothpick, funding was provided to continue an effort initiated last year by several MCA camps to raise the profile of MCA presence at "Camp Ministry Days" at various U.S. Mennonite colleges.

· entering into a relationship of mutual fellowship and learning with camp ministries from outside of North America.

The raft of planks with its cargo of toothpicks is sailing on. We welcome your questions or comments, MCA "sailors"!

* * *

Behind the camp and retreat center's directors and administrators are the large number of board members that by their wise counsel and overall support determine the direction and viability of their institution. Not often visible on the binational scene, many do however attend binational meetings.

As Seen Through the Eyes of a Board Member

Arlin Buller, board chair, Rocky Mountain Mennonite Camp, writes about the 2000 convention in the MCA Newsletter, October, 2000.

"Vision, planning, and support are an ever-present ingredient of effective board function."

Wow!! What an experience! What a fountain of inspiration! There aren't enough ways to express the good things that we were privileged to be a part of at the 2000 MCA Convention at Camp Hebron. The MCA meetings have always been open to board members from MCA member camps. However, at the Fortieth Anniversary MCA convention a one-day session was specifically programmed for board members.

History indicates that in the past a limited number of camp board members have attended. This year MCA included Lee Schmucker from Wichita, Kans., as a resource person to lead us in a workshop entitled "Developing a high performance board."

The reasons for a workshop like this include:

· Camp boards are the voice of the constituency and as such bring ownership of the constituency to the organization.
· Vision and values of the camp are developed on the board level.
· Long-term direction must be planned.
· Effective planning guides the vision and enables the camp to deliver services consistent with its purpose.

Five board functions were discussed. Boards should:

· Establish vision and direction.
· Develop/adopt policy.
· Guide the organization.
· Guide and support the executive director.
· Develop good board performance.
· Vision, planning, and support are an ever-present ingredient of effective board function. Issues include board member code of ethics, board member job descriptions, board member training, effective meetings, and communication.

With respect to meetings and communications, the following guidelines are a must:

· Effective meetings have clearly defined goals and agendas.
· The agenda is determined by the desired goal, and discussion should lead to the realization of that goal.
· The goal drives the agenda.
· The wise use of time to achieve the desired results enables everyone to take satisfaction in the process.
· All issues need dialogue and good communication to enable everyone serving on the board to take ownership in the conclusion.

The importance of good communication cannot be overstated. Some of the characteristics of effective board communication include confidentiality, trust, confrontational skills that don't threaten, diverse perspectives, shared vision, and humor. Everyone must strive for good communication.

Evaluating executive performance and being evaluated as a board member help focus the time and energy of the organization. Affirming the CEO and promoting open and honest communication between board and executive enable each to avoid difficulties that need not take priorities away from goals and vision.

Camp development and support are closely tied to ownership. Ownership is both legal and emotional. Ownership is the heart where support is most loyal. Boards are very tied to tangible or monetary support but we should never neglect emotional ownership. Involvement and sweat equity give ownership to the constituency.

"Every camp needs to be represented at the MCA conventions by staff and board members."

I was privileged to attend the entire MCA convention and encourage all camp board members to attend the entire Tuesday evening through Friday morning convention. The worship opportunities, the hymn sing, the musical contributions, the prayer groups, the workshops, the mealtime discussions and the special interest groups are all a demonstration of how Christian/Anabaptist/Mennonite camping sets its rudder and trims its sails.

The enthusiasm of staff members from camps all across the continent builds during these four days. We as board members must catch this tremendous dedication and enthusiasm. Every camp needs to be represented at the MCA conventions by staff and board members.

* * *

Mennonite camping is dynamic, fueled by creative minds. It may also be distinctive as discussed in the following article by Mary Jane Eby, past president of MCA, in the MCA Newsletter, *April, 1999.*

Let's Talk About....Caution!! Mennos in Process

Darryl Kutz, director of outdoor recreation at Columbia Bible College (CBC) in Abbottsford, British Columbia, facilitated three group interactive sessions relating to Anabaptist-Mennonite camping with the basic question, "What is distinctive?"

At beautiful Camp Squeah, (site of the Western Regional Convention) twenty-five persons actively participated in worship, "Let's-talk-about" sessions, acquainting ourselves with Camp Squeah's camping/retreat ministries, as well as biking, canoeing, and rock climbing. All Canadian provinces west of Ontario were represented (Manitoba, Saskatchewan, Alberta, and British Columbia) as well as the western states (California, Oregon, Colorado, and Arizona). As people working with camp retreat centers we were warmly hosted and invited to experience the meaning of living the church of Christ in a holistic way.

Discussion Focused on the Questions
· Is your Mennonite camp unique?
· Where is your camp in relation to all others in Christian camping?
· How are you different?
· Does it matter?

Listing Core Values
Listing core values became a fun way to begin to focus on what might be unique at our Mennonite camps. Among the core values we cited:

· a high view of God's Word, centrality of Christ, ministry
· community, separate (from the world), simplicity, mutual aid
· discipleship, peace, justice, respect for God's creation
· stewardship in all of life, people of the land.

127

In asking, "Is there Anabaptist theology in camping ministry?" the choice of curriculum, especially for summer camp, was of crucial interest. This developed into discussion about what we mean by "curriculum" and who chooses the theme for summer camps.

Pacific Southwest Mennonite Conference has developed a retreat ministry board that gives overall direction to the development of a six-year curriculum. Pastors and camp staff are contributors to the development of materials.

Other discussion focused on the concern about the importance of connecting with supporting churches, issues of accountability, and the continuation of nurturing after a week at camp.

And let's Talk About...
What we may not be doing so well—areas of camping ministry where we need to do much work.

- conflict resolution-campers, staff, and board members
- simplicity—modeling a Jesus lifestyle
- retention of church support
- nurture and care of young adult staff
- emphasis on living faith daily
- Creation care—a biblical directive
- invitations to faith—a free choice.

Community was a common theme throughout our time at Camp Squeah. One of the ways in which the image of community became a reality for each of us was in the fact that we represented several different church conferences (Mennonite Brethren Church, Conference of Mennonites in Canada, General Conference, and Mennonite Church) yet we all shared common visions.

The word images for community that came to mind included care, support, bonding, accountability, belonging, shared vision, worship, conflict (not necessarily negative), and team ministry.

Yes, God is interested in community (Galatians 6:1-10, 1 Corinthians. 12:12).

Darryl summarized our time together and sent us on our way with these words: "As you go, actively make disciples, drawing, nurturing people toward God."

"So what?" and "Who cares?" were echoed at various times throughout our days together. We were reminded that God cares and God's people care.

* * *

High on the agenda of any Mennonite camp and retreat center should be the concern, "How is the theology we express in our mission and/or vision statement true to the Bible and our Anabaptist heritage?" At times this was a major item on the MCA binational agenda as well. In the MCA Newsletter, Summer, 1994, editor Jim Penner tells of the 1994 North American convention.

Theology for Mennonite Camping
Dana and Donna Sommers, together with an energetic and capable staff, provided an enjoyable and warm atmosphere for the biennial convention of the Mennonite Camping Association (MCA) representatives from Mennonite camps across North America gathered at Camp Amigo, Michigan, March 21-24, 1994, to share visions and ideas and to challenge each other.

With informal dinner conversation, small group discussion workshops, and excellent keynote addresses by Gayle Gerber Koontz and Perry Yoder there was plenty of grist for any mill. The weather cooperated perfectly giving us the entire spectrum from a nighttime thunder storm to an afternoon any July would envy. Music provided by Tom and Lois Harder (Friedenswald) and The Road Less Traveled—Doug and Jude Krehbiel (Mirror Valley) brought color and life to the week.

Tim Lehman's book, **Seeking the Wilderness**, formed the backdrop against which we explored the theme,"Seeking God's face: Forming a theology for Mennonite camping." It was apparent at the convention that there was a tension between two perspectives of camping ministry and its applications. In spirited discussion the question of emphasis and focus were bandied about. Which comes first, "environmental caring or evangelism"? It was exciting to see firsthand that we indeed were moving in the direction of forming a Mennonite theology for camping.

Both Gayle and Perry made it clear that in creation we can find God. Just as the pot tells us about the potter, creation tells us about God – creation as God's handiwork uninterpreted. If we do not explore, try to understand, and nurture it and let it nurture us, we will miss God's most immediate message to us. It also became apparent that when we go into the wilderness to seek God, we find God seeking us in ways not possible in our cities of concrete and steel.

"Just as the pot tells us about the potter, creation tells us about God— creation as God's handiwork uninterpreted."

The convention concluded Thursday morning with a time of silent individual reflection followed by a communion service. It was perhaps fitting that we shared both solitude and togetherness that morning, Seeking God's face is an individual pursuit that finds validation within the community. This convention provided a new vantage point from which to rediscover our Anabaptist theology and how it finds expression in camping ministry. Hopefully we have "set our faces towards Jerusalem." Hopefully we will follow our spirits as we are led towards a renewed understanding of camping ministry from a Mennonite perspective, even though it may fly in the face of conventional wisdom, or, horror of horrors, our own preconceived notions.

"Before setting out on your journey to find this great treasure, rid yourself of all you possess. Go empty-handed...or else you will not be able to carry back what you will find."
— Michael of Grantham

* * *

Another article, this one from the MCA Newsletter, Summer, 1997, *about the 1996 biennial MCA convention held at Lakewood, also considers camp program on a practical basis. The invited speakers were Jim and Helen Reusser, longtime Mennonite camping leaders and thinkers. Jim and Helen are referred to elsewhere in this book.*

Jim and Helen Reusser of Kitchener, Ontario, were the keynote speakers at MCA's 1996 biennial convention at Lakewood Retreat outside of Brooksville, Florida. Aside from the fact that those from the Northern States and Eastern Canada missed a terrific blizzard, the location was perfect. The staff and volunteers at Lakewood did not miss an opportunity to meet the needs and offer their assistance to the Mennonite Camping Association.

In their first address to the convention, the Reussers paid homage to those who influenced their lives and the lives of their children at camps. They reinforced the concept that the basic camping unit is the counselor and a group of campers. This is not an age-specific model. It was the model used by Jesus. Jim Reusser challenged us to see in the counselor-camper relationship everything that is needful at camp. The rest are extras. There is no

need, he said, to provide a camp with all of the amenities of home. Rather we should be doing just the opposite and strip away the outside world so that, in our less encumbered state, we may find God.

Helen echoed these sentiments but with a different tack. She challenged camps to do what they do best. From an educational perspective, there are many things that can be done in the home, at church, and in youth groups. At camp there are educational opportunities that exist nowhere else in the present day Christian experience.

> *"Camp ought to be the setting where campers find innovative solutions to everyday problems, solutions where everybody wins."*

Specifically, in the counselor-camper group setting we have the chance to model Christ-like living twenty-four hours a day, seven days a week. Camp ought to be the setting where campers find innovative solutions to everyday problems, solutions where everybody wins. Camps should reuse, recycle, reduce, compost, and garden. Caring for the environment is not fashionable, they said, it's biblical.

As Jesus lived and taught with his disciples, he was concerned with their transformation. He lived with them so that they could become more like him. Are we willing to let the campers in our care become like us? The question that comes before this, Jim reminded us is, "Are we modeling the life of someone transformed by the Spirit?" If so, we need to invite others to live with us and allow them into our lives so that they may see the hand of God at work in us.

Consistency in action, doctrine, camp policy, and operations are keys to this goal, a challenge to every camp staff and volunteer.

* * *

In her role as director of children's education with the Commission on Education with the General Conference Mennonite Church, Eleanor Snyder was a representative from that group on the MCA board. She also was a curriculum developer and writer of Christian educational materials, including that for camps. What follows is one of her contributions appearing in the MCA Newsletter, Summer, 1997.

Beyond the Printed Word: The Reality of Camp Curriculum
By Eleanor Snyder

I can think of no better Christian education experience for children than a week at summer camp. A child who goes to Sunday school every week in the summer receives thirteen hours of formal education. Add a week of vacation Bible school at fifteen hours and you have, at the most, twenty-eight hours of Christian nurture over the summer. Compare this with a live-in camping experience for an entire week! What an opportunity for growing in faith and meeting God in new ways.

Camp staff have the privilege of helping children to know and meet God in a number of ways. I call this the "curriculum of camping." Curriculum is much more than what one finds in a book. However, the printed resource materials are important.

When you look for Christian resources to enhance your chosen theme, keep in mind there is a theological bias to it. Does it concur with the Anabaptist theology of our denominations? Does it compliment our theology? Does it respect the age-appropriate faith of a child without demanding an adult-type faith response to God's invitation to God's reign? For a better understanding of the Anabaptist approach to learning and theology with children, read **Jubilee Guidebook!** a leader's piece for the Sunday school curriculum, Jubilee: God's Good News.

Far more important than the theme or printed materials is the curriculum of camp staff. An old Irish proverb says, "What the child sees, the child does; what the child does, the child is." Children learn from what they observe much more readily than from what they hear.

How staff relates to each other and the children speaks volumes. If the children experience love and compassion, if they are respected and treated fairly, they will know what a Christian looks like. When staff can articulate their own faith easily and freely, children will know what a Christian sounds like. Staff, by action and words, reveal the character of Jesus for children who may or may not have any knowledge about God. And staff, by actions and words, facilitate "moments of grace" in children's encounters with God.

"An old Irish proverb says, 'What the child sees, the child does; what the child does, the child is.'"

God's creation is a third curriculum for children in camp settings. It provides natural opportunities for children to meet God through exploration of the great outdoors, through experiences of prayer, singing, playing, journaling, sitting in silence, and observing God's world. Show them the wonders of nature, remind them of the vastness of God's universe, and celebrate with them the joy of a mysterious creation that includes them. Help them to hear God's invitation to love and show compassion to everything that God has created.

Children learn what they live. The combination of committed Christian staff, theologically sound printed resources, and an idyllic camp setting is hard to beat for helping faith come alive and grow in children.

It is my prayer that, in teaching and learning together, children and staff will experience God's vision of healing and hope for themselves and the world so that God's Word does not return empty but is transmitted effectively and faithfully in the days to come.

* * *

The MCA Newsletter *was often a place to share ideas about the meaning of the Christian camping experience. In 1993, Orv Gingerich, a Highland Retreat board member and program coordinator of Rocky Mountain Mennonite Camp, Colorado, shared about camping as a temporary community, an idea implied in much of the writing in this book. His article follows...*

Building a Stronger Church

"Temporary community" is a helpful way to understand the value and importance of camping in the life of the church. Although there is intrinsic value in Christian camping, its ultimate value lies in something larger than itself—the church. Mennonite camping is important only if it builds up and strengthens the church through its ministries which nurture, educate, evangelize, prophesy, heal, and release gifts of the church to minister to people.

A camp or retreat can be viewed as a "temporary community" which provides a place and time where people experience the wholeness of Christian community through worship, fellowship, education, play, and working together. This "temporary community" can strengthen and energize God's people to return to their routines of home, church, work, and school better able to live faithful, victorious, balanced, and joyful lives. According to Gordon Dahl, author of **Work, Play and Worship**, Americans have a strong tendency to "worship their work, work at their play, and play at their worship." The temporary community is a setting where these skewed values can be adjusted.

Our contemporary culture tends to isolate us through our self-sufficiency and busyness; therefore, the church needs to be intentional about building community if it is to be a reality. Community implies relationships, or more specifically close relationships, in

which there is trust, mutual caring, and accountability. The community experience is fostered in a variety of ways in the congregation through forming small support groups, Sunday school classes, family clusters, mission groups, and the like. Church camps and retreat centers can provide a place for these groups and larger groups to experience a more intense "temporary community" which strengthens these organic units of the congregation.

A retreat is by definition a short-lived experience, usually only overnight or a couple of days. It cannot replace the other ways a congregation experiences community in an ongoing way. Nevertheless, a concentrated experience of temporary Christian community can be a powerful catalyst for the church. A small group can experience in two days of retreat what it may take three-to-four months to accomplish in weekly one-hour meetings. It's important to be realistic and thoughtful about how a retreat can maximize the benefits of a "temporary community" experience.

"...a concentrated experience of temporary Christian community can be a powerful catalyst for the church."

The cumulative effect of a day or two of retreat accelerates the growth of mutual concern, understanding, and love within the church. Retreaters get beyond talking about the weather and see each other outside their usual roles within the church.

A different schedule, a new environment, a leisurely pace, an informal social setting, and an around-the-clock situation are the benefits of a retreat or camp event which provide a congregation with new opportunities for experiencing and building its common life and ministry. This strengthening of the local church through experiences of "temporary community" is the purpose of Christian camping.

The idea of temporary community was borrowed from **The Temporary Community** *(Albatross Books, 1984) by Tom Slater.*

As anyone knows who has spent time in the wilderness or been involved in camping, especially in an administrative role, "initiative" is invaluable in dealing with the challenges presented on a day-by-day basis. Following is an article from the MCA Newsletter, Spring, 1996.

Initiating Creativity: Facilitating Growth in an Initiatives Area

By Jen McTavish, Silver Lake Mennonite Camp

In a small corner of Silver Lake Mennonite Camp, it appears that someone has sneaked in and installed a random assortment of ropes, cables, boards, and wooden logs. To our campers and staff, however, this is the initiatives area, a world of rancid yogurt floods, peanut butter swamps, bottomless canyons, giant spider webs, and rubber chickens in need of rescue. But it is more than just a world of fun and imagination.

It is a place where we challenge campers and staff to develop their abilities to work as members of a group. Through communicating, cooperating, and lots of trial, error, and perseverance, these groups work together to reach a seemingly impossible goal. They balance, hug, and giggle their way to success. Afterwards they cheer for themselves and congratulate each other for their good ideas and hard work.

Their experiences at initiatives stretch beyond the completion of the challenges at hand, however. Before the group attempts any serious problem solving, all members must agree to three basic points contained in what we call a "full-value contract."

They agree to:

· work together as a group towards both group and individual goals

· adhere to all safety and behavior guidelines (which includes the promise not to devalue nor put anyone down, including oneself)

· give and receive feedback, and to try to change their behaviors where appropriate, according to that feedback.

The discussions which occur throughout the initiatives sessions often involve issues which reach beyond those activities and into the rest of our lives. We (the campers and staff) talk about setting goals and accepting challenges. We talk about risk-taking and openness within the group. We talk about putting ourselves in someone else's shoes. We talk about getting along with each other. In other words, we talk about lots of things that are truly important in real life. And we hope that through this program we can continue to encourage the growth of individuals at camp and for the rest of their lives.

"They balance, hug, and giggle their way to success."

How We Began

We constructed the initiatives area at Silver Lake in the spring of 1993. Ten staff members assisted two friends of the camp who were quite knowledgeable in the construction of initiatives elements. It took only one full day of work to construct ten initiatives, and cost the camp about $2,400 (Cdn). This program area was truly a bargain for us, and the staff involved in building it developed a special ownership for the program.

Although the materials were not expensive, we did not cut any corners where safety and risk management were concerned. We used good-quality wood that would withstand our harsh winters, and used only galvanized bolts and screws where metal hardware was required. All rope parts were constructed from soft, durable, nylon rope, and installed so that they could be removed and stored indoors for the winter. The importance of using high quality materials can not be stressed enough, as it helps to ensure a safe program, and minimizes wear and tear.

All staff wishing to lead the initiatives program attend professional development workshops that provide hands-on experience with proper group facilitation and sequencing of activities, safety considerations, and care of equipment.

Getting your Camp Started

Initiatives programs can add new life and variety to the summer experiences of your campers and staff. However, it is important to realize that this is not a "miracle" program that runs itself. Before introducing initiatives to your camp, make sure that you can guarantee the following:

· The construction of the initiatives equipment must take place under the supervision of qualified builders who have experience in building such structures (many such contractors are available in the US and Canada, usually listed as "Adventure Programmers" or "Ropes Course" builders).

· High quality materials must be used and, wherever possible, protection from the weather, especially from the sun and from snow/frost.

· Enough staff must be available to run the program once it is constructed. These people must have professional training in the areas of group facilitation and ropes course initiatives instruction, especially with respect to physical and emotional safety issues.

· A system must be put in place to carry out regular safety checks of all equipment, and a regular evaluation process of the program and its effectiveness with campers and staff must also take place.

In other words, consider adding this program to your camp facility, but only if you can ensure that it will be constructed and facilitated professionally and with the support of an ongoing evaluation system.

Good luck with starting an initiatives program at your camp! If implemented properly, it will bring you and your campers years of challenge, enjoyment, and group building experiences.

Information about initiatives programs can be obtained from Project Adventure, Inc., P.O. Box 100, Hamilton, Massachusetts 01936. Also, Karl Rohnke has written several excellent "must-read" books for anyone who is serious about adventure programs and initiatives. These include Silver Bullets, Cowstails and Cobras, and Bottomless Bag.

* * *

In the Spring, 1996 MCA Newsletter, *the staff at Black Rock Retreat contributed an article on program selection. Following that is an earlier article in the Spring, 1992,* MCA Newsletter *about a special camp held at BRR. Arranged in chronologically reversed order, the second one shows how some of the programming vision of the first is applied.*

Black Rock Retreat: Where Programs Serve the Vision

Why Do We Choose to Run the Camp Programs We Do at Black Rock?

Programs are like the tools that carpenters use for their trade; the choice of a specific tool is determined by the task that needs to be done. Our programs are some of the most versatile tools we possess at camp, and choosing the proper programming tool ensures that our guests will have the experiences they are seeking in coming to Black Rock.

"We run programs that meet the various needs of people in society, whether those needs are academic, social, spiritual, or physical."

We run programs that meet the various needs of people in society, whether those needs are academic, social, spiritual, or physical. The programming staff sees itself as an arm of the church since they aim to provide mountaintop experiences, introduce new concepts or review or reemphasize existing ones, offer encouragement and challenges, all in a simple and peaceful atmosphere. In this sense, one of our program goals is to supplement church experiences rather than duplicate them.

Another of our programming goals is to work together as an entire staff to provide quality programming for a reasonable rate. Our resource persons are local people who are experts in their fields. These people included musicians, storytellers, drama groups, college professors, and naturalists. Since we offer quite diverse programming, including Elderhostel, outdoor education, golden years retreats, home school family camps, a challenge ropes course, family music camp, and a Memorial Day open house, we have been able to make use of a variety of local talent while continuing to meet the needs of our guests. In this way, we endeavor continually to adapt and adjust our programs to meet the needs of an ever-changing society while remaining true to our original mission and vision.

Discovering the Creator – As a Family
By Dale and Sue Jones, program directors, Black Rock Retreat

Q: What is a family creation encounter, a family excursion to the local zoo?

A: Well no, not exactly.

Q: Well, then, what is it? What do you do on one?

A: You explore various aspects of God's creation such as plants, animals, rocks, and water, up close and personal. Basically it's studying science in the outdoors.

Q: OK. I get the creation part now, but why is it called a family encounter?

A: Because it's something done together as a family. You know, Mom, Dad, Johnny, and Susie all out walking through the woods together smelling the wild flowers and catching salamanders along the way.

The purpose of a family creation encounter is to discover the Creator through the creation. It says in Romans 1:20 that the invisible attributes of God are clearly seen, being understood by the things that are made – creation.

Family encounters are an opportunity to spend time together learning about God by studying the great textbook of nature. Families can pull away from the high tech distractions of the world to explore the simple, yet incredibly complex and beautiful, world God has given us. Family creation encounters, as described above, were a key part of the program during home school family camp this past October at Black Rock Retreat. Many families who have chosen to educate their children at home came to spend four days together, drawing closer to each other and God by learning more about the natural world.

Each morning began with a time of organized family devotions, studying a biblical concept revealed through creation, and then applying that concept by working on a family project together. The remainder of the day was given to a variety of family creation encounters led by Black Rock staff – everything from discovering the amazing design of a snake, to listening for the rocks to cry out and sing praises to God.

"Family encounters are an opportunity to spend time together learning about God by studying the great textbook of nature."

Parents also had the opportunity to attend workshops on home education. Each evening featured a session on creation science presented by Dr. Bob Goette of the Associates for Biblical Research, then more nighttime nature fun through games, hikes, stargazing, and a good, old-fashioned, campfire with singing and s'mores.

All in all, home school family camp was a great time for families to draw closer—closer to each other, closer to new friends with common interests, and more importantly, closer to the Creator—all through the creation.

Starting the camping experience at an early age can make a lasting impression on a young child. Following is an account of a camp that encourages campers to join their parents in a camp for first-timers. The story could be told with variations by many of our member camps. It was a "minicamp" in more ways than one.

Camp Valaqua Holds Family – Style Minicamp

By **Tim and Danita Wiebe-Neufeld**, *former directors of Camp Valaqua in Alberta in the MCA Newsletter, Fall, 1994*

After thirty-five years, Camp Valaqua experienced a first this past July 1-3, our first minicamp. The three-day camp was aimed at campers ages six to eight, and their parents. Parents who registered their children for the camp also registered themselves, as the camp provided a summer camping experience for parents and children alike. The response was quite positive, with over forty people attending this inaugural event.

Campers were placed in cabin groups, and spent much of their time experiencing many of the general camp activities, such as canoeing, nature, games, and camp skills. Other activities included singing, skits, and a wagon ride around the camp property that was met with enthusiasm that even a torrential downpour could not snuff out. Meanwhile, the parents had the opportunity to attend a workshop on parenting, learn water color painting, go on a nature walk, and relax.

There were also times when everyone came together for joint events. Morning worship services and evening campfires were enjoyed by all. During meal times, cabin groups sat together while their parents visited at adjoining tables. At bedtime, the campers returned to their parents to sleep, providing time for them to relax and share the experiences of the day.

The minicamp provided a relaxed and secure atmosphere for young campers to savor their first summer camp experience. It was good to have parents there to deal with the problems young campers often have when attending camp for the first time, such as homesickness. By giving the campers the security of seeing their parents occasionally throughout the day, they were able to spend more time enjoying the camp atmosphere and less time missing their homes and families.

The minicamp also gave parents and children time to do summer camp together. It also provided an opportunity for parents to experience some of the skits, songs, and activities their older children enjoy throughout the summer. Camp Valaqua's first attempt at a minicamp was a resounding success. Positive feedback from parents was encouraging.

In summer 1972 while we (Larry and Mary Jane) lived in Puerto Rico, we sent our two oldest children to Eastern Pennsylvania to the Spruce Lake wilderness camp where we joined them later for the annual Mennonite Medical and Nurses' Convention. As the brief account below tells, our sons had the privilege of being part of a long tradition.

Camp... For the Children's Sake!

What is the mission of Spruce Lake wilderness camp?
The very reason we have been here since 1963 is to make an impact on the lives of young persons with the reality of Jesus Christ, all in the context of the great outdoors where the quiet voice of God seems most audible.

Former and first directors Al and Kass Detweiler dedicated twenty years of their lives to this vision over forty years ago. Then, as now, they saw God miraculously providing for material needs and human resources again and again.

"The vision then, as now, was that a shortage of money should never keep a child from experiencing camp."

From the Start, Wilderness Camp Was Dedicated to the Children
The vision then, as now, was that a shortage of money should never keep a child from experiencing camp. "We never wanted to be an exclusive camp that provides excellence at the cost of who can attend," said director Kent Kauffman.

So How Does Wilderness Camp Make This Possible?
Wilderness camp has chosen to seek support from ministry-minded friends and to stimulate volunteerism to keep tuition down, the experience up, and the doors wide open to people of any socioeconomic background.

The Campership Fund was established as a way for folks from the broader Christian community to share with those who, in stating their circumstances, ask for economic support. Spruce Lake's ongoing mission has been to guarantee support for approximately ten percent of applying camper households in any one year.

Then God said, "Let us make humankind in our image, to be like us. Let them be stewards of the fish in the sea, the birds of the air, the cattle, the wild animals, and everything that crawls on the ground." Humankind was created as God's reflection: in the divine image God created them, female and male, God made them. Genesis 1:26-27, The Inclusive Hebrew Scriptures.

Mary Lou Farmer, administrator, Crooked Creek Christian Camp, Washington, Iowa, shares the following account of what they are doing that perhaps does not make the most economic or practical sense in order to live as God's stewards on some of their land (from the MCA Newsletter, May/June 2004). This also fits well with the formal position stated in our Mennonite confessional as noted at the end of the story.

Camp Restoring Prairie Habitat to Pre-European Status

Several years ago, Crooked Creek Christian Camp purchased about fifty-five acres of farmland adjacent to the camp, including the field north of the camp's entrance drive. (Prior to this, the camp owned only the drive into camp and no land on either side.) The fifty-five acres were rented to a farmer for corn and soybean production for the past few years.

We Have Open Land ... What Shall We Do?

In 2002 and 2003, the board of directors spent a significant amount of time discussing what the camp's goals were for this land.

The goals of preventing erosion, creating habitat for wildlife, more educational opportunities, and a more natural appearance prompted the board to return the land to plant species that were native here years ago.

Planting Instead of Building...

Six grasses and sixteen flowering forbs (herbs other than grasses) were planted in November, 2003, on about half the farmland. Upland wetlands will comprise another portion of the land. Eight thousand trees and shrubs were planted as windbreaks and field borders in April 2004!

"We hope our guests, too, will join us in watching the prairie come to life, and the trees grow and mature."

By enrolling this land in a fifteen-year program offered by the U.S. Department of Agriculture, the camp will receive an annual payment for returning land to prairies, wetlands, and trees.

Restoration Benefits All ...But Takes Time

Forests and prairies do not sprout up overnight. The prairie areas were mowed during 2004 to control weeds. Some growth and flowering was observed in 2005, but the prairie will continue to come into its own for several years.

The board is excited about this venture! Within the camp's boundaries, we will have large areas of both prairie and timber, the habitat that existed before European settlement. There will be educational opportunities for camp visitors as they get to know and appreciate the prairie. We will be completely able to control soil erosion naturally!

We hope our guests, too, will join us in watching the prairie come to life, and the trees grow and mature.

Called

"As stewards of God's earth, we are called to care for the earth and to bring rest and renewal to the land and everything that lives on it ... We are to commit ourselves to right use of the earth's resources as a way of living now according to the model of the new heaven and the new earth."

Confession of Faith in a Mennonite Perspective (1963), pp. 78, 80

Some of the member organizations have multiple campuses, often with unique programs depending on their ministries. One such is Willowgrove Farm, a fusion of Fraser Lake Camp and Glenbrook Daycamp. Kyle Barber, executive director, shares their story in the MCA Newsletter, Winter, 2000.

Anatomy of an Amalgamation

When the term amalgamation comes to mind, most minds jump to large-scale business such as banks, insurance companies, or AOL & Time-Warner. The amalgamation trend is certainly alive and well and has been a significant theme over the past five years as businesses jostle for market share and overhead efficiency. Amalgamation, though, is not only for the large, profit sector. It has now occurred within the Mennonite Camping Association. This is how it happened.

Fraser Lake Camp, a residential camp in the Kawartha region of Ontario began in 1955 and had a long history of providing Christian summer camping for children. A private Mennonite association camp based in York region, Fraser was plagued by low registrations through the 1990's and had serious financial shortfalls over a seven year period. Programs and facilities suffered as the camp struggled to stay afloat. Something needed to be done or the 257 acre, well-equipped facility would be lost.

In December 1997, Fraser Lake Camp approached Willowgrove Inc. to seek a relationship that would allow Fraser Lake to continue. Willowgrove, a private Christian, not-for-profit charity is located in Markham, Ontario and is a Mennonite association. Willowgrove runs diverse year-round educational programs (a Primary School, an Outdoor Education program and an Agricultural Education program) and Glenbrook Day Camp . . . the only Mennonite Day Camp in the MCA! It was clear after initial discussions that a relationship was imminent and specifics would be addressed by a combined panel of board members from the two organizations. A process would be put in place that would address the short-term needs of managing camp but also the long-term goal of transferring camp ownership over to Willowgrove.

The first step in the process was for the Fraser board to allow Willowgrove entire control over the camp operation while remaining financially liable. It was agreed that the Fraser board would serve as a program committee that was available for consultation but that the Willowgrove board would have final authority. Based on the trusting and prayerful nature of these two partners, legal contracts were not written.

With a management agreement in place, the combined panel then focused on legally joining the organizations. This process would need to be communicated clearly to both associations and sensitive feedback was welcomed at regular intervals. It was crucial to amalgamate the associations as well as the operations. The goal was to have all members, supporters and alumni from Fraser become part of Willowgrove. The panel also had to consider the legal processes of governing bylaws and provincial law. These things take time!

The verdict is almost in. In December, 1999, both memberships voted unanimously in favor of the amalgamation and the papers have been filed under the Corporations Act. It was the first amalgamation of non-share corporations that our experienced law firm had processed.

On the program front, the management contract gave Fraser Lake a new lease on life. Fraser & Glenbrook were blessed with exceptional summers in 98 & 99. The year-round management team of Willowgrove has allowed for a more complete and specialized approach to "marketing, program planning, volunteer recruitment and maintenance while reducing the significant overhead costs of staffing. Cross marketing, central purchasing, public relation considerations and synchronized staff. Recruitment/hiring are other strengths of this new company. The complete service of operating a day camp as a feeder system to a residential camp is a unique combination....sort of a camping "farrow to finish". Christian seed planting at Glenbrook is leading to a more direct ministry at Fraser and allows for a more significant impact on those who remain in the succession. Willowgrove with Fraser is far less regional and welcomes the interest of a wider participation.

Many have commented that the process has resulted in an excellent marriage. Some have joked that it is an excellent marriage because the camps lived together for two years.

"The complete service of operating a day camp as a feeder system to a residential camp is a unique combination....sort of a camping 'farrow to finish.'"

Anyway, we are thankful for God's leading through this process and are excited by the new opportunities that we have been entrusted with.

Other amalgamations are Camps with Meaning in Manitoba and Adirondack Mennonite Camping Association in New York.

The following article appeared in the MCA Newsletter *in Summer, 1992. Although no longer a member of MCA, Tel Hai is a part of the history of that time and still a vital Mennonite-connected camp.*

"Tel Hai: A Light on the Hill"
By Paul J. Smith, *administrator*

Many people ask me what the name Tel Hai means. This unusual name grew out of the camp's original purpose of providing a summer camping program for inner-city Jewish children from New York City. Abner Zook, who was an active witness to Jewish people, had a vision of providing a camping facility, a "Light On The Hill," to Jews. That is where the Hebrew name Tel Hai came from. This 60 acre facility, nestled in the heart of rich Amish farm land in Southeastern Pennsylvania started its humble beginnings in 1950.

Tel Hai. .. the name is unique and unknown to many. Many people have yet to discover this wonderful place with its unique characteristics. We offer many things which only much larger camps & conference facilities seem to have. A large swimming pool, beautiful new gymnasium, and an 18 hole mini-golf course under a roof are ready and waiting for the camp's guests. The grounds also include a five-acre lake, complete with covered bridge to a small island, which is home for boating and canoeing. It's also inhabited by a resident population of Canadian geese. We offer a horse program in the summer as well as RV camping.

For many years Tel Hai was strictly a rental facility. In 1992 the board is taking monumental steps toward expanding the ministry focus of the camp. I was hired in January of this year as Camp Administrator and a Program Director position has been added as well. The future plans for Tel Hai include programs for all ages, outdoor education and a new adult retreat facility, all created for the purpose of affecting as many lives as possible for God's Kingdom.

"Tel Hai. .. the name is unique and unknown to many. Many people have yet to discover this wonderful place with its unique characteristics."

Tel Hai... the name is unique and unknown. Tel Hai's future? May it continue to be unique and life changing while it's name becomes known for God's glory.

Without volunteers, what would we do? The most visible are the vast number of summer youth camp counselors who dedicate most of their summer at little or no pay. But there are other persons as well, illustrated in the next three articles.

The first of these, by Matt Kauffman Smith for the GCMC and MBM news services, is reprinted by permission from **The Mennonite**, *July 28, 1998.*

Youth Group Members Find God and their Way Through Wilderness Service Assignment
Lincoln City, Oregon.

Driving more than thirty minutes uphill on a gravel road, the youth group members from Metamora (Illinois) Mennonite Church didn't know where they would end up or what sort of service opportunities would be found in the wilderness.

"I thought this place was going to be a dump because when we came up it was really dark and we couldn't see anything," says Sam Bonnell. "All I saw was this gravel road, and I said, 'Great, what am I getting myself into?' "

What the thirteen youth and four sponsors got themselves into was a week of experiencing God in nature at Drift Creek, a Mennonite camp near Lincoln City, Oregon. The group spent June 11-18 clearing hiking trails, painting cabins, cleaning, and helping prepare meals for the rush of summer campers.

"I think the youth group members learned about God and God's creation," says Metamora youth sponsor Susan Surratt. "Being out here, it's so peaceful. They don't have to worry about any of the things they usually do."

" '...you never really know until you get away from it that you don't need it in your everyday lives.'"

As is the case for many Mennonite youth groups, Metamora takes a trip every year, alternating between the Mennonite Church youth convention and a weeklong service trip. Two years ago, the group served in Toronto, working in agencies and learning about urban living.

"In Toronto we worked more with people, and here we work with ourselves," says youth group member Brad Rogers. "The work's different, but it's all for the same purpose."

For each excursion, the Metamora youth group turned to Group Venture, a joint program of Mennonite Board of Missions and the Commission on Home Ministries offering short-term service assignments for high-school-age youth at thirty-to-forty sites in North America.

"They get a chance just to get away from the stuff of life, the busyness of life," says Ron Sears, who administers Drift Creek Camp with Jeanne, his wife. "They're still busy, but there's no television, no radio, there's no phone where they're staying, and it's thirty-five-to-forty-five minutes to McDonald's. "It's a great place to experience God. You can allow God's Spirit to work in you and God's voice can be heard."

The Metamora youth say they welcomed a break from remote controls and stereo systems. "I can do without that stuff," says Rachel Sutter. "But you never really know until you get away from it that you don't need it in your everyday lives."

* * *

Camp Deerpark in New York State was where Anna and Byron Zimmerman did SOOP. Following are Anna's.

Reflections on Serving at Camp

On August 28, my husband Byron and I left our home in Lancaster County, Pa., to begin a SOOP (Service Opportunities for Older Persons) assignment at Camp Deerpark in the lower Catskills, eighty-five miles northwest of New York City. There are some fifty organizations throughout the United States and Canada that welcome older persons to volunteer. We chose to come to Camp Deerpark.

Our term of service will be ending on November third. These last few months have given us a new appreciation for the ministry of Camp Deerpark and the New York City Mennonite Churches that sponsor the camp. We came wanting to be a blessing to the staff and the program. We will leave richly blessed because of our experiences here. This article is our way of saying thanks for providing a place like Camp Deerpark where persons of all ages have the opportunity to learn and grow.

Join me on the front porch at Camp Deerpark. Look across the lawns and down to the tree line that skirts the perimeter of the grounds. Notice the many colors, sizes, and shapes of trees. The people who come to this place are as diverse and beautiful as the trees dressed in their autumn colors.

We found that this is a place where city children sit with shining eyes and for the first time in their young lives roast marshmallows around a real campfire. They experience the joy of raking leaves, then tumbling into the colorful mound. Budding young scientists find awesome bugs to add to their collections. The stars and the moon are brighter here and family bonds are strengthened while gazing through a telescope at the heavens. Here children experience God's marvelous creation.

This is a place where God is praised. One evening I came from the chapel after finishing some housekeeping duties. I was surrounded by music as I walked. The group that was meeting in the chapel sang in Spanish. The voices of a group of men up on the hillside by the cabins resounded through the trees. Another family group sang together while gathered on an opposite hillside. Although the songs and the languages were different, there was a unique harmony as many voices were raised in praise to God.

"The people who come to this place are as diverse and beautiful as the trees dressed in their autumn colors."

We found that this is a place where prodigal sons and daughters celebrate their return to the Father. Life's experiences and spiritual journeys are shared while swinging on the front porch or sitting around the table with cups of coffee. Here we were called brother and sister.

Voluntary service brought Mike Yordy to Little Eden in Michigan in 2001. Read his...

Reflections on Voluntary Service at Little Eden

The Little Eden mission statement states, " Little Eden, a member of the Mennonite Camping Association, offers families and friends an affordable place where they may gather as brothers and sisters in Christ to be inspired, to share, and to grow while relaxing among the beautiful nature created by God."

The Little Eden board and employees are committed to keeping Little Eden affordable for families, as demonstrated in the mission statement. This can only occur through volunteerism, which this camp is built upon. Since the summer of 1998, young couples have volunteered their time serving here at Little Eden.

Patrick Morley, the author of **Man in the Mirror**, writes about issues relating to men. However, the following quote from his book is pertinent to all of us. He writes:

"...Focus on personal peace and affluence has largely replaced deeply held, self-sacrificing convictions (and the resulting community-building causes) which benefit the human condition. The path to significance is bigger than the individual. We often only spend our energies to satisfy ourselves, rather than to serve others. Significance is not possible unless what we do contributes to the welfare of others.

"Serving others is difficult and humbling, especially when you are serving others who are vacationing. Yet I firmly believe that voluntary service here at Little Eden is very beneficial for those who are called to participate. The jobs can be difficult, hard, and tiresome. However, Little Eden offers an atmosphere where you will grow emotionally and spiritually, and where you will learn more about yourself and your relationship with God. It is a refuge for young couples wanting and needing a couple of months or year or two before going into the world and tackling other tasks God has intended for them to do.

"This has also been my experience here at Little Eden, first, in the capacity of voluntary service, and now as a full-time employee. No matter where you are in life, this is a place of refuge allowing you time for reflection to align yourself with God in preparation for the next step in life."

A person who dedicated her considerable talents, energy, and interest to Christian camping, Lily Loewen was for many years the Mennonite Brethren Church liaison on the MCA board of directors. The following article in the MCA Newsletter, Winter, 1998, was reprinted with permission from the September/October, 1997, Christian Camp and Conference Journal (a Christian Camp and Conference Association publication).

Lily Loewen – Lady of the Lagoon
By Lloyd Mattson

Lily Loewen is one of Christian camping's grand women: a versatile, articulate, innovative veteran, who owns a legacy of changed lives. To discover what makes her so valuable, join her and a cluster of campers around the sewer lagoon at Camp Arnes on huge Lake Winnipeg in Manitoba, Canada.

"How deep is the lagoon?"
"Optimum depth, five feet, so sunlight can penetrate every molecule of water."
"Sunlight, why?"
"To cleanse the water-sunlight produces a cleansing action."
"Hey! There are two pools!"

"Cleansing comes in two stages. First, the collection pool that receives effluent from every drain in camp. Then the refining pool. Eventually, the water becomes so clean it is allowed to flow into the lake, where we swim and play."

Lily talks about the fence—a protected area for cleansing: the underground pipes—hidden influences that channel effluent to the lagoon; and patience as cleansing takes place. Finally the results: cleansing fits the water for the purposes God intended. If the lessons haven't grabbed you, take a refresher course in Metaphor 101!

You probably never thought about spiritual truth from a sewer lagoon, but Lily Loewen did. And she thought about an enchanted forest trail for little kids, and dozens of other fun ways to teach about the creation, the Creator, and responsible earth stewardship. With a nature lady like Lily on the staff, it's little wonder Camp Arnes enjoys a waiting list summer after summer.

"If the lessons haven't grabbed you, take a refresher course in Metaphor 101!"

Lily earned her undergraduate degree at the University of British Columbia, then taught school for several years in Columbia, South America. In 1973, she completed a master's program in outdoor education at Northern Illinois University, which included a summer in Germany, Austria, and Switzerland.

In 1987, the outdoor teacher education faculty at Northern Illinois University's Laredo Taft Field Campus recognized Lily's contribution to environmental education and leadership by naming her the "Outstanding Out-of-State Alumnus" for the year. And Lily's laurels extend beyond Canada and the United States. She was much appreciated as a lecturer or consultant on Christian camping and outdoor education as she toured Japan and Taiwan.

But Lily devoted most of her career to Camp Arnes, where her brother Dave was director. She developed and implemented a year-round resident outdoor education program that attracted thousands of students from Winnipeg and public schools in the surrounding area. She developed a leadership training program (LTP) for senior high students to prepare them for assignments as cabin counselors or members of the support staff. LTP looked beyond camp leadership, guiding students in basic Christian living and life-sharing among peers and throughout life. Now in semiretirement, Lily keeps in touch with many of her former students to encourage or counsel them.

Lily gave generously of her time to the Manitoba Outdoor Education Association as an officer and member of the executive board. She also frequently presented workshops at local, national, and international conferences, including Canadian and U.S. Christian camping association gatherings.

In addition to outdoor education leadership, Lily coordinated the Camp Arnes rental groups and helped them plan programs. Her ministry spanned the generations as she developed activities for seniors at three levels: active adults (the fifty-to-sixty-five-plus retirees); super seniors (less-active folks sixty or older); and an Elderhostel program. Lily also developed a German family camp for younger immigrant families in the area.

Camp Arnes' stature, as one of Canada's premier camps can be attributed in no small part to Lily's innovative leadership and commitment to Christ.

Though slowed by encroaching arthritis, Lily continues to travel and counsel camps on outdoor education and retreat programs. An able writer she has been urged to preserve her *Seize the Moment* discovery guides, and hopefully she will do that. When you know how to look, you can find spiritual truth almost anywhere, even in a sewer lagoon!

The following article was adapted from the MCA Newsletter, *Winter, 2000.*

Twenty-Three Horses Killed in Barn Fire

Animals Touched the Hearts of Children at 50-Year Old Camp

Nearly two dozen horses, which had touched the hearts of hundreds of disabled and disadvantaged children, were killed yesterday in an early morning fire at a Christian camp west of Winnipeg.

"It was quite a shock," said Bob Wiebe, executive director of camps for the Conference of Mennonites in Manitoba as he met with reporters in the main lodge of Camp Assiniboia. The 50-year-old camp, on Lido Plage Road about 16 kilometres west of Winnipeg, plays host yearround to hundreds of children and adults, including many who are sponsored by the Free Press Sunshine Fund and other charitable organizations.

A motorist on the Trans-Canada Highway spotted flames from the barn in the night sky and called police just after 4:30 a.m. Firefighters from the Elie and Headingley fire departments arrived a short time later, but it was too late to save the animals.

Headingley RCMP Const. Gord Goresky, who investigated the blaze along with the fire commissioner's office, said it appeared the fire was accidental. "It looks like a horse blanket fell in close proximity to a portable baseboard heater and the radiant heat caused the blanket to ignite and set the barn ablaze," Goresky said. "Call it fate – it's just too bad all the animals were lost."

Staff that live at the camp were awakened by a neighbor who also saw the fire. "There was nothing we could do at that time," said Wiebe, adding that a number of smaller animals, including several cats, a peacock, chickens, a goat and sheep – part of a small petting zoo – were also killed in the fire. The total loss is estimated at about $120,000.

Tragically, the horses aren't usually kept in the barn, which included a tack shop and riding arena. They had been rounded up Tuesday and placed in stalls in preparation for an appointment with a faurier yesterday, said Wiebe. "If it hadn't been for that, the horses would, at least, still be here," he said ruefully.

The 23 horses, all of which were named, were a major part of the camp experience, said Wiebe, adding groups use the camp yearround. In fact, another group had been booked for the end of the week. There were no guests staying at the camp when the fire broke out.

Standing near the twisted steel roofing and smoldering hay bales, camp manager Ron Wiebe (no relation) said he hopes the barn and the horses will be replaced. An insurance agent was to come out yesterday to survey the damage.

"Many so-called tough kids are brought to the camp," said Ron Wiebe, "and when they come face to face with the horses, they're instantly quiet."

Mealtime, snack-time, sometimes it seems we are always eating at camp. Perhaps it's the fresh air, the exercise, the camaraderie, the good food. But good camp food is not accidental, nor a guessing game. Before the food reaches the table or plate, there is much planning and the executing of plans.

And nothing is more important than the menu as told in the MCA Newsletter, *Fall, 1989, by Elaine Frey, a registered dietitian and food service director at Camp Hebron...*

Menus, More Than a Guessing Game
Seven factors to consider when planning a menu

Good menus don't just happen. Food items are not randomly picked when menu planning. Much thought and consideration should be given to writing menus for adult retreats or children's camp.

Of the many factors taken into consideration when writing menus, I have chosen to focus on seven. Of equal importance, they are not listed in any particular order.

1. Nutritional balance

    As a registered dietitian I feel offering guests meals that provide all essential nutrients over the course of a day is important. Although they may choose not to eat their vegetables or drink their milk, we have at least made it possible for them to eat nutritionally.

    Daily menus should include 6 oz. meat or alternate protein source, 4-to-5 servings of fruit and/or vegetables, 2 servings of milk, 4 servings of bread and/or grain products.

2. Cost

    To maintain a fairly constant daily raw food cost (the cost of food without labor or energy), it's necessary to balance an expensive meal with one less expensive. For example, a roast beef banquet could be offset by a lunch of chicken noodle corn soup, muffins, and salad.

    In addition, an expensive food item may be balanced with a cheaper food item at the same meal. For example, the cost of a rich cream cheese dessert could be offset by serving a cheaper salad such as applesauce. Raw food cost shouldn't be more than 30% of the price charged for meals. If $6.25 is charged for an evening meal, then raw food cost should be $1.88 or less.

    The next three factors are important for eye appeal. Meals that look appealing are generally better received than bland ones.

3. Color

    Meals should consist of foods with a variety of colors. Having a plate of all white, or brown, or green foods set in front of us does not create an interest in eating. Complimentary colored foods should be served together. White foods should be offset with brightly colored items.

If you had the choice of the following two menus, which would you choose?

Broiled haddock, mashed potatoes, buttered cauliflower, applesauce, vanilla ice cream or broiled haddock, baked potatoes, whole baby carrots, tossed salad, dressing, strawberry ice cream.

Although similar in content, the brown potato skin, orange carrots, green salad, and pink ice cream create an attractive, colorful accompaniment to the white fish.

4. Texture

Meals should consist of foods with a variety of textures. Combining crunchy, soft, smooth, and grainy foods makes a meal more enjoyable to eat. Look at the above mentioned menus again. Notice how everything in the first is soft or mushy, whereas the second adds the crunch of tossed salad and chewiness of potato skins.

5. Size, Shape, and Potpourri

Menus should contrast mixtures of foods with single foods; small pieces with large; round foods with square foods; chopped with whole foods. The following example illustrates this:

Chicken casserole, mixed vegetables, tossed salad, fruit cocktail

or

Chicken casserole, green beans, tossed salad, peach halves

In the first, everything is chopped into small pieces and mixed together. The second menu is similar in content, but incorporates foods that are not chopped or mixed.

6. Flavor

Complimentary flavors should be blended in a menu. Bland foods help to temper spicy foods; mild dishes temper ones which are strong-flavored. If a meal contains too many of one type, your guests may be displeased. For example:

Roast pork, harvard red beets, sweet pickles, sauerkraut, lemon meringue pie

A better choice would be:

Roast pork, sauerkraut, applesauce, mashed potatoes, cherry crumb pie

"...remember, serving good food is a key ingredient to a successful guest group ministry."

7. Variety

Variety is the spice of menus as well as the spice of life. Food items should not be repeated from one meal to the next or even from one day to the next (i.e. applesauce for lunch on Monday and applesauce for supper on Tuesday). Nor should foods that are made from the same basic ingredients.

The following should be avoided:

Lunch:
Chili, carrots and celery, cornbread, apple crisp

Supper:
Taco salad, applesauce, cornmeal cookies

Both entrees are tomato-based with hamburger. Two items are made with apples; two are made with cornmeal. Foods that are too easily repeated are tomatoes, apples, hamburger, pasta, cheese, and chocolate. This situation may be harder to avoid when writing menus for children because they tend to like similar foods (pizza, chili, taco salad, etc.), but it is possible with a bit of creativity and finagling.

Others

Other considerations are the food preferences of our guests, the number of people to be served, the season of the year, the equipment available for use, and kitchen personnel. Good menu writing comes with practice. Putting all the pieces together is not always easy. Writing a "perfect menu" and having the guests love it is even harder. But remember, serving good food is a key ingredient to a successful guest group ministry.

As a result of the repeated interactions of the Mennonite camping community through MCA gatherings, the camping staff can become like an extension of the closer "family" of each member camp. Sometimes this family is impacted by personal tragedy as told in the following two accounts in the MCA Newsletters, the first in 1986.

Woodcrest Directors Killed in Car Accident

Woodcrest Retreat, Ephrata, Pennsylvania co-directors Charles "Chuck" and Joyce Brubaker were killed in an auto accident on March 28. The couple's baby daughter, Carmen, escaped serious injury. Eric, their four-year old son was not involved in the accident.

Chuck and Joyce had lived at the camp since August, 1983. Chuck, a schoolteacher and Joyce, a registered nurse were camp caretakers and directed the summer day camp program.

Woodcrest Retreat is owned by Woodcrest Retreat Association. They provide facilities for one-day retreats along with their day camp outreach to local youth. We trust God will continue to bless the Woodcrest ministry in spite of this tragic loss.

Don Rittenhouse was anticipating serving as president of Mennonite Camping Association. A great loss to his family, but to all of us, plans were tragically changed as told by Jon Welty Peachey in the MCA Newsletter, October, 2000. *The following is an edited version...*

MCA President Dies in Tragic Accident – Family and Friends Say Good-bye

Don Rittenhouse, age 43, executive director of Laurelville Mennonite Church Center, died as the result of injuries sustained in a two-car accident Friday afternoon, July 28. He was returning to Laurelville from Harrisonburg, Va., when the accident occurred near Addison, Pa., on Route 40.

Rittenhouse was life-flighted to the West Virginia University Trauma Center in Morgantown, W. Va. He died in surgery several hours later. The memorial service for Don Rittenhouse was held at 1:30 p.m. on Tuesday, August 1 in the Shenandoah building at Laurelville Mennonite Church Center. More than 500 people joined together in memory of Don and in celebration of his life.

Don is survived by his wife, Jane, and their two daughters, Leah, 11, and Krista, 8, his parents, and three brothers.

Doug and Wanda Roth Amstutz, pastors at the Mennonite Church of Scottdale, where Don was chair of the congregation, guided the service. Doug served as worship leader, and Wanda delivered the meditation entitled "The Lord Is Near." Members of the congregation also paid tribute to Don with special music throughout the service.

Many MCA members and camp directors attended the memorial service.

Finally, there are some who found a long lifetime of service in the Mennonite Church camping ministry. Many persons could be used as illustrations. But perhaps none are more exemplary than the following team as told by Grace Nolt from Spruce Lake Retreat in the MCA Newsletter, Spring, 2000. *What follows is an edited version...*

Faithful Leaders in Camping Ministry

Paul and Leanna (Kauffman) Beiler spawned a legacy of faithful commitment to the church through Christian camping, 1973-99, at Spruce Lake Retreat in northeastern Pennsylvania. In 1973, W. Paul Moyer and fellow board member, Ernest Alderfer, interviewed the young pair of teachers just back from three years in Botswana under Mennonite Central Committee. Spruce Lake was looking for a full-time director to start a year-round program.

In Leanna they saw a young woman full of creativity and energy. She emerged from the Shenandoah Valley farm fields and the sanctuary of Lindale Mennonite Church, where she led the entire congregation in singing. Her family had moved from Goshen, Indiana, to Harrisonburg, Va., so the children could attend Eastern Mennonite High School as day students.

In college, "Tall Paul" strode into Leanna's life on legs that left her standing below his shoulder. But when she exploded up court for a lay-up, he took notice. He was an accomplished basketball player. They were married between Leanna's junior and senior year.

Paul had grown up in Morgantown, Pa., not far from Conestoga Mennonite Church, where the Beiler family went to church. From his dad, who ran a car dealership, he inherited a handyman's knack for fixing almost anything.

Mennonite camping, booming in the 1940s and 50s with seventy-five new programs throughout the U.S. and Canada, affected Paul's life significantly. Several siblings and he would ride with their parents to Laurelville Mennonite Church Center on the far side of Pennsylvania for family camp. Paul also attended boys' camp and junior high camp at Laurelville.

Paul later worked at Laurelville and at Tel Hai Camp in roles as varied as counselor, waterfront director, and activity leader. After marriage, Paul and Leanna worked together several summers at Highland Retreat, Camp Hebron, and Tel Hai Camp, Leanna's first camp experiences. Soon they were convinced the camp setting is one of the most effective avenues of ministry within the church. Why? They had both seen for themselves what happened to people there, freed to discover who God was in their lives.

As early camping trailblazers, loneliness often affected the small Beiler family those first years. Accepting the challenges, they kept working, though not knowing what would arise from these arduous beginnings. Pushing little Mary Jo atop a cart piled high with laundry, maneuvering the backhoe to carve out basements beneath existing buildings, preparing meals, organizing volunteers, taking reservations, they planned it all while keeping an eye on Mary Jo and later son Ryan.

Each began to sense a huge personal satisfaction as they exercised their hands-on, creative gifts. Paul's flair for photography and birding led to slide shows and spring nature retreats. He could run heavy equipment as well as take reservations, wash dishes, or negotiate a sale. Leanna's "green thumb" contributed much to Spruce Lake's aesthetic ambience, demonstrated in arranging landscape, flower beds, and seasonal floral arrangements in the dining and reception areas. She also discovered an artist's delight in designing new buildings better using existing space.

Leanna and Paul often searched for ways to make Spruce Lake's "arm" more effective for ministry. As with many camps in those decades of expansion, Spruce Lake first focused on the spiritual needs of children and youth. Today, not just 400 but approximately 1,400 children each year see Christian integrity, faith, and love expressed with tremendous opportunities for discipleship through wilderness camp and expeditions, an American Camping Association accredited program.

They noticed the trend for modern folks to lose touch with the natural world. From Paul's love of nature, and training as a biology teacher, grew the dream of an outdoor school where all ages could rediscover awe of God's creation—where adults could learn to communicate a godly respect for nature and humanity's place in it. Today, Spruce Lake

"...they were convinced the camp setting is one of the most effective avenues of ministry within the church."

Paul and Leanna (Kauffman) Beiler

outdoor school's professional teacher/naturalists educate more than 3,000 students, teachers, and home-school families each year.

Respect for the earth was also integral to administrative policy. When the situation demanded a new method of wastewater treatment, an environmentally sound spray irrigation system was built, one of the first in the Pocono region. All-camp recycling was enacted. New buildings and renovations added to facilitate ministry were planned with an effort to preserve the natural, attractive outdoor environment.

Paul and Leanna insisted that Spruce Lake's programming remain the driving force of ministry. Christ-centered teaching and guided recreation do not "just happen." Intentional spiritual and educational programming is essential to the integrity of mission, so that Spruce Lake does not simply become a "nice, Christian resort."

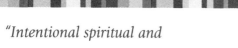

"Intentional spiritual and educational programming is essential to the integrity of mission."

"Building muscle" for the church also meant sacrificing personal time for staff needs. For example, when the work load began to prevent staff from leaving the grounds for church, Beilers started their own service-Anabaptist-style in their living room. They also initiated a thriving children's Sunday school. In 1983, the small group of worshipers drafted a covenant, and Spruce Lake Fellowship was adopted into Franconia Mennonite Conference. Now participants could relate to the larger Mennonite Church family. Leanna and Paul remained pivotal persons in the congregation's life, honing its unique strengths of flexibility, creativity, and lay leadership.

Today, Spruce Lake Retreat is ranked in the top five percent of the 800-plus member camps in Christian Camp and Conference Association. It is also one of the largest of forty-seven member camps in Mennonite Camp Association.

The Beilers feel a little uncomfortable when such facts are highlighted, as if they'd had much to do with it. They feel that the story belongs, instead, to hundreds of staff, volunteers, donors, and friends. To an unusually supportive board. To an Almighty One in the midst of them all.

The following is by Britta Williams, *Baltimore, Maryland...*

I am continually amazed at Jesus' intense desire to gather his children in retreat. For me, the graces of the 2004 retreat at Camp Andrews became more present in the days which followed it; a testimony to Christ's ability to transform us from the inside out, and working in the depths of our souls without us even aware of his powerful move. Amazing.

And this by Kaitlin Dyck, *Youth Farm Bible Camp*

Last year, attending camp for my first time, I really didn't know what to expect. I had no idea it would have such a great impact on me in every way. I want to leave camp this summer feeling like I did last year: spiritually stronger, emotionally happy, and able to get ready in five minutes flat in the morning.

I loved the way the girls in my cabin looked up to me, and I especially loved leading devotions, and being able to talk to them about anything. I hope to lead some more kids to Christ, make more amazing friendships like last year, and I also want to grow spiritually. I think camp is one of the most unique and unforgettable experiences, and I can't wait till this summer!

* * *

To help meet the challenges of the Mennonite camping leadership in the future, Goshen College and the Mennonite Camping Association have launched the Camping Inquiry Program. The following two articles describe the program and the participating camps and the experiences of a young woman who participated.

College, Camps Start Internship Program
Goshen, Ind.

Goshen College and the Mennonite Camping Association have launched an internship program to encourage students to consider ministry in camping and retreat programs. Called the Camping Inquiry Program, it parallels Goshen's current programs for congregational ministry and church-sponsored voluntary service.

Goshen residents Larry and Janet Newswanger provided a grant through their family foundation to start the program. During a two-year trial period, six Goshen students per year will have opportunity to spend six months at one of three Mennonite Camping Association-member facilities: Amigo Centre, Sturgis, Mich.; Camp Hebron, Halifax, Pa.; and a third location yet to be determined. Responsibilities could range from counseling to administration to food service to maintenance. On-site mentors will teach and work with participants.

"The Camping Inquiry Program will give participating students firsthand insights into the multifaceted operations of our church camps and retreat centers," says Stuart Showalter, Goshen's director of career services. "We hope that some of these students will graduate to become the next generation of leaders."

After two years, Goshen and the camps will evaluate the program. Organizers hope it can eventually be extended to other Mennonite colleges and Mennonite Camping Association members.

Reprinted by permission from The Mennonite, *March 5, 2002*

Canoes, Bugs, and Meeting God
By Anita Yoder, assistant director of career services

Lauren Metcalf learned how to hoist a fifty-pound canoe onto her shoulders, to use a map and compass, and to pack gear efficiently this summer. As part of Goshen College's Camping Inquiry Program (CIP), she taught similar camping skills this summer to individuals participating in five-to-six day overnight canoe trips into the Boundary Waters Canoe Area Wilderness in northern Minnesota – an area bordering Canada featuring one million acres of protected land and hundreds of lakes and rivers.

CIP's goal is to expose students to the mission and programs of Mennonite camps and retreat centers, with an eye toward future outdoor ministry. A 2004 graduate, Metcalf (a senior from Dalton, Ohio) interned at Wilderness Wind, an organization that offers wilderness experiences for individuals and groups, based near Ely, Minnesota.

Preparing participants for overnight sojourns requires a lot of instruction and careful attention to detail. Metcalf oriented participants with a day of teaching canoe strokes on a nearby lake, how to portage, backpacking, food preparation and safety. She emphasized developing wilderness ethics: reducing the human impact on the environment and creating an awareness of the interdependence of all life.

Metcalf also learned that facilitating a trip requires patience, flexibility, good communication, and sound decision making. "We're always checking in with people to see

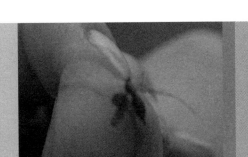

how they're doing," she said. "They may be tired and not want to say anything, or eager to continue exploring."

An emphasis on spiritual reflection is one aspect that differentiates Wilderness Wind from other outfitters. Metcalf facilitated opportunities for contemplative awareness by encouraging time spent in prayer and reflection. Just as she led others in wilderness awareness, Metcalf also appreciated how the experience has enriched her. "I love being out on the water, interacting with people, and listening to the silence. It's been very spiritually refreshing for me," she said.

Goshen College Bulletin, *September, 2004*

* * *

Nightfall on the Siletz River
By Larry Eby, November, 1996

> *Scattered leaves like feathers after plucking*
> *blown in random scatter*
> *cling to the steep riverbank*
> *riverine bushes hug the edge draping over*
> *reaching toward grey current*
> *fading autumn remnants*
> *of bright yellow, orange, red, heliotrope*
> *a benediction as night falls*

Chapter 9

The Place of the Mennonite Church in the World of Christian Camping and Retreating

"Receiving God's Love in Christ"

The Mennonite Camping Association vision statement declares, *"God calls us to be followers of Jesus Christ and, by the power of the Holy Spirit, to grow as communities of grace, joy, and peace so that God's healing and hope flow through us to the world."*

The brochure goes on to say that member camps give expression to this vision by leading their camp and church communities on a journey of transformation through:

· Seeking God's face in creation
· Receiving God's love in Christ
· Radiating God's Spirit in the world

The brochure further states that our camping and retreat ministries offer well-rounded experiences of Christian community through:

· a loving circle of acceptance and healing that supports growth in faith
· a place where the gospel is both heard and seen
· a sense of belonging that invites personal commitment to Jesus Christ and discipleship and opportunity to recognize and express gifts

In the book you now hold in your hands, Tim Lehman speaks of the "love story" created by Christ, lived by Christ, continually written by Christ, a love story for us to participate in and share with others. He suggests we can change the world only as we are fixed to that continued story. By taking the life of Christ upon us and living it ourselves we become God's image. This appropriation of the life of Christ as crucial to our understanding of discipleship can set us apart as Mennonite camping people.

We share God's image. This implies that we share God's concern for the well-being of creation in a nurturing attitude, not to exploit it as a commodity to be consumed. Place is important in knowing God in a deep way. Mennonite camps are "knowing places," different for each of us in our settings and different to us at different times. We can turn our encounters in nature into a life text for salvation as Jesus did in his parables, giving in to all the moments of real life.

So where do we as Mennonites find ourselves in the comprehensive picture of Christian camping? Do we fit best in the larger scene of mainline evangelical camping as illustrated by Christian Camp and Conference Association, the large ecumenical Christian camping organization that many of our camps are members of? Or is there something about us that sets us apart? Tim Lehman suggests that appropriating the life of Christ in our understanding of discipleship sets us apart. If so, how are we doing that?

We asked each of the forty-six MCA member institutions for their mission or vision statements and some reflection on how these statements are used and supported in their programming. We also paid attention to how their statements and programs correspond to the vision statement of MCA. Almost all responded with information that appears with their listing in Chapter 6. We are pleased to see a clear connection with what is expressed in the MCA vision statement. This is especially evident in hospitality and service, something that is ingrained in our heritage. Also pervasive is a commitment to spiritual nurture and growth, an emphasis on biblical teaching and living and discipleship, and presenting the

message of Jesus. True, most of this would be on the vision page of any Christian camp. So we do have much in common with the non-Mennonite member institutions of Christian Camp and Conference Association.

One-third of our members mention care of the earth and appreciation of nature as things to be cherished and protected. They see the natural setting as relief from the ordinary crowded spaces and schedules of living, the outdoor environment as a refreshing place to get away to study God's Word and see God in nature. Some include the concept that nature itself can speak to us of God, the Creator present in creation. Of the *"still small voice"* (KJV) or *"sound of sheer silence"* (NRSV) that Elijah heard.

Persons throughout this book reflect on what makes camping and retreating different from the rest of our church and living activities. Perhaps as camping leaders and participants we need to give conscious thought to that in our programming. And on the list of things to consider is to what extent we want the programming and other activities to portray and enhance the appropriation of the life of Christ as crucial to our understanding of discipleship that can set us apart as Mennonite camping people presented by Tim Lehman.

"Perhaps as camping leaders and participants we need to give conscious thought to that in our programming...on the list of things to consider is to what extent we want the programming and other activities to portray and enhance the appropriation of the life of Christ as crucial to our understanding of discipleship that can set us apart as Mennonite camping people."

Is it enough to go to a place apart for Bible study and evangelism without recognizing "God in this place," as an actual Presence in the fleecy clouds, the babbling brook, the majestic trees, the jumping trout, the rolling waves, the moonlit, starry skies, the loon's cry, the snow-clad mountain peak, the physically or mentally challenged child, as well as the gathered celebrators of the joy of life in the outdoors?

Mennonite camping as envisioned by our forbearers and current thinkers and writers incorporates all of these. An environment and program that respects and acknowledges the Creator and creation, a salvation way of life that addresses our individual and societal needs along with preservation and redemption of the natural environment, and a recognition of God's voice in the universe that is God's gift to us "In Harmony with Creation."

The future of camping and retreating carries both a challenge and a hopeful direction. It would be easy to follow a popular model of camp as a place of recreation, of exploiting the natural environment, in creating modern places of comfort not much different from our home setting where we can enjoy beach, mountain, lake, or stream and have Christian fellowship, worship, and evangelism.

Or should we be challenged to another model? Of consciously having our camps and retreats be places where God is not only in the activities and structures but also in planned places and programs? And in these programs the gifts of God's nature can speak directly to our senses, connecting us to the sounds, sights, tastes, touches, and smells of this good earth and the created things of which it is comprised and that occupy its environment.

As faithful caretakers of God's creation, the answer seems clear.

Appendix

A Vision for Mennonite Camping

In a busy fragmented world, the camp/retreat environment offers all participants, staff and volunteers an opportunity to experience the meaning of living the church of Christ in a holistic way. Our camp/retreat programs and settings provide, within a limited space of time, a fully integrated experience of being the church.

We attempt to model Jesus' teachings and way of life in every dimension of daily life at camp. We also help campers/retreaters see how these teachings connect with their life in the church, in society, and in their relationship with nature. For us, care of the earth has become an extension of Jesus' ministry. Our camps and retreat centers directly reflect an Anabaptist/Mennonite theology of Christ's peace and love as central to the gospel.

Mennonite Camping Association (MCA) claims the overall statement of Vision: Healing and Hope adopted by the Mennonite Church and the General Conference Mennonite Church. This vision states:

"God calls us to be followers of Jesus Christ and, by the power of the Holy Spirit, to grow as communities of grace, joy and peace, so that Gods healing and hope flow through us to the world."

Member camps give expression to this vision by leading their camp and church communities on a journey of transformation through:

> *Seeking God's face in creation,*
> *Receiving God's Love In Christ,*
> *Radiating God's Spirit in the world.*

Seeking God's Face in Creation

In a world often detached from nature and from spiritual reality, our camping and retreat ministries offer a way to reconnect with the created order and invite us to experience God through:

- prayer, solitude and worship
- scripture study and reflection
- outdoor discovery and play

Receiving God's Love in Christ

Our camping and retreat ministries offer well-rounded experiences of Christian community through:

- a loving circle of acceptance and healing that supports growth in faith
- a place where the gospel is both heard and seen
- a sense of belonging that invites personal commitment to Jesus Christ and discipleship
- an opportunity to recognize and express gifts

Radiating God's Spirit in the World

As a place where the power of the Holy Spirit is seen and known, camps and retreat centers offer inspiration for faithful, creative ministry in God's world enabling participants, staff and volunteers to:

- be peacemakers, servants and witnesses of God's Love
- be caretakers of the earth - God's garden,
- be prophets who, from a creative distance, call the church to faithful living in a materialistic, violent world
- live in harmony with God, nature, each other and the world beyond our camp or retreat center

Therefore we are committed to provide programs and places for people to meet God face to face, to put the complexities of life into perspective, to make choices and commitments and return to the outside world with renewed energy and vision.

This Vision Statement was accepted by the MCA membership at the Biennial Convention held in March, 1998 at Camp Arnes, Gimli, Manitoba.

MENNONITE CAMPING ASSOCIATION BOARD MEMBERS 1980-2005

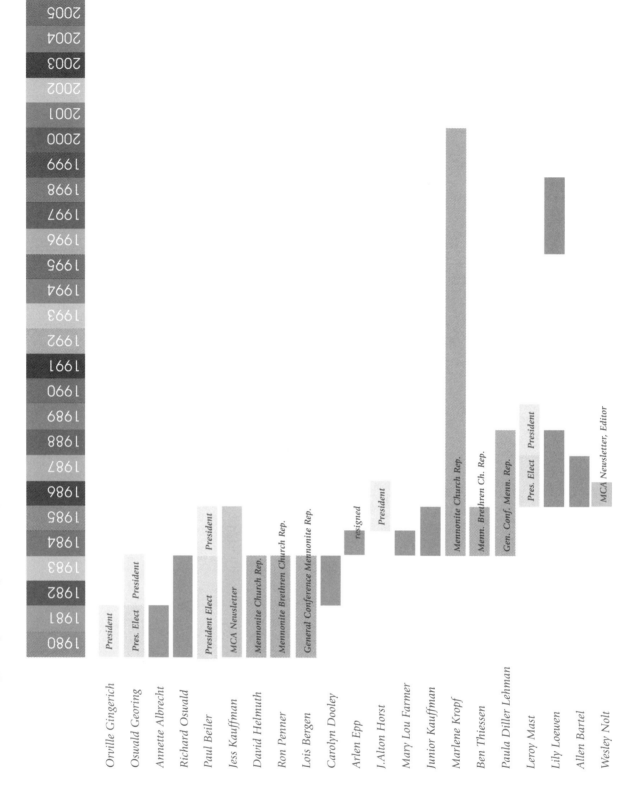

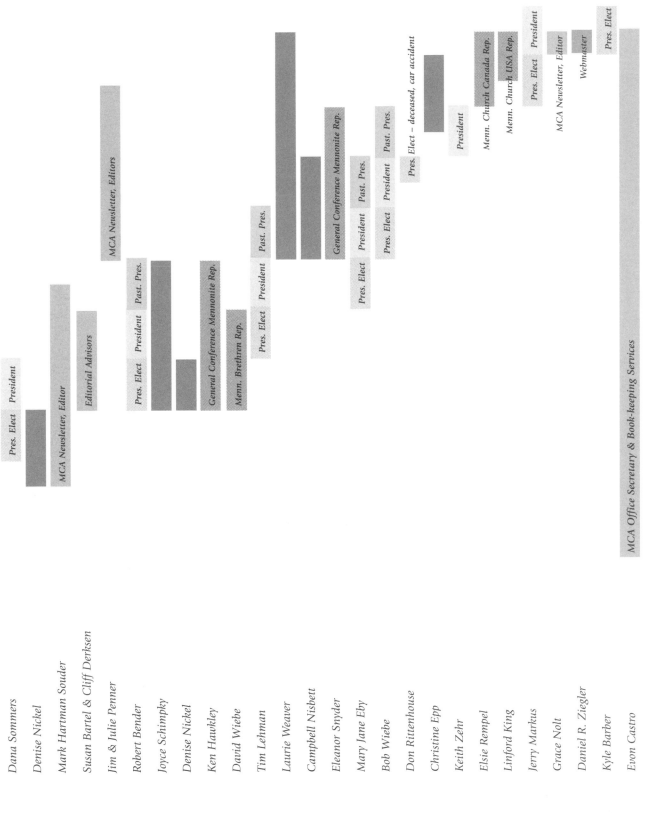

Dana Sommers — Pres. Elect / President

Denise Nickel — MCA Newsletter, Editor

Mark Hartman Souder — Editorial Advisors

Susan Bartel & Cliff Derksen

Jim & Julie Penner — MCA Newsletter, Editors

Robert Bender — Pres. Elect / President / Past. Pres.

Joyce Schimpky

Denise Nickel

Ken Hawkley — General Conference Mennonite Rep.

David Wiebe — Menn. Brethren Rep.

Tim Lehman — Pres. Elect / President / Past. Pres.

Laurie Weaver

Campbell Nisbett

Eleanor Snyder — General Conference Mennonite Rep.

Mary Jane Eby — Pres. Elect / President / Past. Pres.

Bob Wiebe — Pres. Elect / President / Past. Pres.

Don Rittenhouse — Pres. Elect – deceased, car accident

Christine Epp — President

Keith Zehr

Elsie Rempel — Menn. Church Canada Rep.

Linford King — Menn. Church USA Rep.

Jerry Markus — Pres. Elect / President

Grace Nolt — MCA Newsletter, Editor

Daniel R. Ziegler

Kyle Barber — Webmaster

Evon Castro — Pres. Elect

MCA Office Secretary & Book-keeping Services

Authors, Producers & Designers

Mary Jane Breneman Eby and Larry Eby, currently retired from careers in medicine, nursing and other careers, are parents of six children and grandparents of eight, all of whom have acquired through years of family camping a love of the outdoors. Additionally, they served for five years as directors of Drift Creek Camp in Oregon. Out of that experience they previously edited and wrote *Spirit Roots*, a forty-year anecdotal history of Drift Creek.

Jennifer Gingerich is a graduate of camping at Drift Creek Camp and Goshen College with a major in Bible, Religion and Philosophy. She is currently employed as a Youth Pastor and Community Center Coordinator at Salem (Oregon) Mennonite Church.

Dave Helmuth is a retired pastor in Goshen, Ind., who served in Puerto Rico and Indiana. He also was a staff person with the Board of Congregational Ministries (Mennonite Church) and from that position was a board member of Mennonite Camping Association. He loves to fish and canoe in the boundary waters and other parts of Canada with family and friends.

Tim Lehman, husband of Susan, pastor of Jubilee Mennonite Church in Bellefontaine, Ohio, has spent much of his life in camping ministry. A co-founder of Wilderness Wind in Minnesota, he authored *Seeking the Wilderness: A Spiritual Journey*, a notable publication in the genre of spirituality and nature.

Darryl Neustaedter Barg is Director of Media Ministries for Mennonite Church Manitoba (Canada). His wife is Krista and they are parents of two children, Joshua (10) and Natasha (7). While his musical gifts are used in his employment, in conferences, workshops and other musical events, his favorite place to be is leading singing with a few dozen junior highs at camp.

Ozzie Goering served for years with the General Conference Camping Committee in the 1950s, one of the forerunners of MCA. He has a Doctors Degree from Indiana University in Recreation with an emphasis on Camping. Professor of Outdoor Teacher Education at Northern Illinois University for 21 years, he is now involved with Heifer International and lives with his wife, Elaine, in Moundridge, Kan.

About the Producer

Paul M. Schrock, Harrisonburg, Va., worked for 40 years at Mennonite Publishing House/ Herald Press, Scottdale, Pa. He participated in the creation of more than 700 books there. A native of Oregon, he attended Western Mennonite School, Eastern Mennonite College, and Syracuse University. Married to June Bontrager, Alden, New York, they are the parents of Carmen Schrock-Hurst, Brent Schrock, and Andrea Wenger and the grandparents of five.

About the Designers

Kauffman & Associates is a company whose mission is to create elegant, effective communications. K&A has over 20 years of experience with design, illustration and photography, doing award-winning work for a large base of local business clients as well as national corporations.

Wilbur Kauffman, Creative Director
Melissa Vu, Art Director
Vanessa Kauffman, Illustrator

MH/B
CLASS   ACC.

Breneman Eby, Larry & Mary
(LAST NAME OF AUTHOR)   Jane

In Harmony with Nature
(BOOK TITLE)

0805482741
CLS-3   MADE IN U.S.A.
                                        SUPPLIES